**W9-AYO-750**

DISCARD

# Get Serious About Getting Married

SERIOUS TIPS FROM
A SUCCESSFUL MATCHMAKER

# Get Serious
# About Getting
# Married

365 PROVEN WAYS
TO FIND LOVE IN LESS THAN A YEAR

## JANIS SPINDEL
with Karen Kelly

**1❂ ReganBooks**
**Celebrating Ten Bestselling Years**
*An Imprint of HarperCollins Publishers*

NOTE: The names of clients and friends mentioned in this book have been changed for privacy reasons.

GET SERIOUS ABOUT GETTING MARRIED. Copyright © 2005 by Janis Spindel. All rights reserved. Printed in the United States of America. No part of this book may be used or reproduced in any manner whatsoever without written permission except in the case of brief quotations embodied in critical articles and reviews. For information, address HarperCollins Publishers Inc., 10 East 53rd Street, New York, NY 10022.

HarperCollins books may be purchased for educational, business, or sales promotional use. For information please write: Special Markets Department, HarperCollins Publishers Inc., 10 East 53rd Street, New York, NY 10022.

FIRST EDITION

Designed by Kris Tobiassen

Printed on acid-free paper

Library of Congress Cataloging-in-Publication Data has been applied for.

ISBN 0-06-057873-4

05 06 07 08 09 RRD 10 9 8 7 6 5 4 3 2 1

For Allen, Carly, and Falyn

# Contents

Acknowledgments *ix*

Introduction: The Evolution of a Matchmaker *xi*

## Part 1: Preparation Is Everything

1. Get Serious About Who You Are and What You Want So You Can Get Ready to Find *Him!* *3*
2. Look Great and Feel Great *35*
3. Healthy Is as Healthy Does *77*
4. Breaking Up Doesn't Have to Be Hard to Do *99*

## Part 2: Widening the Net and Increasing Your Chances

5. Get in the Mood and Become Date-able! *117*
6. Your Life as a Dating Venue—
   Where to Go to Find "Him" *133*
7. Going to the Pros *163*

## Part 3: Dating Toward Marriage

8. The Big Date: Ready, Set, *Go!* *183*
9. Relationship Building and the Three Stages of Dating *209*
10. True Love: Commitment and Marriage *239*

Resource Guide *261*

Personal Favorites *275*

# *Acknowledgments*

First and foremost I would like to say that there is only ONE person responsible for making me who I am today: my father, Norman Siderman. He taught me the value of people and nurtured my "gift of gab" from day one. At eighty-seven, he's still talking to everybody, everywhere, every single day! Thanks also to my beautiful mother, Luba, for giving me life. Of course, I can't forget my wonderful siblings Warren, Ilene, and especially Marsha. She's the Cupid in Ralph Lauren who runs my New Jersey division and has been my eyes and ears at many a party and continues to be an invaluable asset to my business!

I would also like to send my deepest love and appreciation to my husband, Allen Spindel, and to my daughters Carly and Falyn for allowing me the time go out and pursue my passion for matchmaking.

My gratitude also goes to publisher Judith Regan and editor Aliza Fogelson for recognizing the need for this book and for giving me such freedom in imparting my knowledge to singles everywhere! Many thanks to the great women in my office, Shula, Alex, Jaime, and Annie. They keep Janis Spindel Serious Matchmaking, Inc. humming while I'm constantly on the run!

I would also like to thank the wonderful professionals I work with and the men and women who belong to Janis Spindel Serious Matchmaking, Inc., for sharing your expertise and experiences with me. It has been a pleasure!

Finally, I would like to thank my writer, Karen Kelly. Karen, I invited you into my sometimes hectic, a little crazy, but always interesting world and you have represented me, the nature of my business, and my philosophy beautifully! I cannot thank you enough!

# *Introduction*

## THE EVOLUTION
## OF A MATCHMAKER

hy would anyone become a matchmaker? *How* does anyone become a matchmaker? I get asked these questions all the time. My ability to make lasting matches is half "born-with-it instinct" talent and half practice. Specifically, I have paid attention to and focused on people my whole life, and studied how they relate to others. As a result, I have what I call "flashes" about potential couples. Putting the right man and the right woman together is really more of an art than a science. Making matches isn't something you can learn in law or business school.

You're still probably wondering who I am and where I came from, too. Well, my transformation into a matchmaker didn't happen overnight. But it has been percolating inside me all my life. . . .

I grew up one of four children in Westfield, New Jersey. My father owned a chain of nine furniture stores, and I started working for him when I was nine years old, helping on the floor and showing customers merchandise. I'd also observe the way he comfortably chatted with the huge variety of people who came through the doors. Watching him taught me how to talk to people and set them at ease. I thank my father for giving me the gift of gab and for teaching me that every single person deserves to be treated with respect and compassion.

But he was more than a just charming raconteur. He was also a savvy businessman and taught me his complex system of inventory and order codes. Nine furniture stores meant *a lot* of upholstery and end tables to keep track of. The business and organizational strategies he taught me help me to this day in running a successful company in a very competitive city.

My high school years added more to my matchmaking foundation. At sixteen I was juggling three jobs, attending school, and having fun socializing with friends. My ability to multitask (the hallmark of every good matchmaker) was definitely shaped and honed then! I made a little history by being the first girl ever to work at the Baskin-Robbins ice cream parlor; I was an executive secretary for a local attorney and I was also the top salesperson in the lingerie department (what else?) of the great, bygone department store B. Altman.

I may not be a Rhodes scholar, but in the high school year book I was voted best dressed, girl with the cutest nose, shortest skirts, and most popular. If that's not laying the groundwork for matchmaking, I don't know what is!

But seriously, each work experience put me in contact with all kinds of people. I had to understand and connect to them in order to do a great job. I learned how to think on my feet and turn challenging situations into fruitful opportunities and to make demanding customers feel relaxed and well cared for.

After high school I attended Marjorie Webster College in Washington, D.C., which was at the time the equivalent of New York City's Fashion Institute of Technology. My older sister Marsha was a fashion editor. Right before school ended for the year I would accompany her to showrooms in New York in hopes of landing a summer job. After junior year I secured a job as a showroom model for a manufacturer's representative. That meant trying on the various makers' clothing for potential buyers, usually department stores.

One afternoon in particular really changed my life. All the salespeople had gone to lunch. Casual Corner's owner and his entourage of general managers and buyers came in—unannounced. Casual Corner was a *major* retailer at the time, and a sale to their stores would make a difference to the small manufacturers my company represented. It was unheard of in the industry for a buyer to walk into a showroom without an appointment, but when you were as big as Casual Corner was at the time (think *HUGE*), you could pretty much do whatever you wanted to do.

Without missing a beat I took the executives through the collection. I certainly knew it very well, having tried on each piece more times than I could count. I was completely honest and told them which pieces I thought would work for the stores and which items I thought were dogs. They were impressed with my frankness—and my accuracy too, as it turned out. The items sold like hotcakes for Casual Corner, which was a good thing, since Casual Corner had written a $150,000 order on the spot. When my boss came back he could not believe his eyes. Or his sales book.

As you may have guessed, I didn't go back to Marjorie Webster.

Long story short, that sale became legendary in the garment industry and I got job offers from reps and manufacturers all over town. I stayed in New York and worked in the fashion business as a national sales rep for another firm. I traveled the world, managed a staff of eleven men, and had the time of my life. Working in the fashion business developed my eye for style and offered me further proof that appearance and clothing can really change a person's whole demeanor and attitude. Great personal style can also change how others view you.

After a few years, I got burnt out on the fashion business and I was selling corporate memberships to the New York Health and Racquet Club. It was a great way to meet men, by the way (if you're thinking about changing careers). I met my future husband, Allen, when I went to the office in the garment district where he was working and tried to sell his bosses a membership. I spotted him in his office and thought, "*He is cute!*" At the end of the sales call, I approached Allen and told him I was walking home and asked him if he wouldn't like to accompany me. I was wearing linen shorts and a blazer. It was the height of fashion at the time, but not to Allen's liking, as I found out later. But ever a gentleman, he walked me home anyway, enduring both a stop at a photo store and the subsequent show-and-tell description of the family pictures I had picked up. When we arrived at my building, I told him I would give him my number if he promised to call. He took it and promised—but of course he never did call.

About six months later I was at the gym waiting for an aerobics class. I was at the top of the stairs and, as it turned out, Allen was at the bottom with his friend, waiting to get into the same class. I had on a pink bandanna and white sweatpants with my hair in pigtails, tied in pink ribbons. Pink is my favorite color, if you haven't figured that out by now. The outfit was a far cry from the blazer-and-linen-shorts getup. I saw Allen but didn't recognize him. He saw me, too—but he didn't realize I was the girl he'd walked home. I overheard him say to his friend, "See that tall girl up there with the white sweatpants? I'm going to marry her." Yeah, right! I looked at this guy and thought, "*Who the heck is that?*" Only later did it dawn on both of us that we had met six months earlier.

After class, Allen asked me if I wanted to grab a "light bite." I found out soon enough that light bite to Allen meant inexpensive meal! He took me to the steak chain Tony Roma's of all places! But I survived and we soon started dating seriously and exclusively.

All I ever really wanted was to get married and have babies. Even though I had been a successful fashion executive and had the time of my life as a single woman in New York, in my heart I really craved the family life—and I didn't really care whether I ever worked again. Before I met Allen I had been in a very painful four-year dead-end relationship. "Jim" was a great guy in many ways, but he simply could not commit to one woman. I trailed along after him like a silly schoolgirl, always hoping I could change him (lesson number one: A leopard does not change his spots). Allen was completely different from Jim. He is what is known in Yiddish as a *mensch*. Translated, that means a real man, a great guy, and as I knew it would turn out, a wonderful and true husband and father.

One morning while we were still dating Allen shoved the *New York Times* in front of me and I kept pushing it away.

"I don't want to read the paper, Allen, I have to get ready for work!"

"Read it, read it, there's something important you should really look at," he begged.

Finally, I relented and looked at where his finger was pointing, at the very bottom of the front page. There, in tiny capital letters read: JANIS WILL YOU MARRY ME? ALLEN.

I looked up at him and said, "I don't know." I know, I know. What kind of a thing is that to say? But really I was totally flabbergasted. Needless to say, we did get married, and twenty-one years later we are still together, enjoying life with our two beautiful daughters, Carly and Falyn.

We moved to New Jersey after I had my first daughter, Carly. I wasn't happy about it, but there I was, stuck in the suburbs. I had quit my job (Allen says he retired me when we got married). My sister Marsha was still a fashion editor so I would spend time going with her to showrooms after Carly was born. My dream was always to have a little girl so I could dress her up, and now, with my sister's help, I indulged every fashion fantasy I had for little Carly. In order to get those fabulous styles home from the wholesalers I had to buy multiples. So I figured I would sell the extras to my girlfriends.

Every time I went to the park or into a store with Carly dressed in one of her unique ensembles, women would stop me and ask, "Where did you get that *adorable* outfit?" And I would say, "I sell them." So another business was born and soon I had three locations of clothing stores, which I called Mommy and Me. Even after we all moved back into the city, I was still running the stores in New Jersey. I actually started out selling only children's clothing but when one of my customers visited me at home and saw some dresses of mine hanging in my basement to dry she wanted to buy them. *Voila!* I was back in the women's fashion business.

Meanwhile, I still had a lot of single friends and I was always putting them together with each other. Every time I met someone single, I'd have a flash about which of my other friends he or she would be perfect for. Even when I was single I would always fix up ex-boyfriends with my girl-friends (to great success—a lot of them are married).

One of my single girlfriends suggested that I have a dinner party for all the single people I knew and all of their friends. I thought, "Yes, I would love to do that!" A neighborhood restaurant was willing to close on a Friday evening for the party. The first dinner was a huge success and people started asking to be put in my database. What *database?* But I called every-one I knew, word of mouth led to more people, and pretty soon the restau-rant found itself accommodating dinner parties for 100 people!

I formed my first singles' dinner party business with a partner and called it One Man, One Woman. When my partner decided to take a break I ran the parties on my own. Being the hostess with the mostest, I would make sure people met each other and circulated. After I got a call from the fourteenth woman saying that she was going to marry a man she had met at one of my parties, I looked at the phone in amazement, then looked at Allen, and said, "Honey, I think I'm a matchmaker."

Janis Spindel Serious Matchmaking, Inc. (JSSM) was born. Twelve years and over 700 marriages later, I have a staff of seven and a database of almost 10,000 *fantastic* singles. And I still love every minute of it. Bring-ing people together in marriage gives my life a dimension of happiness I can't describe. I get a jolt whenever I learn that two of my people (as I call them) are tying the knot.

Business really exploded after the *New York Times* did a story on JSSM in February 1999. Due to the enthusiastic response to the first story, the paper did a follow-up about a week later. My second gorgeous daughter, Falyn, was just born so I was obviously just a little bit busy and didn't even know about the second story. I remember checking my phone messages at some point and hearing that my voice mailbox was full. Odd, I thought to myself. How could I have more than 100 messages in less than a day?

There I was, three days later, simultaneously nursing little Falyn and returning 200 messages from eligible bachelors and bachelorettes. Need-less to say, my youngest daughter thinks her mother has a telephone attached to her ear. But she and Carly and Allen know that family always comes first for me, and I thank them all for letting me bring that message to other couples.

I'm good at matching couples because I adore people and I have good instincts about them. I also know and truly believe that every one of us has something valuable to offer another person. I'm not a scientist or an adver-tising executive or a Harvard MBA. I am an old-fashioned, modern-day matchmaker who understands what it takes to find a soul mate. And I will do just about anything to find the right person for a client. I have literally run down the street after men and women. I've stopped cabs, chased buses, gone shopping when I didn't need a thing, and walked into restaurants after I've already eaten—all in an effort to find wonderful people.

This book represents many years of learning what works and what doesn't work for women who are seeking a man to call "my husband." And why do I think you can make that happen in a year or less? I'll go into detail in the book, but the basic idea is that once you're ready to get out there and find your match, it doesn't take very long at all to figure out if someone is right for you or not. And I don't believe in long engagements—if you both want to get married, go for it! There's no good reason to wait. It really can be accomplished in a year, if you're focused and you follow the right steps.

My business is unique from other matchmaking companies I know of. First of all, the majority of my clients are men, not women. I screen the men who come to me very carefully to ensure that they are truly marriage-minded. I spend a great deal of time with my clients, getting to know their preferences and taste. Home visits give me an insight into their personal lives, their taste, and their level of sophistication. Lunch and dinner "dates" with these men show me how they will treat a potential mate when out on the town. Finally, listening to and observing my male clients has given me an enormous amount of insight into what men like and dislike about women.

Most of you should start at the beginning of the book and follow my tips and advice from beginning to end. I have ordered them in sequence for a reason: You have to prepare yourself well before you are ready to meet your mate. All the tips, techniques, and advice collected here are proven ways to help you realize your dreams of meeting Mr. Right and living happily ever after. It *can* happen, if it's what you truly want.

Good luck and happy hunting!

Love,
Janis

# *Part 1*
# PREPARATION
# IS EVERYTHING

*I* am not going to lie to you. In order to find a man whom *you* want to marry and who wants to marry you, you have to be your best self. You are simply not going to meet a fantastic person who is your equal unless you are in top condition. Today's dating environment is highly competitive and potentially stressful. Before you begin your quest, you must take some time to prepare yourself psychologically and physically. In Part 1 I'll take you through the steps you need to follow before you get out there. It's called *laying the groundwork*. You may want to rush ahead and just begin meeting people and dating. But hold on! My private clients have to go through the preparatory process, and so should you. It's worth it.

First, it's essential to prepare yourself mentally to make a good match. This means you have to focus on what's important to you in a relationship and in a man, and it means getting serious about priorities from children and pets to religion and politics.

Together, we'll prepare you physically as well. Appearance and health are two of *my* non-negotiables when it comes to being ready to enter the dating and mating scene. You have got to look and feel great! My favorite image consultants, beauty and makeup experts, doctors, diet and nutrition gurus, and I will share our secrets for assessing your look, style, and well-being—and we'll show you what you can do to improve them. We'll give you loads of tips on making changes that will result in a new, sexy, fashionable, fit, and fabulous you! Even details as seemingly minor as white teeth, shiny hair, and well-pedicured toes shouldn't be forgotten, so we'll deal with it all—from head to toe.

# One

# Get Serious About Who You Are and What You Want So You Can Get Ready to Find *Him!*

*I* assume you're reading this book because you want to fall in love and get married. How great is that? That's a wonderful, honorable goal. That's why I am not going to mess around. This book will take you through each step that gives women the best chance of meeting Mr. Right (as opposed to Mr. Right Now). For most women, Mr. Right is a man who is smart, successful, funny, kind, and attractive—a man of intelligence and quality—whether he's a stockbroker, a lawyer, fireman, or cowboy.

I think marriage is one of the greatest things on earth. Having someone to love, cry with, talk to, share life, and grow old with: *That's* sexy. *That's* wonderful. *That's* hip and cool and stylish. Don't let anyone tell you it's not. Some people scoff at those actively searching for a loving mate. I don't, not only because it's my business to help find people their soul mates, but also because I believe love and marriage are sacred. So don't, for a single second, feel embarrassed about making a conscious decision to look for a marriageable mate.

There's a lot of advice floating around about what women can do to meet and be attractive to men. Some of that advice I agree with. For example, being as pretty as you can be is classic wisdom and we'll deal with that later. But there's one aspect of meeting and enticing men that often gets overlooked, and it may be the most important part of preparing to go from single to married. And that's *you*.

The single biggest mistake women who want a committed relationship make is to look for someone without knowing what they themselves want from a man and from marriage. I *know* that you will not be successful in your search unless you have your priorities straight and you are very clear about the kind of man you will be happy with. That's because finding the right person to marry—to love—isn't all Kismet. It's not 100 percent magic. Yes, chemistry is important. But there are qualities and issues of character and even appearance in a man that are important to you and to every woman I know. Only after you have determined what's important to you—and what's not—can you begin your search honestly and seriously. You may think you know what you want in a man; you may even be positive about it. But take the time to do as I ask in this chapter anyway. You may be surprised! Determining your likes and dislikes and your hopes and dreams before you embark on this journey is time well spent!

This book is not about helping you get married just for the sake of getting married. I have known women and men who have done it that way, and the marriage usually doesn't end up very well. The tips and worksheets will help clarify what you're looking for. They will help you consider how important a host of issues are to you: values, goals, money, religion, politics, looks; even smoking and drinking. Once you have determined how you feel about these issues, you can move forward in your search with a lot more confidence. If a date or someone you meet doesn't match up with what I call your "non-negotiables," he probably isn't husband material and you can move on. What a relief that will be! No more wasting time on the wrong person.

Look, I know this attitude may sound a bit harsh. But I've met many women who have wasted *years* in relationships with the wrong man, hoping they will change. *They don't.* So don't rush ahead to the section on beauty and appearance. You may be saying, "Janis, I know what I want in a man, I don't have to think about it." I require each of my clients, both male and female, to fill out the detailed questionnaire you'll find in this chapter. It makes a difference to put your ideas in writing because seeing your preferences on paper will really help keep you focused. Making a promise to yourself about what you want in a relationship will make it that much harder to veer away from the standards you've set for yourself.

## 1. DETERMINE WHAT YOUR "NON-NEGOTIABLES" ARE

Qualities or attributes you've determined are essential for another person to possess are what I call your "non-negotiables." Be clear about them, because knowing what they are is a very important step in finding a mate. Your list will likely be diverse and include feelings about height and weight (physical appearance), smoking and drug-taking, religious affiliations, drinking and eating habits, and other general interests. A single redeeming characteristic doesn't add up to Mr. Right. If you meet someone who does not possess your non-negotiables, you should seriously consider moving on. You can't change a person's essential beliefs and behaviors. You might be able to polish superficial characteristics, such as a lack of personal style or clumsy social skills. But non-negotiables are permanent or may be extremely hard to change. Compromising on them usually leads to unhappiness, discontent, and even relationship disaster.

The questionnaire at the end of the chapter (pages 19–33) will help you figure out what your non-negotiables are.

## 2. ESTABLISH YOUR LONG-TERM GOALS

What do you want to accomplish in five, ten, even fifteen years? Where do you want to be living? What do you want to be doing professionally? The answers to these questions will help you determine the kind of person you want to be with. This step is as important as figuring out what your non-negotiables are. Your long-term goals must match those of your potential mate's. If two people have very different goals, it's going to be very challenging for them to make their relationship work. Once you admit to yourself what those goals are, you can bring them to bear in your search for a mate. One of my women, Alana, thirty-four, realized she wanted to move out of the city to the "country," Connecticut, to be specific. A lot of the guys she had been dating were committed New Yorkers—the rolling hills of New England didn't hold much interest for many of them, even in the guise of a weekend house. Alana knew she would eventually go nuts by being stuck in the concrete jungle. So she focused her efforts on meeting men who lived in Connecticut or outside of the city. She did this by traveling Metro North to commuter towns where she was interested in living, during rush hour! This put her in contact with a

## UP CLOSE AND PERSONAL
### *The Non-negotiable Disaster*

A client of mine, Rochelle, now a very young fifty, fell hard for Ron. And they were compatible—on the surface. They held many of the same values and political beliefs. They even shared the same passions for sports and opera. *How great is that?* One thing was missing, though, and it was one of Rochelle's "non-negotiables." She wanted the commitment of marriage and children, and that desire was also tied into her value system. But Ron didn't want marriage. He had been married once before and that was enough for him. I told Rochelle that a man with those feelings was not apt to change, and I begged her to let me introduce her to men who did share those non-negotiables with her. (Rochelle is a dead ringer for Elizabeth Taylor—it would have been no problem for me to find a fantastic man for her who *wanted* to marry her.) Rochelle didn't listen. She was in love with Ron and thought she could change him. After seven years of living together, it finally dawned on Rochelle that, sadly, Ron really wasn't going to marry her. She was now too old to have biological children of her own. Thanks to fertility treatments and adoption, Rochelle can still have a child. But she had to break up with Ron and start over. Rochelle is a beautiful woman and I know she will find someone who shares her passion for marriage and children. But it would have been easier and less painful eight years ago.

lot of men, both married and single. But the married men had single friends. As Alana chatted up her fellow riders, she made friends. She actually met a single guy (investment banker, I might add) on Metro North and now they are on the marriage train, headed for Connecticut.

## 3. DON'T BE TOO RIGID

*Not looking for your mate will result in not finding him.*

The flip side of figuring out your non-negotiables is pinpointing qualities you can live without. If your must-have-in-a-man list includes too many requirements, as in, "He must be a rich artist/broker with a penthouse apartment and a fantastic beach house, leather jacket, motorcycles, limousine, . . ." you *might* have to reevaluate! The point is to figure out what's important to you and lose everything else. Become open-minded—once you meet someone who has those non-negotiables going for him, chemistry *can* happen. For instance, I had to turn down a woman who came to me, since her requirement was "fifty-year-old widower with two children." This requirement narrows the field so drastically that it would have been almost impossible to find her a match. And the qualities of being a widower or having two children don't really define a person's character or personality, so I was not even sure why this specific profile was so important to her.

## 4. BE CANDID ABOUT YOUR VALUES

The two things that have to be in sync in order for a relationship to succeed are common goals and shared values. Values are somewhat different from non-negotiables, in that values define your very essence. For example, a non-negotiable can be something like never been married, non-smoker, and Jewish. Non-negotiables are attributes. Values, on the other hand, go deeper: They have to do with beliefs and ideas. For example, religion can be both a non-negotiable and a value. I have met women who want to marry only a Catholic man (or a Jewish man, etc.) and it's a non-negotiable. Some care about the degree to which the man practices his religion and some don't. I define that as a value. As one woman said to me, "I want to meet and marry a Catholic man, but I don't care whether he attends church every Sunday or is deeply religious. I am more concerned that he share the same background as I do."

If two people's values conflict, it will be very difficult for them to sustain a long-term, loving relationship. Physical attraction alone isn't going to hold together a couple who don't share the same hopes and dreams and the same cultural, social, and religious convictions. Not in my experience, anyway. This is why it's imperative to be honest about the "big questions": children, religion, sex, money, politics, and what you consider to be right and wrong. The questionnaire at the end of this chapter will help you. If you have conflicts with your mate about things that really matter to you, you may find it very difficult to reconcile these differences. If you do share goals and values with your partner, you'll be able to reach great heights together and accomplish many things, and your relationship will likely grow stronger with time.

## 5. LIST ALL THE PEOPLE YOU LIKE AND WRITE DOWN WHY AND WHAT YOU LIKE ABOUT THEM

The people you care about will have many of the qualities you want in a man. Don't you want your future husband to be both your lover *and* your friend? You may not think so during the first blush of passion—but a committed relationship requires that you find your mate sexually attractive *and* attractive on an intellectual and spiritual level, too. I have *never* met a happily married couple who only had sexual passion in common. Recognize the qualities you really love about your friends—it will help

## JANIS FACT

### TOP THREE THINGS THAT WOMEN WANT IN A MAN:

1. Intelligence
2. Sense of humor
3. Character and integrity

you see why they are important in a potential mate. And I guarantee you will find some surprises once you start thinking about why your friends are your friends. Some might be good listeners, and some may laugh at your bad jokes; some may always be willing to go to the movies with you when you're feeling low and lonely. Now, wouldn't all of those qualities be nice to have in a husband?

## 6. RECONNECT WITH YOURSELF

Get to know yourself! This is especially important if you have recently broken up with someone (more on that in Chapter 4). Sometimes, especially after a bad relationship, you might have a tendency to lose sight of yourself and your own needs. That's particularly true when you have been in a relationship that catered to the whims of your partner (which is a real no-no, by the way). Start spending time with *yourself* doing things *you* like to do—an extra bonus for later on, when you're ready to start a new relationship: You'll learn that being involved in things you enjoy can be a great way to meet men! Whether you enjoy old movies, crafting, cooking, antiquing, or reading, indulge yourself. You're in for some changes, so above all, be nice to yourself.

## 7. FABULOUS YOU

Create a list of your best qualities (preferably on a pretty pink sheet of paper) and tape it to the mirror where you do your hair and makeup. That way, you can read it every morning and be reminded of how great you are!

## 8. PUT THINGS IN PERSPECTIVE

First, things are never as bad as you think they are, and second, things can always get better, especially if you work at it. These are two ideas you should live by—especially when you are on the search for a mate, which *can* be overwhelming. It can also be overwhelmingly *wonderful.* That's why you have to keep every turn of event, every setback and accomplishment, and every opportunity, gained or missed, in perspective. Everything you are going through right now and in the future is just part of the larger picture. Each experience you have can be used to your advantage if you don't blow it out of proportion and you learn from it instead. For example, if you talk to a guy and he doesn't respond with interest, don't be dissuaded from trying again. He's just one person and not representative of the entire male species.

## 9. CREATE A "MEET AND MARRY THE MAN OF MY DREAMS IN ONE YEAR OR LESS" GET SERIOUS BUDGET

That's right—make a budget. (In Chapter 2, I will ask you to create another related budget for beauty and health changes.) If you really want to meet someone in a year or less, you are going to have to commit some funds to the project. It's not going to happen overnight and it won't be free. There are a lot of things you are going to have to do and participate in to improve your appearance and to meet new people. That can include traveling, attending social events, changing jobs, moving to a new city or state, hiring a matchmaker or other matchmaking service, getting beauty and cosmetic treatments, and so on. What can you afford to spend? How will you allocate it? Use the Get Serious budget worksheet in this chapter to get started.

## 10. STOP NEGATIVE THINKING—THIS SECOND

"I have no time to meet people." "There's no one at work or anyplace in my life that I'm interested in." "I just don't feel like putting myself out in the singles scene." "Single women are everywhere; I can't compete." "Men always gravitate to younger women." *ENOUGH!* I have heard it all before, and it's a waste of time to:

1. Put yourself down.

2. Think that you're a hopeless case.

3. Believe "the one" for you isn't out there.

Negative thinking affects your looks, general attitude, and demeanor. Pessimism will have a detrimental impact on your chances of meeting

# THE GET SERIOUS BUDGET

What I can spend now                              $ _____

What I can spend _____ months from now            $ _____


Total overall estimated budget                    $ _____
*(See below for specifics, which should add
up to the total overall budget, above.)*


## ALLOCATION
*(Note: Some of these items may not apply to your
particular circumstances, so please allocate
according to your own situation.)*

Travel                                            $ _____

Changing jobs                                     $ _____
*(Take wardrobe, increase or decrease in salary, and
commuting changes into consideration.)*

Move to new city                                  $ _____

Matchmaking services                              $ _____

   Internet                        $ _____

   Matchmaker                      $ _____

   Classified ads                  $ _____

Beauty services                                   $ _____
*(Take this total from Chapter 2 beauty budget
worksheet, page 39.)*

Clothing                                          $ _____

Therapist                                         $ _____

Social events                                     $ _____
*(This can include any "public" event where you
will meet people, from sporting events to dinners
out to charity benefits.)*

someone new. Banish bad thoughts *NOW!* In fact, every time you start thinking negative thoughts, consciously stop yourself and replace them with happy, positive thoughts. Avoid watching too much bad news because it can waste time better spent elsewhere and can have a negative effect on your mood. For example, read one newspaper to keep abreast of current events, but don't get bogged down by watching news show after news show. Listen to music that makes you happy. Engage in activities that are productive and energy increasing, such as walking, swimming, and dancing.

## 11. DESCRIBE YOURSELF

In the questionnaire at the end of this chapter, I ask you to create a personal "word photograph." This is an important exercise because it allows you to think about what you like and dislike about who you are. Describe both your appearance and your inner being. Keep this description in a notebook, where you can update or revise it as you go through the steps in this book. As you work on your appearance and as you get to know yourself and what you're looking for, that "word photograph" may very well change. It will be enlightening and encouraging for you to see how this reflection evolves as you make changes in your attitude, appearance, and health.

## 12. LIST THE THINGS YOU DON'T KNOW HOW TO DO BUT WOULD LOVE TO LEARN AND EVEN MASTER

Do you want to know how to make a soufflé? Sail a boat? Ski? Paint? Draw? Operate a hot air balloon? It doesn't really matter how wild your dreams are. Write them down. Once you have made the list, you can use it as a starting point to try new things. Later on, in the dating section, I am going to ask you to try some new things in order to get out and meet people. Figuring out what intrigues you now lays the groundwork for adventures later on. Plus, taking the time to dream about all the things you would like to accomplish is a great way of learning a little bit more about yourself and the kind of mate you are looking for.

## 13. KNOW WHAT MAKES YOU REALLY HAPPY

Write down all the things you really love in the world—sunsets, champagne, chocolate, scary movies, cashmere sweaters, and sleeping 'til noon. The sky's the limit here. I want you to focus on all the things that make you *purrr* with joy. Then, I want you to indulge in a few of them (but watch the calories, please!) whenever you're feeling a little overwhelmed.

## 14. KNOW WHAT GETS YOU CRAZY

Write down all your pet peeves. Rude people, nasty waiters, snobby colleagues, nosy neighbors, polyester, blue eyeshadow, fat-free ice cream. *Whatever!* Seeing what you don't like will help you avoid it later on. Life's too short to waste on annoying people, places, and things!

## 15. REFUSE TO BE A VICTIM

Make it a priority right now not to stay in a relationship for more than five minutes with someone who doesn't treat you well and with respect. It doesn't matter how physically attractive you find a person, or how much he *seems* to be smitten with you—if you are "doing for him" and he is not "doing for you," there's something wrong. And if he is rude, disrespectful, or God forbid, violent or nasty, don't waste another second with him. Being a victim in a relationship doesn't lead anywhere worthwhile. Too many women stay in abusive relationships or they settle for what I call *psychological starvation.* And then they get into a vicious circle of playing the victim with their friends, families, and themselves. Make it a priority to spend time with only those people who honor your self-worth, whether they be boyfriends or potential boyfriends or friends in general of either sex.

## 16. BE A HERO

Being heroic means directing yourself outwardly, not inwardly. Do something nice for a stranger, smile more, bring a co-worker a cup of coffee, volunteer at the local food co-op or hospital. Giving of yourself in generous ways can expand your spiritual horizons. And frankly, making someone else happy, even if it's just for an afternoon, will have the added benefit of making you feel good about yourself and giving a huge boost to your self-confidence. And doing something for someone else, especially someone new, opens up your world and puts yourself in a different "place" emotionally and physically—and it might be just the place where your future husband resides!

## 17. GET HELP!

Look, I'm not saying you're nuts. Far from it. I *am* saying that we all have "issues," especially surrounding relationships. So if you aren't seeing a shrink, find a good one now. If you are already seeing a professional and feel you aren't making enough progress, consider changing therapists.

A therapist can help identify those characteristics that might be holding you back, and can help you work through these mental blocks. She (or he) can also help you work through insecurities and fears that may be keeping you from being attracted to the right person. A good mental health professional can also help you define and zero in on the things that are really important to you. Why not bring your list of non-negotiables in for review for your next visit? Start discussing your desire to get married with your doctor if you haven't already.

There's a temptation to depend on friends for "therapy," but it's not a good idea. Friends have their own agendas, aren't trained, and have a tendency not to be honest with you. A "disinterested" third party such as a psychotherapist has the dispassion, education, and experience to give you the support you need.

## 18. TURN ON YOUR INNER LIGHT

Single people are like taxicabs. If their lights aren't on, no one is going to hail them. So make sure your light is on! That means looking your best (see Chapter 2) and exuding confidence and energy! Smile! Be friendly, open, and considerate. Make sure everyone you meet knows you are available—not in a sleazy or sexual kind of way, but in a way that says, "I'm friendly and approachable and if you say hello to me I'll say hello back."

## 19. MONEY MATTERS

Many men, I am sorry to say, still think women are interested in them for their money, but in my experience that couldn't be further from the truth. Most of my female clients have great jobs and interesting careers. They don't need anyone to buy them dinner, take them on a vacation, or help them financially. They don't need a man for his money. They have their own. But women *do* want security. And most successful women want to be with a man who can hold his own and be on the same financial plane as they are. It can be difficult to be with a man if he is making substantially less money than you are. That situation can be harder on him than it is on you (you may not care—but he will!). The resentment or insecurity it may breed in him can be damaging to a relationship. So you have to do some hard thinking about the financial qualities you are looking for in a man. Think about where you are in life financially, and where you will be five or ten years down the road. Do you want your partner to be at the same place? If it really doesn't matter to you, fine. But remember that it may matter from his point of view, and that could kill an otherwise great relationship.

If you do end up dating someone substantially less well off than you, be prepared to reassure him if any insecurity pops up. Susan, thirty-seven, a savvy and sexy TV actress, makes lots of money and lives a very sophisticated life. Her beau, Joseph, a slightly younger man (thirty-four, but who's counting?) is a television producer and makes a lot less money. Susan never hesitates to buy gifts for him or treat him to dinner. But he takes Susan out, too. And she doesn't make the salary difference an issue by going out of her way to impress her earning power upon Joseph. "I don't deny myself anything," says Susan, "but I make it clear that everything that Joseph offers me in terms of love, companionship, and romance is beyond price."

Dating or marrying a man whose means far outweigh yours isn't as dreamy as it sounds. You have to be prepared to live up to the expectations of that lifestyle. Ask yourself if you are ready, willing, and able to cope with many different social functions and obligations. If expectations are too high, you may find yourself in too deep.

## 20. BE REALISTIC

Indulge in dreams, fantasies, and flights of fancy once in a while as a way to expand your imagination. But you also have to come down to earth at some point and really look at your life. After you have assessed where you are and where you want to be in the future, you have to accept that you may have to make some changes—to your appearance, your lifestyle, maybe even where you live and what you do for a living! You also might have to come to grips with the fact that you might not meet that Brad Pitt look-alike. I am *not* suggesting that you "settle" for anything less than what you want. I *am* saying that you have to realize that images of love you see on TV and movies and read about in books are fairy tales. Real life offers challenges not always considered in fiction.

## 21. BE HONEST

You have to be honest about what you want from a relationship (marriage, children, lifelong companionship, etc.). From the outset, you have to make a commitment to be honest with potential mates about yourself and your feelings. That doesn't mean telling everyone what you think all the time. It *does* mean that you should not tell someone you love him if you don't. Don't carry on in a relationship if you *know* it's not going where you want it to go. You should not do things you don't feel good about doing (like having sex too early in a relationship). It means not leading someone on just to be "nice" when you are not interested in him. And it means being honest with yourself about where you are in life and what you can do to change it.

## 22. FORGIVE, FORGET, AND *MOVE ON*

Sometimes when a relationship ends badly or you've been "dumped" by a boyfriend, you can hold yourself back from finding a new, healthy, and happy relationship. You simply can't forgive him, forget him and the pain he caused, and move on. But unless you can let go, you'll have trouble being open to enjoying new friendships. If you've had that experience, don't believe you can never go out with a man again. Don't punish yourself by overeating, drinking, taking drugs, working without looking up, or closing yourself off. I've seen it happen, and it's ugly. Believe me, *he's* not going to suffer because you're angry and taking it out on yourself. *Get over it! NOW!* If this is a situation you currently find yourself in, please read Chapter 4 right away.

## 23. GET BUSY!

"When you stop looking, you'll find him." Since you can't see me, I'll tell you right now I am rolling my eyes and groaning. This is the single worst, most inaccurate "truism" I have ever heard. Not looking for your mate will result in not finding him. You have to actively participate in finding yourself a mate. If not, you will not be in the right place at the right time. You will not look your best or feel your best when "it" happens. Everywhere you go and everything you do from now on presents an opportunity to meet someone. If you are busy, involved in life, and, most of all, out there "looking," your chances of finding a mate increase 1,000-fold. I don't mean coming on strong or pouncing on every single man you meet. Being busy and involved in looking doesn't mean you should be desperate or obsequious.

Do not put off your search until some indefinite time when your life changes. You've heard it before: "I'll do it when I lose twenty pounds," "I'll do it when I find a new job," "I'll do it next week, after the work deadline is past." And on and on it goes. You can procrastinate until you wake up one day and realize you're fifty-five, have never been married, and are *still* waiting for the work deadline to pass. It never does. Seize the day! Don't waste time. You'll find loads of suggestions on how to do just that in the following chapters, so having no imagination is not an option. There are plenty of ideas here to get you started.

## 24. CLEAN UP YOUR ACT . . .

Now's the time to get your "life house" in order. Make sure you have no nagging responsibilities to take care of, and if you do, complete them and get them off your plate. Ensure that you have the time and psychological space to go on your quest for the perfect mate. If you have major tasks and obligations hanging over your head (a big project that's due at work, reciprocating visits to friends and family, or getting your taxes done), take care of them so you can be free and clear to devote your energies to finding a mate. Unnecessary distractions will only hold you back.

## 25. . . . AND YOUR HOUSE

And while you're at it, clean out your closets, re-cover shabby furniture (or buy new if you can afford it), donate mismatched glasses and dishes, and keep only the things you love around you. Your home is going to become dating central one of these days, and you might as well get it cleaned up now. It's also the time to get rid of any vestige of past relationships. That means photos, his clothes or furniture, or anything that reminds you of *him* and your life together. If you can't bear to sift through it, donate what you can and put the rest in a box in an out-of-the-way place. In a few months, check back and see if you're ready to toss it!

## 26. SAY BYE-BYE (TO ANYONE WHO MAKES YOU MISERABLE)

Clear your Palm or Rolodex of friends who aren't really friends, colleagues who make you crazy, old boyfriends who won't stop calling, and annoying cousins (or other relatives) who ask *way* too much of your generosity and time. When someone looks like trouble or just keeps you from doing the things you need to do to be happy, delete them—from your address book, your computer, your Palm, and your life!

## 27. LOVE YOURSELF!

Finally—and this is a big one—love yourself. Treat yourself with respect. Eat food that's good for you, wear clothes that are flattering to your figure, listen to beautiful music, and spend time with friends you love. Be good to yourself every day.

# JANIS'S QUESTIONNAIRE

The more honestly and completely you answer this questionnaire, the better you'll understand exactly what you want in a man. Your chances of finding the right match will increase and your chances of wasting time on men who don't fulfill your criteria will decrease. If something is unimportant to you here, make a note of it. When you have completed this form, you will have a pretty exacting picture of what you really want in a man! Keep your answers in mind, along with your non-negotiables, whenever you meet someone. Go back to it and review whenever you feel you're slipping into old patterns or making big compromises.

## YOUR GENERAL PREFERENCES IN A MAN

1. I prefer to date a person whose age is between_____ and _____.

2. I prefer someone who is:
   - ☐ Divorced/separated
   - ☐ Single/never been married
   - ☐ Widowed

3. How close in miles should a prospective partner live?
   - ☐ Far away (I like to travel!)
   - ☐ In another city
   - ☐ In my neighborhood, within walking distance
   - ☐ In the same city or town as I live in
   - ☐ Within driving distance (one or two hours away)
   - ☐ Doesn't matter

4. I prefer a man's height to be _____.

5. I prefer a man's build to be:
   - ☐ Average
   - ☐ Doesn't matter

- ☐ Heavy
- ☐ Muscular
- ☐ Slightly overweight
- ☐ Slim

6. I prefer a man's hair color to be:
   - ☐ Blond
   - ☐ Brown
   - ☐ Black
   - ☐ Red
   - ☐ Gray
   - ☐ Doesn't matter

7. I prefer a man's eye color to be:
   - ☐ Blue
   - ☐ Brown
   - ☐ Green
   - ☐ Gray
   - ☐ Hazel

8. I want a man to be very physically fit.
   - ☐ Yes
   - ☐ No
   - ☐ Doesn't matter

9. I like a man who:
   - ☐ Doesn't have an interest in sports
   - ☐ Is active
   - ☐ Is athletic and loves sports
   - ☐ Is sedentary

10. My racial/ethic preferences are:
  - ☐ Caucasian
  - ☐ African-American
  - ☐ Asian-American
  - ☐ Latino
  - ☐ European
  - ☐ Other
  - ☐ Absolutely does not matter to me

11. My religious preferences are:
  - ☐ Catholic
  - ☐ Jewish
  - ☐ Muslim
  - ☐ Protestant
  - ☐ Other
  - ☐ Doesn't matter

12. How religious should a man be?
  - ☐ Moderately
  - ☐ Not at all
  - ☐ Very

13. It is okay if a man:
  - ☐ Drinks moderately/socially
  - ☐ Gambles
  - ☐ Smokes
  - ☐ Takes drugs

14. I prefer a man who:
  - ☐ Has children living with him
  - ☐ Has children who do not live with him full time

□ Has no children

□ Doesn't matter

15. Which, if any, of the following living arrangements would you find *objectionable*?

□ Lives alone

□ Lives with children

□ Lives with parent(s)

□ Lives with pets

□ Lives with roommates

□ Lives with sibling or other relative

16. Minimum income level that would be important to you:

□ $30,000–$50,000

□ $50,000–$100,000

□ $100,000–$200,000

□ $200,000–$300,000

□ Over $300,000

17. Preferred occupations (if it doesn't matter, make a note of it):

_____

_____

_____

_____

_____

18. A man should be:

□ Analytical and good at debating or making a convincing argument

□ Artistic

□ Good with numbers

□ Interested in museums and culture

- ☐ Mechanically inclined and/or knows how to use power tools
- ☐ Musical
- ☐ Scientific-minded
- ☐ Able to call a repairman

19. Education level completed:
    - ☐ High school
    - ☐ College
    - ☐ Graduate school
    - ☐ Law school
    - ☐ Medical school

20. Is there anything else that's important to you?

    _____

    _____

    _____

    _____

    _____

## QUALITIES QUIZ

Please circle or list, from the qualities list on page 25, your top ten *essential* qualities in a man (seeing them in black and white may prompt you to realize important qualities that you may not be conscious of!):

1. _____
2. _____
3. _____
4. _____
5. _____
6. _____
7. _____

8. _____

9. _____

10. _____

Please list the ten qualities that would be nice to have in a man, but are not essential:

1. _____

2. _____

3. _____

4. _____

5. _____

6. _____

7. _____

8. _____

9. _____

10. _____

Please list the ten qualities that are completely unimportant to you in a man:

1. _____

2. _____

3. _____

4. _____

5. _____

6. _____

7. _____

8. _____

9. _____

10. _____

# QUALITIES LIST

Absent-minded
Adventurous
Affectionate ·
Aggressive
Agreeable
Anxious
Arrogant
Attentive
Brave
Calm
Capable
Cautious
Charming
Common-
   sensical
Communicative ·
Competitive
Complimentary
Conceited
Confident ·
Conservative
Controlling
Conventional
Creative
Critical
Cynical
Decisive
Defensive
Demanding
Dependent
Depressed
Disorganized
Domestic
Dominant

Doubting
Down to earth
Easygoing
Emotional
Enthusiastic
Ethical
Excitable
Extravagant
Flexible
Forceful
Forward
Friendly
Funny ·
Fussy
Generous
Gentle
Good listener
Good
   personality
Happy ·
Honest ·
Hot-tempered
Idealistic
Imaginative
Impatient
Impersonal
Impulsive
Independent
Inhibited
Intellectual
Intelligent
Inquisitive
Jealous
Kind

Lenient
Liberal
Loud
Loving
Loyal
Macho
Mellow
Moderate
Modest
Monogamous ·
Moody
Naïve
Neat
Opinionated
Organized
Outgoing
Outspoken
Passionate ·
Passive
Patient
Perfectionist
Pessimistic
Physical
Physically fit
Playful
Positive
Possessive
Prudish
Punctual
Reserved
Responsible
Restless
Rigid
Risk-taker

Romantic ·
Sarcastic
Secretive
Self-conscious
Self-effacing
Selfish
Self-sacrificing
Sense of humor
Sensitive
Sensual
Sentimental
Serious
Sexy
Shy
Snobby
Sophisticated
Spoiled
Stern
Straightforward
Street-smart
Stubborn
Style-conscious
Submissive
Sweet
Talkative
Thoughtful
Thrifty
Tough
Trusting
Unconventional
Uninhibited
Warm
Wild

## INTERESTS QUIZ

Using the list below, please write down ten interests it would be important for a man to have and the top ten interests you have that would be important for a man to understand or take part in:

His interests:

1. _____
2. _____
3. _____
4. _____
5. _____
6. _____
7. _____
8. _____
9. _____
10. _____


Your interests:

1. _____
2. _____
3. _____
4. _____
5. _____
6. _____
7. _____
8. _____
9. _____
10. _____

# INTERESTS LIST

Acting

Adventurous
  or extreme sports

Antique cars

Antiques

Art (painting, etc.)

Astrology

Ballet/dance
  performances

Ballroom
  dancing

Baseball

Bicycling

Bird-watching

Board games

Books/literature

Boating (speed-
  boating/yachting)

Bowling

Bridge

Camping

Car racing
  (seeing/doing)

Card games

Cars (new/sports)

Casinos/gambling

"Cat person"

Charity or
  volunteer work

Classical music

Comedy clubs

Computers

Concerts

Cooking

Country &
  Western music

Crafts

Cruises

Dining out

"Dog person"

Entertaining

Filmmaking

Fishing

Flea marketing

Flying

Folk dancing

Gardening

Going to the beach

Going to the city

Going to the country

Health food

Hiking

Horse racing

Horseback riding

Hunting

Ice-skating

Jazz

Jogging/running

Languages (speaking)

Latin dancing

Lifting weights

Motorcycles

Movies

Museums

News

Opera

Partying

Pets/animals

Photography

Playing instrument

Politics

Pool

Pop/rock dancing

Racquetball/squash

Rock/contemporary
  music

Roller-skating/
  -blading

Sailing

Scuba diving

Shopping

Sight-seeing

Singing

Skiing

Soccer

Square dancing

Swimming

Talking on the phone

Tennis

Theater/plays/
  musicals

*This Old House* pro

Traveling abroad

TV

Volleyball

Walking

Water sports

Wine tasting

Working on cars

Working out

Woodworking/
  carpentry

Wrestling/boxing
  (as a spectator)

Wrestling/boxing
  (as a participant)

Writing

Yoga

# RELATIONSHIP ATTITUDES QUIZ

This quiz will give you a good picture of how you think a relationship should evolve—and what you really expect from a date. Sometimes women tell themselves one thing but really believe another. If you're honest, this little test will help you see what you would really like in a man. Later, we'll talk about attitudes that you might think about loosening up as well as those that you should not.

1. Who do you feel should pay for a date?
   - ☐ Share expenses
   - ☐ The man
   - ☐ The woman

2. Do you think the man should always ask the woman out?
   - ☐ No
   - ☐ Yes

3. Sex is appropriate:
   - ☐ In a long-term relationship, regardless of commitment
   - ☐ When you are attracted to someone
   - ☐ Within a committed relationship
   - ☐ Only after marriage

4. You are sexually:
   - ☐ Moderate
   - ☐ Somewhat disinterested
   - ☐ Very passionate
   - ☐ Warm

5. Sex in a relationship is:
   - ☐ Everything
   - ☐ Not important at all

☐ Somewhat important

☐ Very important

6. When you are in a relationship, how much time do you like to spend with your partner?

    ☐ All the time

    ☐ Most of the time

    ☐ Only on weekends

    ☐ Some of the time

7. You are a person who can be described as:

    ☐ A homebody—you enjoy spending time at home, cooking, doing things around the house, yard, etc., and are not particularly social (unless it's required)

    ☐ A person who wants to be out and about a lot—on the town, shopping, visiting friends, socializing, going to the movies, theatre, etc., and who does not like to do things around the house

    ☐ A combination—you enjoy being at home and going out

8. In a relationship, you like to see your friends and do things without your partner:

    ☐ Never

    ☐ Often

    ☐ Sometimes

9. What else can you say that's "essential" or key to your lifestyle right now?

_____

_____

_____

_____

10. Your stage in life right now is:
    - ☐ You are just beginning to build a career
    - ☐ You are on top of and actively involved in your career
    - ☐ You want to start raising a family
    - ☐ You have a settled lifestyle that you are happy with
    - ☐ You are still raising children and are newly divorced/separated
    - ☐ You have completed raising a family and want to start on a new lifestyle
    - ☐ You are looking for someone who can enjoy your retirement with you

11. As far as children are concerned, you:
    - ☐ Have no children and would like to have a child (children)
    - ☐ Have a child (children) and do not want more
    - ☐ Have a child (children) but would like to have more
    - ☐ Would like to adopt a child (children)
    - ☐ Have no children and have no interest in having children

12. Your long-term goals are:

    _____

    _____

    _____

    _____

    _____

This last question is *extremely* important because it will give you an idea of the kind of man you have been attracted to in the past. Awareness of similarities between them will help you recognize patterns that you may wish to avoid. Please choose (using the qualities list on page 25, if you want) the first five qualities that describe your last three romantic partners, including ex-husband(s):

Partner 1: _____

_____

Partner 2: _____

_____

Partner 3: _____

_____

## "ME" QUIZ

These questions will show you what you like or dislike in life on a personal level. Your answers will come in handy later, when we get to the dating section of the book (and your life!):

My most avid interests are: (Use the interests list on page 27)

_____

_____

My dream vacation is:

_____

_____

My favorite restaurants are:

_____

_____

My favorite magazines are:

_____

_____

My all-time favorite movies are:

_____

_____

My favorite plays or shows are:
_____
_____

My favorite musical groups/musicians are:
_____
_____

My favorite spectator sports are:
_____
_____

My favorite sports to play are:
_____
_____

My favorite vacation spots are:
_____
_____

My favorite cities in the world are:
_____
_____

Things that make me really happy are:
_____
_____

What gets me completely crazy:
_____
_____

In my free time, I like to:
_____
_____

How I feel about my career/profession:

_____

_____

How I feel about my relationship with my family:

_____

_____

My greatest assets are:

_____

_____

My greatest shortcomings are:

_____

_____

A verbal/word photograph of how I see myself (personality, beliefs, values, who I am):

_____

_____

I would describe the person I'd really like to meet as someone who is:

_____

_____

Two or three people I admire most:

_____

_____

If I could have three wishes granted, they would be:

1. _____

2. _____

3. _____

Now that you've completed the questionnaire and exercises in this chapter, put your answers away for a day. After twenty-four or forty-eight hours, take a look at your answers. Now that you're "fresh," the clear picture of yourself and the kind of man you are really looking for will be evident. You should have a good handle on the values and qualities that you want. Stick to your guns and don't compromise on the big stuff, and be willing to overlook the unimportant qualities that do not contribute to a man's true character. Now you are in a better position to make good decisions about potential mates. And you will be better able to teach yourself to find diamonds in the rough.

Refer to this questionnaire throughout the process outlined in the book. See if any of your desires and opinions have changed or evolved and make a note of them. This way, you can see your own progress as someone who has started to take love and life seriously.

# Two

# Look Great and Feel Great

I've been on breakfast, lunch, and dinner dates with more than 7,600 men. That's a lot of food! When I first consider taking a man on as a client, I require him to take me out. It's a good test of potential clients because it shows me how a man thinks, acts, and will most likely treat a woman when they're on a date. By looking at everything he does, from how he treats the waitstaff to how he deals with me, I am able to predict a lot about his dating savvy and manners—in other words, how he will treat *you* on a *real* date. (Luckily, my husband doesn't mind—he knows that going out with men is part of my business as a matchmaker. Plus, I have an *adorable* husband, and I'm crazy about him, so no other man can hold my interest the way he does!)

From those thousands of dates and meetings with men, and the post-mortem conversations I've had with men (and women) after they've gone on dates I have arranged for them, I've learned what makes men tick—and what they want in women. Here it is, the unvarnished truth: Men are attracted to pretty women. It doesn't matter where you live—New York City or Salt Lake City, town or country, high-rise or ranch—men want to meet, date, and marry women they find attractive. There it is, I've said it. *LOOKS COUNT.* Along with a whole lot of other things, of course. Many men also want to be with smart, sophisticated women from good families—women who have strong values and can hold their own in any situation.

First and foremost, though, men are visual. Even men who have a casual style want their dates to dress up and to look beautiful. Looks are what all the men I have ever met say they notice *first* about a woman. Women, on the other hand, are much more tolerant and flexible about men's looks and move beyond them more quickly than men do. A man has to feel some aesthetic pull from a woman—he has to find her attractive first. Of course, beauty is in the eye of the beholder, and different men define beauty differently.

In order to compete in the dating world you have to do *everything* you can to look your personal best. Your appearance has to be one of your top priorities. It's not shallow, frivolous, or silly to care about the way you look. Even naturally great-looking, stylish women can stand to update their wardrobe or hair. And there are other benefits to looking your best all the time: Not only will you be more likely to attract the kind of man you are looking for, you're likely to see a difference in other areas of your life—your self-image and even your job. Studies show that attractive people are thought of as smarter, more successful, and nicer than people who aren't perceived as attractive. Some people may feel this is a sad fact of life. Perhaps, but I don't think so. The good news is that improving your appearance is within your reach.

If you are reentering the dating game after a breakup or a divorce, it's especially important to do an appearance revamp. You may have become as comfortable with your "old" look as you were with your old relationship. That's because some people in relationships feel they can stop doing the little things that enhance their looks. Over time, they may have gotten comfortable looking messy or sloppy. I disagree with this concept, by the way—I think it's important to always look great for your boyfriend or husband, too!

Creating an attractive look by enhancing your best features needn't be time-consuming or fussy. In fact, it shouldn't be. Your style and beauty routine can and should be fairly simple. Men don't like a lot of frilly, complex clothing or makeup that is applied with a heavy hand. Men like classic, sexy, up-to-date styles—and most women look best in these kinds of clothes. They also want women to look polished but natural and unmade-up. Ironically, you can only achieve this look by using makeup! (Later in the chapter, I'll explain how.) Most trends are for teenagers, not adults. Looking fashionable and stylish, however, *is* for grown-ups, and there's no reason why you can't look terrific and up to date without being a fashion victim. Remember that great style is individual: The clothes worn on the iconic television series *Sex and the City*, for example, are not for everyone. In fact, very few women can carry off extremely fashion-forward, highly sexy clothes, especially if you work in a traditional office. Those kinds of clothes work for very specific lifestyles. And by the way, the "hooker look" is never popular with men seeking a serious relationship. Most men I know use that *specific* expression in describing the appearance of women they *don't* want to date.

I also believe that every woman, no matter her age, can look age-appropriate, "youthful," and sexy. Coco Chanel once said that there are no ugly women, only lazy ones. You have to take the time to learn how to enhance your best features, minimize your figure flaws, and wear the right makeup and hairstyle for your face and age. I'll go back to my original conviction—looks count! See that *awesome* guy at the newsstand? He could be your future husband, and you'd better look good the next time you run into him.

## 28. MAKE A BEAUTY BUDGET

You have to devote serious resources to your fashion and beauty redo. There are a lot of improvements that are free (smile more, stand up

JANIS FACT

**TOP THREE QUALITIES THAT
MEN LOOK FOR IN A WOMAN:**

1. Great looks
2. Thin body
3. Younger than they are (but not necessarily "young")

straight), but makeup, hair care, beauty treatments, and cosmetic procedures cost money. And some of them present a substantial investment. That means you have to make a financial commitment to make yourself look as beautiful as possible—and it's worth the price. Creating a budget (using the worksheet provided) will allow you to see exactly how much you can spend now and how much you need to save for other expenditures. Don't have any qualms or guilt about spending as much money as you can afford on your appearance—it's your calling card.

Please note that this budget is a subset of the overall budget in Chapter 1 (page 11). The grand total here should be transferred to the Beauty Services section of that worksheet to help you calculate your meet-a-man grand total.

## 29. THROW IT OUT!

Check out the questionnaire at the end of this chapter, graciously provided by my image consultant Elena Castaneda. It will help you assess your look and figure out what you might need to do to change it. Professionals can help overhaul your wardrobe—but you're smart. You know something about your own taste, lifestyle, and comfort level. Now is the time to look at your clothing and ruthlessly edit. You can make a *huge* difference in your wardrobe simply by throwing out anything that is damaged, stained, ripped, or otherwise worn out. Next, try on everything remaining and get rid of clothes that don't fit—whether they're too big or too small. (See **Tip 31. The Fit's the Thing,** for advice). After that, discard all items that are out of style (for example, wide shoulder pads and pleated pants are dated and can be unflattering). By the time you are through you will have the bare bones of your wardrobe. At this point you can more easily judge what you need to buy.

## 30. BUY CLOTHES FOR THE BODY YOU HAVE, NOT FOR THE BODY YOU'D LIKE TO HAVE

Midriff tops, low-slung pants, spaghetti strap T-shirts, and white jeans are great, but they don't look good on everyone. Image consultant Elena Castaneda says that when you are considering buying new clothing, be sure

# BEAUTY BUDGET WORKSHEET

What I can spend right now                                          $ _____

What I can spend _____ months from now          $ _____

Overall estimated budget                                           $ _____

## ALLOCATIONS

**Big-ticket services:**

Image consultant                                                        $ _____

Professional teeth whitening                                      $ _____

Plastic surgery                                                           $ _____

Other                                                                         $ _____

**Expensive services and products:**

Personal shopper                                                      $ _____

Makeup artist                                                            $ _____

New clothes                                                              $ _____

Contact lenses, new glasses                                    $ _____

Other                                                                        $ _____

**Moderate services and products:**

Haircut and color                                                     $ _____

Pedicure and manicure                                            $ _____

New accessories                                                      $ _____

Massage                                                                  $ _____

Spa treatments                                                       $ _____

Shoes                                                                     $ _____

Other                                                                      $ _____

**Inexpensive items and services:**

Over-the-counter teeth-whitening products           $ _____

Professional blow-out                                              $ _____

One makeup session                                               $ _____

Hose and undergarments                                        $ _____

Casual clothing                                                        $ _____

Other                                                                       $ _____

that it's not only fashionable, but that it looks good on you, too. Clothing should be the right style for your age, height, weight, and build. All clothing should fit you properly. Clothes that are too small will make you look heavier; ditto for clothing that's too big. If you are in the process of losing weight or changing the shape of your body, you should still wear clothes that fit you correctly *now*. Stick to classic silhouettes while losing weight. When you reach your goal weight, or after you've completed any body work you may be doing, *then* you can treat yourself to some new, well-fitting clothes.

## 31. THE FIT'S THE THING

Everyone is unique, and a professional image consultant can help you best judge a good fit. A friend can't be objective, and you cannot always depend on her to tell you the truth. There are basics, however, that you can consider when trying anything on.

Elena says everything you wear should feel comfortable and easy to move in. If a piece of clothing tugs or pulls when you move, it should stay on the rack. Anything too tight should be left in the dressing room. What's too tight? If a skirt outlines your derriere and pulls so tightly you can see lines across your front, it's too tight. If you have to strain or suck in to button pants, they're too small. If a blouse buckles across your chest when you button it, it doesn't fit and you shouldn't wear it. Basically, if something feels taut or doesn't offer you freedom of movement, it's probably too small. Clothes that are too large (if you can fit your hand easily into the waist of a skirt or pants, they're too big) are also unflattering. Baggy pants, "big" shirts, and loose dresses are not particularly fashionable, nor are they terribly attractive or flattering. If you think big clothes are disguising your figure flaws or excess weight, you're wrong. And men don't like them. Clothes should lie flat and skim your body.

## 32. GET RID OF IT!

Regardless of your age, none of the following items should be in your closet, and they certainly should not be part of your dating wardrobe!

These wardrobe wreckers can also wreck your chances of impressing Mr. Right.

1. Novelty socks (kittens and toasters on your ankles just do not make it!)

2. Neon or frosted lipsticks and nail polishes

3. Black lipstick and nail polish

4. Hair bands, headbands, "scrunchies," or elastics, unless you're working out. In that case, make sure whatever you are using to hold your hair back looks pretty, clean, and neat.

5. Fuzzy sweaters that "shed"

6. Heavy, black-rimmed glasses

7. Peg-legged pants that stop above the ankle (the *only* woman they ever flattered was Audrey Hepburn)

8. Baggy sweats

9. White tights (unless you're an on-duty nurse!)

10. Thick black fishnets with seams

11. Oversized T-shirts with sayings on them

## 33. HIRE AN IMAGE CONSULTANT

Hiring a style pro is one of the most important investments in yourself that you can make. I urge you to create room in your budget to hire a professional image consultant. A well-trained style expert can help you develop and enhance self-confidence by improving your overall appearance. She will likely begin by asking you a lot of the questions found in the worksheet at the end of this chapter. Then she will want to go "shopping" in your closet and begin working with the clothing and accessories you already own. Next, she will take you to a department store and boutiques to help you select anything you need to complete your wardrobe. She will also help you choose the best makeup and hairstyle and can recommend appropriate fitness programs and cosmetic procedures if necessary.

Unlike a friend, an image consultant has no agenda other than to help you achieve your best look. She's completely objective and without an ulterior motive. She should be trained in fashion and design so she really does know, from a technical standpoint, what styles work for you. An image consultant can work with your specific needs, body type, and taste to help you find a look that is unique to you. The advice in this section and in any other book on style and fashion is general. It's a start. But working with an image consultant can make dramatic and immediate positive changes in how you look and feel.

Elena says that the best image consultants will ask you a lot of questions about yourself. Finally, they should demonstrate that they are interested in helping you define a personal style. "A lot of consultants have their own sense of style and try to impose it on everyone else in a boilerplate kind of way," says Elena. She suggests finding someone who takes the time to understand who *you* are and who comprehends that you want to both improve your appearance *and* attract the opposite sex.

An image consultant can cost anywhere from $150 to $300 an hour, depending on the service and the city or town you live in.

## 34. LASH OUT AT HIM!

Adding lashes *individually* to your eyes is one of the biggest beauty-boosting secrets I know. It takes skill and practice to add lashes this way on your own, so it's best to visit a makeup studio and have it done by a pro. According to Laura Geller, makeup artist *extraordinaire*, adding flare lashes at the outside corner of your eye makes your own lashes look so much more voluminous—and that's *before* the mascara goes on. Another plus is that when you embellish natural lashes they don't need as many coats of mascara. "Adding a few flares lifts the eyes up," says Laura. "If your eye is small or turned down or if you don't want to wear a lot of makeup, individual lashes will make your eyes look bigger and your face more awake and youthful. All the makeup in the world will not do that," she says. Laura's right—I add individual lashes when I am going to be attending any major event or making a public or television appearance. And I insist that women I work with get them when they go on first dates or attend Janis Spindel Serious Matchmaking dinner parties. You will be *amazed* at the difference such a seemingly small addition to your makeup can make.

Individual lashes are "extremely flirty and elegant and it is never out of style; it's a classic makeup trick," says Laura. "When I whip out the lashes and put them on a client, it's like they had surgery. It adds a level of excitement that goes beyond just beautiful makeup," she adds. Laura says you can expect individual lash applications to last about one week, but some women feel comfortable removing them after one day.

## 35. CHANGE YOUR HAIRSTYLE AND COLOR

Your hairstyle can both date and age you. If you haven't changed your hairstyle in over two years, it may be time for something different. If you haven't changed it since high school, make an appointment with a good stylist *today.* Men prefer long, blown-out hair that's touchable. But if long hair just isn't an option for you, choose a style that has a long appearance that will flatter your face in a feminine, touchable way. The point is that you want movement in your hair. Caroline Lemeda, proprietress of MV Salon in New York, says that having layers cut into your hair increases movement.

Avoid, at all costs, overprocessed styles that require lots of "product." If your hair is super-short, consider growing it out a bit, just to give him something to run his hands through. Color should look as natural as possible. A top-notch stylist or colorist (most good salons have a trained colorist on staff) can give you advice about the best hair color for your skin tone. It's worth seeking professional advice on cut and color, as it takes time to reverse hair mistakes.

Caroline says the number one mistake women make with their hair is being afraid to change it, especially if it's too long and, as a result, weighs down their face. And while it's true that men love long hair, it's also true that hair can be *too* long. At that point, depending on the kind of hair you have, it can lose movement and drag down facial features. "Talk to your stylist. If you trust her, let her work with you to try something different," says Caroline. "Check out other women's hairstyles, look at magazines, and bring images into your salon to discuss." A good stylist will take your lifestyle and profession into account as well as your hair texture and shape when working with you to develop a flattering style. "It's possible to find a flattering style that has a long look while remaining bouncy, touchable, and sexy," Caroline says.

## Caroline Lameda's Hair Care Schedule

**Take care to maintain your color and cut. Here are Caroline's handy maintenance reminders:**

- Highlights: touch up every two months
- Long hair: cut every six weeks
- Deep conditioning: once a week
- Single-process color: redo every four to five weeks
- Double- or multiple-process color: redo every five to six weeks

### 36. GROW, HAIR, GROW!

Some short haircuts can be very cute, gamine, and high style. Unfortunately, most men don't see it that way. Sexy and touchable movement is what appeals to them. So if you have short hair, consider growing it out. Caroline Lameda says that if you want to grow your short hair out into a longer style, the first requirement is patience. Caroline advises you to enlist your stylist to help maintain your resolve. "Women with short hair are used to the fun of getting their hair cut frequently. When you are growing your hair out, cuts will be less frequent and far less dramatic," she says. That's because you will want to limit yourself to trims, no more than half an inch at a time, just to keep your hair in shape while it's growing. In order to keep you motivated while you're waiting to achieve the final length, Caroline says to consider color and highlights. "Have fun while you're growing it out," she says, "and keep it exciting." Having a great cheerleader stylist like Caroline helps, too.

## 37. WHITEN YOUR TEETH

It used to be that only movie stars and millionaires could afford to have perfect, gleaming teeth. With the advent of new teeth-whitening technologies, the process is more affordable and accessible *and* very natural looking. That means everyone can do something to improve her smile. I happen to think whitening teeth is one of the most important aspects of appearance improvement. That's because discolored or yellow teeth are unattractive and a turn-off to the opposite sex. White teeth also make you look younger. Both discolored teeth and silver fillings age you. Silver amalgam fillings are not used that often nowadays, so if you have them you might be showing your age. To get a handle on how dark your teeth may be, take the white T-shirt test. Hold a brand new white T-shirt up to your teeth and see the difference. If your teeth look considerably darker or more yellow in comparison, it's time to do something about your mouth. See **Tip 38** for advice from Dr. Elisa Mello of NYC Smile Design on techniques, from over-the-counter remedies to high-tech treatments that can really make a difference.

## 38. SMILE STYLE

There are lots of options in teeth whitening and restoration today—from conservative at-home treatments to complex procedures that require visits to a cosmetic dentist. Which one will work for you depends on your budget and the quality and condition of your teeth. Before you invest in expensive cosmetic dentistry, Dr. Mello recommends that you make sure the dentist specializes in cosmetic procedures—not all dentists are "smile experts." Here are the most commonly available whitening and restoration products and services, according to Dr. Mello:

**At-Home Whitening.** In just the last few years there's been an explosion of at-home teeth-whitening treatments that many people say offer great (and inexpensive) results. Until recently, you could buy only uncomfortable trays and gels over the counter. They were clumsy to use, and forget about talking on the phone! Now there are strips, paint-on liquids and gels, and overnight products. Since they are the most conservative and the least expensive of all teeth-whitening treatments (about $25 or less for a four-week treatment), try them first. To really see if they make a difference, do only your top teeth first and compare the final result to your bottom teeth. If you see a big difference, congratulations, move on to the bottom teeth. If not, you may have to see a dentist.

**Professional Bleaching.** Power bleaching is a high-intensity light treatment that takes about one hour in a dentist's office. Teeth can become up to eight times whiter and brighter with this process. But the whiteness needs to be maintained with at-home trays and gels your dentist will provide. Avoiding cigarettes, coffee, tea, and red wine will also help keep up those pearly whites. Expect to pay about $500 for power bleaching, plus another $250 to $500 for the custom maintenance trays and gels. The bad news is that power bleaching helps only if your teeth are stained and discolored from food, beverages, and smoking. Bleaching will not change the color of crowns, caps, or fillings. Certain gray "stripes" in your teeth, usually caused by antibiotics taken when you were a child (most notoriously tetracycline) are part of the actual tooth and not on the surface, and bleaching will not have an effect on such discoloration.

**It's Just a Veneer.** If you have a lot of crowns, caps, and fillings or if your teeth are discolored from calcification or antibiotics, you may have to consider getting veneers. Ultra-thin porcelain and ceramic veneers will mask chips, discoloration, spaces, and old dental work, giving your teeth a uniform, white appearance that's still natural and very durable. Modern veneers are also translucent, making them appear more like natural teeth, unlike old-fashioned caps that were both bulky and flat looking (which is why movie stars of old used to look like they were wearing a box of Chiclets!). Veneers require serious chair time, however. Expect to make two to three visits per tooth. The dentist will take some enamel off your natural tooth (or remove a thin layer of existing dental work) with a drill and then she will make an impression of your tooth. You'll get a temporary veneer while you wait for your permanent one. Veneers are an investment: Expect to pay about $1,000 per tooth. The good news is that you don't have to veneer every single tooth in your mouth—only the ones that show when you smile. On average Dr. Mello says you can expect to veneer about ten teeth. And veneers last for fifteen years or longer.

**Disappearing Act.** A mouth full of metal? At your age? I'm not talking about braces (but I'm getting to that). I am talking about those old silver amalgam fillings you've had since you were in college or before. They're not only unattractive, but they can give away your age, since dentists have moved away from using them over the past several years. But you can do something about it, and it is called filling restoration. Tooth-colored porcelain and composite-resin material currently used for new fillings can also be used to replace old silver fillings. Your dentist will numb the area, remove the old filling, and clean away any existing decay. Then he'll line the cavity with a resin or cement filler. According to Dr. Mello, the dentist takes an impression. While you are waiting for your new filling you will get a temporary one, also tooth-colored. These new materials are sturdier than silver amalgam. Another benefit? They actually strengthen your teeth and will last years. Expect to pay about $300 per filling.

**Brace Yourself.** If you missed out on braces when you were a kid, and your crooked teeth are driving you nuts, fear not. Today you can straighten your teeth without embarrassing braces. A removable appliance called Invisalign is made from transparent plastic that fixes your smile while keeping your natural tooth structure intact. It's similar to a retainer, so it is not noticeable when you are wearing it. You can remove the appliance to brush your teeth, so food and plaque will not get trapped like they can with metal braces. A computer will make a three-dimensional image from impressions of your teeth to map out the incremental movements necessary to straighten out your smile. A series of aligners is then manufactured. Your dentist will monitor your progress with office visits every six weeks. You wear each set for two weeks until the six weeks is up and then you start all over again until the process is complete. That can take as long as regular braces—from several months to several years, depending on how many aligners you need to achieve the desired results. Invisalign can also cost as much as regular braces, too—from $5,000 to $9,000.

Lingual braces, traditional metal and plastic braces that are applied behind your teeth, are yet another teeth-straightening option.

Talk to your doctor about other strides in cosmetic dentistry, which include laser treatments that remove excess gum tissue to give your teeth a more proportioned look; gum grafting to improve the appearance of lost gum tissue; and new dental implants for missing teeth.

## 39. FACE IT!

Men love beautiful skin. It's a wonderful calling card, so take care of it. In **Tip 57** (page 61) I'll talk about the advantages of seeking out medical attention for your skin. But you can and should maintain a healthy at-home skin regimen. Never skimp on your skin care! Our skin takes a beating day in and day out—and in all four seasons. It's one of the first parts of the body to show age. On the other hand, soft, supple, fresh, and clear skin is youthful, sexy, beautiful, and healthy. Men love soft skin. You will be amazed at the many new, effective products on the market that you can add to your daily routine.

## 40. THE *SKIN*NY ON INGREDIENTS

Over-the-counter skin products make all sorts of claims. You can avoid making costly mistakes by knowing how to read a label to find exactly what you need to help make your skin kissable. But is there really such a thing as a "miracle in a bottle?" Unfortunately not, but there are ingredients that can make a difference in the way your skin looks. Here's a guide to ingredients and what they do, from New York dermatologist Dr. Howard Sobel, whom *many* Manhattanites trust with their faces. Be sure to check with your own doctor before changing your skin care regimen:

**Alpha hydroxy acids** loosen dead cells from the skin's surface for a smoother, clearer appearance. A good over-the-counter product to try if your skin is dull-looking and superficially rough.

**Antioxidants** fight "free radicals" that can accelerate the appearance of age. Worth using on good skin as a preventative measure.

**Anti-inflammatories** reduce puffiness, especially under the eyes. Good for the day after a late night or to refresh yourself with before an after-work date.

**Emollients** can form a thin protective layer that traps moisture. Good for all-purpose moisturizing.

**Essential fatty acids** can improve skin's health and glow. Wrinkles may appear to lessen. This ingredient also can help return moisture to the skin, so it's a good choice if you have dry skin.

**Exfoliants** remove dead skin cells, but be careful—some can be harsh and scratch the skin. If the exfoliant you use is gentle, it can be an effective way of smoothing and refreshing skin.

**Humectants** attract moisture to the skin from the atmosphere. A good ingredient to look for if your skin is dry.

**Hyaluronic acid** helps skin maintain the appropriate moisture level. Again, it's a good ingredient to look for if your skin has a tendency to be dry.

**Retinol or Retin-A** reduces the appearance of wrinkles and can help reduce acne. This prescription-based ingredient can help reduce signs of sun damage and acne scars over time.

**Vitamin A** is believed to improve skin elasticity and promotes an even texture and cell growth. As an ingredient in skin care products, it can be very helpful. It may also help in the form of a dietary supplement, but please check with your doctor.

**Vitamin C** enhances natural collagen production, so it may be good for thirty-five-plus skin.

**Vitamin E** adds moisture and repairs tissue and, again, may be helpful for thirty-five-plus skin.

## 41. WHAT'S IN YOUR MAKEUP BAG?

Laura Geller is one of my favorite people and one of the *best* makeup artists in the country. She says that one of the biggest mistakes first-time clients make is not to use enough color. "Women have a tendency to use such sheer color that they end up not enhancing their beauty or their features," says Laura. "Your makeup doesn't come first, your beauty does," she says. Instead of brightening with color, Laura says women go overboard by covering up the skin with heavy foundation. "Woman who have beautiful skin cover it up and they end up looking like a painted kabuki doll," she says. "It's about using much less but using the right thing and color," Laura says. She advises women to use something sheer for coverage and consider using brighter lipstick and "blending, blending, blending for a youthful appearance."

Here's Laura's mini-guide to what women of all ages should have in their makeup bags, all starting with more color!

### *Twenties*

Makeup for your twenties is all about enhancing natural beauty. At this age you're not repairing, you're enhancing. It's less about foundation and more about **tinted moisturizer.** When you're in your twenties, you want to enhance the glow to your skin by using a little **pearlescence** on your cheekbones. **Gloss** on your lips is young and fresh and pretty. Colorful eye shadows are also important. When you are in your twenties you can use **colorful fashion eye shadows** and you are never going to look like you are trying too hard. Color on your eyes is very playful and sexy, if it's done right. Avoid dull or matte grays and browns, which may make you look tired or dated.

## Thirties

At this point you want to start defining your features. You should make camouflage your new best friend. **Concealer** in a color that matches your skin tone that you can dab on under your eyes and on blemishes and other imperfections is very important. If your skin is in good condition, **sports tints** will even out skin tone without being too heavy. A little extra coverage in the form of **lightweight liquid foundation** is necessary if you feel your skin is in less-than-optimal shape. The thirties are the time when you have to start using **blush** on your cheeks. The thirties are also about using **defined eyeliner** that follows the shape of your eye and the base of your lashes. **Lip liner** used with **creamy, moist-looking lipstick** also helps to create a fuller look to your mouth in natural colors. But be careful: Liner should *not* be obvious or a different color from your lipstick.

## Forties

Things start to go south in your forties, and you have to start working with colors that make a difference, not just safe choices. It's also time to revamp the colors and products you may have been using since you were in college. Now's the time to find the best **concealer** and a fabulous foundation and use them in tandem. Be sure to use a **light-diffusing foundation** or one that has a very low level of pearlescense. This will reflect the light and give you a brighter, dewy look. How to find one? If the bottle says "illuminating" or "light diffusing," you've found the right product. You can also buy illumination or **shimmer** alone and mix a bit of it with your favorite foundation. Don't go overboard—you want a dewy look, not a slick and shiny appearance! You also want to start **contouring** the shape of your eye. If you have too much skin on your eyelid, taupe or light brown colors will recess it. **Light-colored eye shadows** on your lid will make your eyes appear more open. Fluffy brows are a no-no. **Defined brows** make the eyes look awake and refreshed. A professional wax and tweeze can help get rid of bushy brows. Get rid of orange tones. **Taupe under chin and cheekbone** will add back the angularity or sculpted look to your face and make you look more chiseled. **Brightly colored lipstick and blush** will give you a healthy and youthful glow. Dark colors (i.e., burgundy lipstick and brown blush) will make you look harsh—and older.

## Fifties and beyond

You have to continue to work with color, but you also have to ensure that your makeup is subtle. No one should look at you and think, "She's wearing *a ton* of makeup!" **Taupe** is flattering as a contouring color. But browns on the lips, cheeks, and eyes should be banished. Brown is dull and aging, as is dark red, which can look "old" on anyone who's over thirty. Think **peach, pink,** and **coral** for lips and cheeks. Continue to use **light-diffusing foundation** that offers good coverage. Beige, soft creams, and shadows that brighten instead of adding dramatic color will lighten your look. Brows should be defined with **brow liner** or with a shadow that matches brow color. Be sure to **blend** to avoid the "drawn on" look! Do not use matte lipsticks, which can "bleed" and accentuate lines. Instead, try a **moisturizing cream lipstick**. Avoid thick mascara! Instead, consider having weekly applications of individual eyelashes applied (your eyelashes thin considerably as you get older) and/or dyeing what you have with vegetable-based color.

## 42. CLEAN OUT YOUR MAKEUP BAG

Most women I know have dozens of lipsticks and eye shadows that they bought and have never worn, or wore once and then changed their mind about liking the color or consistency. We also have a tendency to just not want to throw out items we paid a lot of money for. But cosmetics do have a shelf life, and it's not very long—three to six months for most items, especially mascara, which should be replaced every three months, according to Laura Geller. They also have a fashion shelf life, which means that pink frosted or deep purple matte lipsticks just don't make it any longer—on anyone, anytime, anywhere. So empty out your medicine cabinet and grab your makeup bag and get rid of anything that's more than six months old, discolored, used up (I bet you a million dollars you have a near-empty bottle of foundation in your medicine cabinet!), or just plain ugly. Toss anything (even if it's unopened) that you have not used in more than three months. If you haven't used it by now, it's unlikely you ever will. Like cleaning out your closet of useless items, you will be left with the best. Take those items you wear all the time and bring them to your appointment with the image consultant or makeup artist so she can see what you really wear every day and whether you've been on the mark or terribly wrong about color and consistency choices.

*Coco Chanel once said that there are no ugly women, only lazy ones.*

## 43. EDIT YOUR ACCESSORIES

The good news: You don't need a lot of expensive jewelry or drawers full of scarves, belts, and shoes. I think the most important accessory is a great watch. A beautiful, classic watch really says a lot about you: It announces oh so subtly that you have taste, discretion, *and* that you care about showing up on time! Other than that, some diamond studs (real or fake), a great pin, a beautiful scarf, and some awesome shoes can really carry you far in the accessory department.

## 44. HIRE A MAKEUP ARTIST

A professional makeup artist can teach you a flattering and efficient technique of applying makeup. In just a couple of hours you can learn what to use for the office, weekends, and evening or dress-up dates and events. The trick is to find someone who understands that, paradoxically, men like women to look good, but not like they are wearing a lot of makeup. But you can only achieve that look . . . with makeup! Laura Geller says that finding a good professional isn't hard if you know what to look for and you know the right questions to ask. First, avoid anyone who piles it on. That's why salespeople at cosmetic counters or superstores are your worst bet. They generally want to sell you as many products as possible, and often they are not trained. So you run the risk of leaving the counter looking like a neon sign.

A *good* makeup artist, on the other hand, will introduce you to new ideas, looks, and products. "I try to separate clients from their old habits and urge them to be open to new ideas," says Laura. "Even if you go once you will learn some important techniques. You know your face well, but it's sometimes the obvious that you are missing—an outsider can see something that you can add and incorporate into your own routine."

## UP CLOSE AND PERSONAL
### *I'm Not Making This Up!*

If you are tempted to disregard our makeup advice, reconsider. Whenever I give talks to women and bring along makeup artist Laura Geller, I see time and time again what makeup can do for a woman's self-esteem and feelings about herself. I also see the change in attitude other people have toward women when they have had a makeover, with just some simple makeup. During one recent event in New York City, a very brave woman volunteered for a mini-makeover with Laura—right in front of everyone! Janet was short, with short dark hair and no makeup. I would guess that Janet is in her fifties. She has great bones and nice eyes. But you wouldn't know it because she had no makeup on at all. She looked old and tired. After Laura applied some sheer foundation in the right shade, a little blush, some shadow and mascara, Janet was *transformed*. The audience actually gasped in delight when her makeover was done! When the workshop ended, people from the audience (including men) literally *followed* her down Lexington Avenue telling her how absolutely gorgeous she looked—and she did. She was a beautiful woman. And do I have to tell you she floated up the avenue on Cloud Nine—literally? Do you know how long it took Laura to do her makeup? About ten minutes.

## 45. BE NICE TO YOUR HANDS AND FEET

Start getting regular manicures and pedicures *today*. Your hands and feet can really show your age if you don't take care of them. You should have a manicure once a week and a pedicure about once every two weeks or bimonthly. A professional manicurist can get you in and out of the salon in less than forty minutes, so it's not a big time commitment, and it can be very relaxing. Many large cities now have very inexpensive salons that do a great job on your nails, so you don't have to spend a fortune on hand maintenance. If you live in a climate with very cold winters, consider having a monthly hot wax treatment on both your hands and your feet during the coldest months. It feels incredible and can remove a lot of rough, dry skin. One last no-no: chipped or peeling polish. It's unprofessional, grubby-looking, and sends the message that you don't care. And men hate it. (Yes, they do notice your nails!) Be sure to have a polish repair kit in your bag to take care of any nail indiscretions!

## 46. CONSIDER PLASTIC SURGERY

Plastic surgery is a big and serious topic, and entire books have been written on the subject, so I won't go into tremendous detail here. But I would be doing you a disservice if I did not mention it, because it can be an important part of any appearance improvement project. If you believe that aspects of your features are holding you back from looking your best, it might be time to consult with a plastic surgeon. "There are good plastic surgeons in every area of the country," says Dr. Alan Matarasso, a highly regarded New York City plastic surgeon and a good friend of mine. He says the best resources are medical associations such as the American Society of Plastic Surgery. And there is so much new technology that a lot of cosmetic surgery has become less invasive and requires a shorter recovery time than in the past.

Brow lifts, eyelid lifts, under-eye procedures, and chin tucks, among other procedures, are fairly uncomplicated (although all are still serious operations) that can have a tremendous impact on how youthful you look. Dr. Matarasso recommends that single people talk to their surgeon about less invasive treatments that result in minimal scarring and recovery time. He also says, and I agree, to say the very least, that you should not cut corners when it comes to plastic surgery. Don't even consider any procedure until you can afford the best care possible.

## 47. GET SHOE SAVVY

High heels make almost every woman's legs look longer, thinner, and sexier. High heels also make you walk with a certain panther-like sexiness that men love. Anytime you have an opportunity to wear heels, do so. Two-and-a-half- to three-inch heels are best for most women—anything higher will be difficult to walk in and hard on the foot. Really high heels (five inches or more) can make you look somewhat cheap—like a stripper or a foot fetishist! "Extreme heels" can also make you flex your calves, which makes your legs look bigger. If you're uncomfortable in high heels, or if you're tall and don't want to accentuate your height, try high-heel-style shoes, where the heel is wide at the top and narrows on the end, with one- or two-inch heels. A neutral pump, something that matches your skin tone, worn with flesh-colored hose makes your leg look longer.

## 48. DRESS FOR MEN

Dressing for men doesn't mean dressing cheaply or in an overtly sexual fashion.

It *does* mean avoiding really high-fashion trends and styles or anything fussy or obvious (big belt buckles, large prints, anything oversized). Most men like simple, elegant silhouettes (even if they don't articulate it in quite that way). What men *do* articulate, again and again, is *get rid of*

*What's hot:* Seamless, nude fishnets
*What's not:* Heavy black fishnets with seams

*the pants.* Elena says her most frequent piece of advice for female clients is "lose the pants!" If you have great legs, go short (but not too short—and yes, there is such a thing as too short). If you aren't happy with your legs, wear a long, flowing skirt. It's the *idea* as well as the look of a skirt that men love.

## 49. MEN'S TOP APPEARANCE TURNOFFS

1. Dressing in a "slutty" or overly provocative manner in the first few meetings or dates

2. Unshaved underarms and legs

3. Overprocessed, "big" blond hair

4. "Hard" hair (oversprayed or overuse of product)

5. Unstylish, frumpy, out-of-date clothing

6. Chipped and peeling nail polish

7. Overdressing or underdressing for the occasion

8. Wearing sunglasses indoors

## 50. DRESS REHEARSAL

Putting yourself together in the morning or for a date shouldn't be difficult. Once you get a handle on what works and what doesn't work in terms of clothing, hair, and makeup, you should be able to be out the door in less than forty-five minutes, from shower to front door. When you have a routine, you know you can be ready at a moment's notice for last-minute invitations (you-know-who could be there too!). One caveat: Don't think you can get away with "refreshing" the makeup you put on in the morning if you are going on a date or other social event after work. Makeup for dates should be reapplied, from scratch! Better yet, book a thirty-minute appointment with a makeup artist for an after-work application.

## 51. STOP LISTENING TO SALESPEOPLE

Salespeople in clothing and department stores and at makeup counters often work on commission. They generally don't have your best interests at heart, and they really don't care how things look on you. They just want to sell you as much product as possible. And in high-end department stores, they can also be imperious and frankly scary. Don't let that stop you from going into these stores to shop—they are often the best places to find "investment" pieces that will work for you for a long time. You must walk into a store with confidence (remember, even the most imperious clerk still wants to make a sale). Ditto for department store personal shoppers. The services can often be free, but again, this is only because the personal shopper wants to sell you items in the store that she works for. Better to hire a no-commission image consultant or personal shopper who does not have a proprietary relationship with a single store. These pros will be objective and help you select pieces that look good on you and fit your budget.

## 52. WEAR A "CONVERSATION STARTER"

Elena says one way to "flirt" with a man is by wearing one fabulous accessory that offers him an "opening" to talk to you. One great pin, a fabulous scarf, or a stunning necklace not only enhances a simple black dress; such accessories will give him something to talk about. Men, in my experience, are often at a loss for words and are relieved when a woman gives them a conversational opening. If you give them a reason to say "That's a great pin" or "Where did you get that scarf?" or "What's that necklace made out of?," they'll feel comfortable approaching you.

## 53. EVERY WOMAN SHOULD OWN . . .

- A fabulous, classic watch
- Diamond stud earrings (real or faux)

- A high-quality black turtleneck
- Well-fitting yoga pants in dark colors (black, navy, brown, dark gray) for looking good while working out
- A thirty-six-inch square Hermes, Gucci, or Pucci scarf
- A little black dress, in a style that suits your figure
- Black velvet pants
- A black miniskirt (if you have great legs)
- "Nude" seamless finely knit fishnets
- A white silk shirt (and something pretty to go under it, such as a lace camisole)
- Sexy mules (to click around in when he comes over for an at-home date)
- Well-cut white T-shirts (great with jeans or under a blazer)
- High heels that flatter your feet and legs
- A pashmina or cashmere shawl
- A sarong (great for *après* beach or shower)

## 54. AVOID OVERDOSING ON TRENDS AND STEER CLEAR OF THE OBVIOUS

Trends in small doses are fine, especially if they update and amplify your overall look. And trendy pieces, carefully chosen, can also perk up ho-hum basics. For example, a leopard- or geometric-print top paired with a simple black skirt and fashionable black heels looks fun and elegant. Wearing a leopard-print cashmere sweater paired with an embossed leather skirt, chandelier earrings, a large necklace, thigh-high boots, and an animal print scarf will make you look as if you were attacked at the zoo. Obvious accessories and clothing will also be a turnoff. That means anything big and shiny, too low-cut, or too "loud" (think head-to-toe Pucci print) is best left on the dressing room floor.

## 55. TAKE SOMETHING OFF

Accessories are great, and, as I've said, an exquisite pin, necklace, or scarf can even become a conversation starter. But when you pile it on, you look like a jewelry store display. Before you leave for work or for a date, make sure your accessories aren't wearing *you*—do you really need a necklace, pin, earrings, watch, *and* a scarf? No. If you are wearing earrings, you probably don't need the necklace, and there's no reason to wear both a necklace and a pin. So do yourself a favor and take one accessory away or maybe two.

## 56. BE BROW SMART

"Brows and the shape of lips are the two things that I have a hard time twisting my clients' arms to change," says Laura Geller. "I can make them over completely, but the minute I touch their brows they are resistant." That's a shame because brows are an important part of your overall look and they need regular grooming and careful attention—and often updating, according to Laura. Your brows frame your face. If shaped properly, they can give you a wide-awake freshness. If left shaggy, they can ruin the look of even the most carefully applied makeup. Like individual lashes, beautifully shaped and tweezed brows can supercharge your look and no one will quite know why. Brows should run the length of the entire eye and frame it. The arch should begin in the corner, by the nose, and sweep over the eye gracefully to its midsection then sweep gently down on the other side. Most women, unless they are very young, should avoid bushy, thick brows. No matter how shapely, they tend to appear unkempt and they

*What's hot:* **Crème lipstick in soft, natural shades or a fresh color with a bit of shine**

*What's not:* **Harsh matte lipsticks in dark or "weird" colors, or, if you are over thirty-five, super slick, thick lip gloss**

weigh down your face. On the other hand, spaghetti-thin brows age you and look unnatural—especially if you have literally penciled them in yourself!

## 57. GET THEE TO A DERMATOLOGIST

If you haven't seen your dermatologist lately, make an appointment. If you've *never* been to a skin doctor, it's time for a visit. Dermatologists aren't just about acne and skin diseases. A good dermatologist can recommend a prescription-based skin care regimen that will make a difference in your skin's health, feel, texture, and overall appearance. He or she can advise you on treating common skin problems, such as pimples, rosacea (an acne-like rash), dry skin, and wrinkles (some wrinkles can be treated in the dermatologist's office; others require a plastic surgeon).

"People should think of dermatologists in the same way they think of a dentist," says Dr. Heidi Waldorf, director of the Laser Surgery Department of Dermatology of Mount Sinai Medical Center in New York. That means you should go both when you have a problem and to avoid or prevent problems. "Dermatologists are the best people to see for skin, hair, and nail care. They have spent years studying, so people are doing themselves a great service when they see a skin doctor for evaluation, prevention, maintenance, and rejuvenation," she says.

For example, many women think acne isn't worthy of a medical visit. That's a myth, according to Dr. Waldorf. Adult acne is often concentrated in the lower face and there are many plans of treatment to help clear it up, she says. "And what's worse, a lot of women get in the cycle of a pimple: They pick at it and it gets worse. It implodes and puts bacteria into your skin and you get more scarring and more acne. A medical professional can teach you how to change your behavior and take care of your skin to prevent scars or other damage.

## *Rejuvenating Dermatological Treatments*

Dr. Waldorf says many skin procedures performed in a doctor's office can have truly rejuvenating effects. "I am pretty conservative and only use products and procedures approved by the FDA," says Dr. Waldorf. She says to be cautious of any doctor or health practitioner who wants to use unapproved products or treatments on your precious skin.

Here are some highly effective treatments, especially for women over thirty-five. Discuss them with your doctor to find out which one might be right for you:

**Microdermabrasion** is a light peel, done manually using a machine that shoots out crystals at various pressures. The crystals exfoliate the skin.

**Acid peel** is light peel that helps topical medicines get to your skin. The peel can also polish your skin and give it a nice glow without any "downtime." If you think your skin looks dull, you can have acid peels on a regular basis at two- to three-week intervals. Once your skin has revived, you can have a peel once a month for maintenance.

**Botox** is a great way to soften the skin in a very natural way and to reduce frown lines between the eyebrows, if it's done correctly. If it's overdone, it can leave you notoriously frozen looking.

**Collagen** injections can be used on the lines that go from the nose to the corner of the mouth.

**Lasers** can help lighten spots and improve skin texture.

**Deeper peels** can tighten the skin and are ideal for women who are not ready for a face-lift but still need rejuvenation that goes beyond what a light peel can accomplish.

## Hair-Care Essentials

Caroline Lameda says every woman should have the following hair-care products on hand:

- [ ] Two natural-bristle brushes—one "paddle" shaped and the other round, for creating curls with a blow dryer

- ☐ One detangler comb

- ☐ Moisturizing shampoo

- ☐ Conditioner (which you should comb through your hair when you are still in the shower)

- ☐ Professional-strength blow-dryer

- ☐ Shine and hold products

## 58. CONSIDER CONTACTS

If you wear glasses and have never considered contact lenses, start thinking about them now. Glasses can be fabulous (see **Tip 59** for proof!) but many women who have been wearing glasses for years can change their look and attitude by allowing themselves the option of contacts. And these days you can even change your eye color. If you have brown eyes and you've always wanted green peepers, now's your chance!

## 59. INVEST IN FACE-FLATTERING GLASSES!

If the idea of contacts gives you the willies, do a serious assessment of how your current glasses look on you. Glasses can be a great accessory. Carefully selected glasses can hide flaws and play up your eyes or cheekbones. And very few men have told me they dislike women who wear glasses.

Felice Dee of Felice Dee Eyewear in New York says, "Let's face it, how much effort and time goes into picking the right pair of shoes for one outfit or a pair of jeans? And how many pairs of shoes do women have? The same woman might have only one pair of glasses to carry her through every occasion." Felice argues that it's more important to focus on your face and glasses than your shoes. "When you are sitting having a dinner date, your partner is going to be much more cognizant of what is on your face than what's on your feet," she says. And it's true. Women who wear glasses need to make an effort to make sure their specs are spectacular.

"When you are looking for glasses, you are really dependent on the person behind the desk," says Felice. "You can't see yourself until you get the prescriptions in the frames, so you need to trust the person you're working with to help you get the best-looking glasses you can find for your face." A good eyewear person should discuss your style and color preferences, along with your lifestyle and profession. "I would not put rhinestones on a female attorney. It might be her passion, but it's not the right look. She can still defy stereotypes and look appropriate, modern, chic, and updated," says Felice.

You also have to outline your needs when selecting frames. Are the glasses for reading or distance? With reading you have far greater variety in what you can do in terms of size, explains Felice, from tiny specs to oversized shapes. But if you need progression lenses, which have many different distances within the lenses, you'll be somewhat more limited in the kind of frame you can get. Many people think they have to go for the very large frame in that instance and some optical shops push that idea. But Felice says there are new progression lenses that are thin and smaller. Depending on your face, there are more flattering options than big frames.

Large frames age you. "You don't have to look ninety when you are forty," says Felice. Outsized sunglasses can be fun, but many women end up looking dated and old-fashioned with giant glasses. Tints are also off-limits if you want to stay young looking. "Tints can really be dreary—there is no need to use them," says Felice. "Older women use them because they think it hides bags, but it adds years, in my opinion," she says. A better solution: Felice recommends choosing glasses with the lower rim hitting the bag or circle so it disguises it.

## 60. BEST BETS FOR SELECTING FACE-FLATTERING EYEWEAR

- The frame shape should contrast with the face shape. "For example, I would not recommend putting round frames on a round face," says Felice. "Women with rectangular and long faces should avoid a frame that droops down because it makes the face look longer. Those with narrow faces should avoid teardrop effects. You want to counteract that round or rectangular shape so an uplifted cat eye might be nice."

- The frame size should be in scale with the face size.
- Eyes should be centered in the frame.
- Contrast frame color with eye color (i.e., red or orange frames with green eyes, black or copper with blue eyes).

## 61. PROTECT YOUR SKIN

The number one favor you can do for your skin is to wear a good sunblock. It's the best antiaging beauty treatment you can treat yourself to. Dr. Waldorf says you should put sunblock on "before you get dressed so you aren't worried about getting it on your clothes. You'll also put more on that way and you will avoid missing areas." Dr. Waldorf says sunblock should go on thirty minutes before you go outdoors so it has a chance to adhere to the skin. "Reapply within the first hour you are outside and then once every two or three hours that you are outside."

Dr. Waldorf also believes in protective clothing if you spend a lot of time outside. "I wear protective clothing made of lightweight, tightly woven fabric. It will shield you from the sun and you will feel less hot because the sun bounces off the fabric," she says. Such safeguarding items are often available at sporting good stores and on the Internet. Dr. Waldorf likes products from Sun Precautions Company. Check the Resource Guide on page 261 for her contact information.

### *Dr. Waldorf's Top Three Skin Don'ts*

1. No tanning
2. No smoking
3. No picking

*What's hot:* **A boat-neck top that enhances your shoulders and collarbone**

*What's not:* **A too-tight T-shirt and noticeable bra straps**

## 62. TIE ONE ON (A SCARF, THAT IS)

A scarf can add dash to your ensemble, transform a tired turtleneck, and wake up last year's little black dress. This accessory can disguise a not-so-swanlike neck and even help draw attention away from figure flaws. (It can also act as a "conversation starter"—see **Tip 43**).

Elena has some scarf smarts to keep in mind:

- Don't place knots where they will draw attention to your largest parts.
- A scarf tied as a choker should be avoided if you have a short neck—better to tie it so it falls mid-chest.
- Long scarves that fall to the top of the hipbone will make short women look taller.
- Small scarves should sport small prints; large scarves or wraps can handle large graphic designs.
- Match scarf size to your body size—a big shawl with fringe will dwarf a small woman; a tiny scarf wrapped around a large woman's neck will be lost and look awkward.
- Choose scarf colors as you do makeup and clothing—make sure they flatter your coloring.
- A thirty-six-by-thirty-six-inch silk twill scarf (think Hermes or Gucci) flatters most women and is the most versatile.

## 63. HOW FIRM A FOUNDATION: CHOOSE THE RIGHT BRA FOR YOUR BODY TYPE

Even the most spectacular outfit will suffer if your bra doesn't fit correctly. You'll also suffer—there's nothing more uncomfortable and unattractive than a too-small bra or one that creates wrinkles under your clothing. Elena says a good bra is one that is unnoticeable under clothing (unless *you* want it to be seen). Elena says the average life span of a bra is six months—the combination of laundering and stretching with changes in your own body make most bras unwearable after that time. But the bra you are wearing right now may not fit you properly. Do yourself, your clothes, and your prospective date a favor and invest in a new, perfectly fitted bra as soon as possible.

How do you fit a bra? Lingerie specialty shops and better department stores often have professional fitters on hand to help you measure your chest and find the right fit. But you can also do it yourself at home, with a tape measure.

Bra Tenders, Inc., an incredible lingerie shop in New York that serves Broadway and television people, along with just regular folks, fits every customer individually for bras and other under things. Here are some of their tips for finding the perfect fit:

Wrap a soft tape measure around your ribcage just under your breasts, making sure it's snug. Add the number five to that measurement (if the number you get is even, add six) and you will have your size (34, 36, 38, etc.). To calculate your cup size, simply take a loose (not tight) measurement across the fullest part of your braless bust. The difference between the two measurements is your cup size as follows:

> One inch = A
>
> Two inches = B
>
> Three inches = C
>
> Four inches = D
>
> Five inches = DD
>
> . . . And so on.

Even after you have figured out your size, you will still have to try bras on before you buy. That's because sizing is not standard, and different manufacturers (especially European makers) have slightly different sizing. So while you may have measured up to be a 34C, you may find that certain makers consider you a 36B. Trying on is important for another reason: You will have preferences in terms of fabric (lace vs. knit) and underwire vs. no wire. Only having the bra next to your skin will tell you if you like wearing it or not. Try bras on when you're wearing something snug, such as a knit turtleneck. This will tell you if your bra will support you without announcing itself.

## 64. SMILE!

Mother was right: Your smile is your best accessory. A bright, friendly smile says "I'm approachable, I'm nice, and I'm happy." Those are three qualities that *really* turn men on. Besides, frowning creates the wrong kind of facial lines. Laugh lines are beautiful but brow frowns are not!

# ELENA'S MAKEOVER QUESTIONNAIRE

While it's challenging to do a self-assessment of your style and appearance on your own, filling out Elena's questionnaire can be a start. These are the kind of questions a good image consultant will ask you—if she doesn't, you may want to look elsewhere before you take out your credit card. If you can't afford to hire an image consultant right now (although I do think you should make this one of your budget priorities), you can at least start to get an idea of what you believe about your appearance and it will help you identify areas of change.

## GENERAL INFORMATION

Profession_____

Marital status:  Single_____ Divorced_____

Have children: No_____ Yes _____ How many_____

Age _____ Height _____ Weight _____

Hair color_____ Eye color _____ Skin tone_____

Ethnicity_____

Do you wear eyeglasses?          No_____ Yes _____

## Clothing

Apparel sizes: Blouse_____ Pants_____ Skirt _____

                 Dress_____ Shoe_____ Bra _____

Brands you wear now:

Shoes_____

Bras_____

Yearly budget for clothing                       $ _____

## Hair

1. Describe your hairstyle. Do you consider it becoming?

   _____

   _____

   _____

2. When you go to the hairdresser are you often persuaded to change your style or are you definite about what you want?

   _____

   _____

3. How would you describe the texture of your hair? (Coarse, soft, curly, straight, frizzy, thin, thick)?

   _____

   _____

4. Is the length of your hair short, medium, or long?

   _____

   _____

5. Which shampoo(s) do you use daily?

   _____

   _____

6. Which conditioner(s) do you use daily?

_____

_____

7. What styling products do you use daily?

_____

_____

8. Do you blow-dry your hair? If yes, how often?

_____

_____

9. Do you use other appliances on your hair? If yes, how often?

_____

_____

10. Do you color and/or highlight your hair? If yes, how often?

_____

_____

11. Do you or have you had your hair straightened professionally?

_____

_____


## Makeup and Skin

12. Is your makeup too bland, too overdone, or just out of date? Do you feel you are competent when applying makeup?

_____

_____

_____

13. What is your current skin care regimen?

_____

_____

_____

14. Is your skin in good condition or neglected?

_____

_____


## Self-Perception

I want you to sit in front of the mirror with absolutely no distractions. Close your door . . . turn off the phone . . . do whatever makes you feel relaxed. Have a pencil ready to answer the following questions as honestly as you possibly can.

15. If you were seeing this woman (yourself) in the mirror for the first time, what broad adjectives first come to mind to describe her? Pleasant-looking? Pretty? Beautiful? Plain? Unattractive?

_____

_____

16. Do you like looking at yourself in the mirror? Yes _____ No _____
    If not, why?

_____

_____

_____

17. Do you think other people find you attractive? Likable?

_____

_____

_____

18. When you walk into a room do you feel noticeable or invisible? How would you prefer to feel?

_____

_____

_____

_____

19. Do you think your external appearance reflects who you are on the inside?

_____

_____

20. Name the actress or public personality whose style you most admire.

_____

_____

21. What are your best features?

_____

_____

_____

22. What are your worst features?

_____

_____

_____

23. Do you know how to dress to accentuate your best features? If so, how?

_____

_____

_____

24. Do you consider yourself confident? Shy? What are you insecure about?

_____

_____

_____

25. Do you consider yourself sexy?

_____

_____

_____

26. Do men find you attractive?

_____

_____


27. Do you consider yourself intelligent?

_____

_____


28. Do you consider yourself emotionally well-balanced?

_____

_____


29. Are you comfortable in social situations?

_____

_____


30. Do you feel that you have a good personality?

_____

_____


31. Do you have good taste?

_____

_____


32. Do you dress well?

_____

_____


33. Do you dress appropriately for different situations?

_____

_____


34. What changes would you like to see in yourself?

_____

_____

_____

## Body and Fitness

35. Are you happy with your weight? Yes _____ No _____

    If not, explain:

    _____

    _____

36. Do you work out on a regular basis? If yes, what is your routine? If no, what types of exercise do you enjoy (yoga, running, walking, dancing, swimming?)

    _____

    _____

    _____

37. When you are disappointed or saddened, do you eat too much or too little?

    _____

    _____

    _____

38. Are you happy with your normal diet? What type of foods do you favor?

    _____

    _____

    _____

39. Do you consider yourself physically fit?

    _____

    _____

40. Have you had or are you considering any cosmetic procedures? If yes, which ones?

    _____

    _____

    _____

## Personal Style

41. Do you feel more comfortable with your looks fresh from a shower or after you're dressed and made up?

    _____

    _____

42. Given a choice between jeans and a sweater or getting dressed up, what do you really prefer/feel most comfortable in?

    _____

    _____

43. On a scale of 1 to 10, how neat/put together are you, with 1 being not at all and 10 being extremely neat/put together?

    _____

    _____

44. Do you often rely on the opinion of a salesperson to tell you if something looks good on you?

    _____

    _____

45. How much time do you spend dressing in the:

    A.M.? _____

    P.M.? _____

46. List your fashion likes and dislikes.

    _____

    _____

    _____

47. What would you like most to accomplish if you were to book a session with an image consultant?

    _____

    _____

    _____

# *Three*

# Healthy Is as Healthy Does

To meet the challenge of finding and marrying a man in one year (or less!), you'll need to not only have your priorities straight and your appearance in order, but you also have to be in the best shape of your life, inside *and* out. When you're healthy you feel good, you exude vitality (*very* sexy), and you have the stamina and confidence you need to be "out there" and "findable."

I've touched on some health matters (seeing a shrink in Chapter 1; getting your hair, skin, and teeth in good order in Chapter 2), but now we're going to focus on tips dedicated to creating good health. You know how great you feel when you're eating right and how sexy and alive you feel when you're exercising and active. You also know how crummy your mood is when you're sitting around watching TV and eating junk food (plus, if you're at home watching TV, it's highly unlikely you're going to meet your future husband). So you understand that the effort it takes to get in shape and eat right is absolutely *worth it*. For women over thirty-five, concerns around weight and health are even more profound because it becomes even more difficult to lose excess weight and stave off signs of aging. The realities of daily living can also interfere with the decisions we make concerning food, nutrition, and exercise. For example, when some of us are overwhelmed by everything that life throws at us, we may see food and eating as a substitute for living a fuller life. Our efforts to balance commitments to family, friends, work, and self and to deal with unrealistic media images of beauty don't make staying in shape any easier! We're under a lot of pressure—some of which we put on ourselves.

Women of all ages also face self-confidence issues. That can influence our ability to maintain a happy attitude and healthful habits. How joyful we feel, how well we are able to cope with stress, our ability to maintain perspective, and whether what we feel on the inside is reflected in our physical appearance are all directly connected to our relationship with food and fitness. Being and feeling healthy are reflections of our engagement with life.

You will see positive results by practicing the tips in this chapter and learning more about food and fitness (I'll provide you with some wonderful resources). Everything you read here promotes healthy living, which will boost your confidence. That's important for the coming chapters, which will put you in unfamiliar situations, encourage you to meet new people, and get you going on dates. None of that is easy! Being your best self is a requirement.

I'm not a doctor, but I do count among my friends and colleagues a variety of medical professionals. I know from working with them and making healthy changes in my own life the importantance of each one of the tips in this chapter. They are starting points. Research, read, and see your doctor and nutrition specialist. Seek out fitness experts. Pay attention to your health. It's your greatest and most appealing asset!

*Note: Before starting any dietary and exercise regimen, please check with your doctor.*

## 65. QUIT IT!

First things first, everyone. If you smoke—*stop right now*. Easier said than done, I know. I have heard doctors say that getting off nicotine is tougher for smokers than it is for a drug addict weaning himself off heroin. That's pretty intimidating. But if you have a cigarette habit, you absolutely have to kick it. It's *never* too late. Not only is it one of the major turnoffs for men, it's also unbelievably bad for your health. Smoking accelerates the aging process, terribly damages your skin and teeth, and looks really *ugly* (*not* glamorous), especially as you get older. Simply put, your life is going to be cut short if you continue to smoke.

Today, there are numerous new products and programs designed specifically for people who want to quit smoking. Many can be used alone or combined with other products. See your doctor right away about your options. I am sure he or she has been nagging you about your habit and will be thrilled to supply you with all the information and support you need. The Resource Guide will also get you started (see page 261).

Overuse of any other mind-altering substance, including alcohol and drugs (legal or otherwise), should also be banned from your life. A glass of wine or a cocktail before dinner is one thing, and evidence shows that moderate use of alcohol may offer important health benefits. But drinking too much will have a bad effect on your overall health, and specifically on your skin, hair, and teeth. Drugs such as sleeping pills also wreak havoc on your system. Better to eat right, tire yourself out with exercise, and get a good night's sleep naturally. Take stock of what you're putting in your body and eliminate anything that it not essential for good health.

## 66. LOSE IT!

You knew this one was coming, didn't you? Looks go hand in hand with weight as far as men are concerned. The majority of men I meet say they are attracted to thin, fit women. This doesn't mean you have to be model skinny. It's an inappropriate, unattainable, and unrealistic goal for most women. You *should* find the right weight for your size and body type, though, and then achieve that weight through diet (not dieting) and exercise. There are tons of weight-loss clinics, health clubs, and fitness centers all over the country—I suspect there are several right in your own neighborhood. Getting off those extra pounds should be resolution number one for you if you're overweight. You'll be more attractive to men, you'll look terrific, you'll feel lighter and more energetic, and you'll be better off in general.

## 67. GET RID OF IT NOW!

Oz Garcia, author of *The Balance, Look and Feel Fabulous Forever*, and his forthcoming book, *The New 50: From 50 to 35 in Nine Months*, says there are certain foods, mainly simple carbohydrates, that you can and should live without. Oz says there's even evidence that these foods can cause depression or worse. Reason enough to give them up. You should consider removing these items from your cupboard and eliminating them from your future grocery lists:

- Sugary sodas and juice drinks
- All caffeine—that means coffee, diet colas (diet sodas without caffeine, such as ginger ale and lemon-lime varieties are okay but not ideal)
- Decaf coffee in particular can make the stomach secrete acid, and the result is you wind up hungrier
- Everything that is wheat-based, especially whole wheat—all breads, bagels, crackers, including sunflower seed bread, flaxseed bread, most sprouted grains and whole wheat–based products
- Cakes and cookies
- Sugary muffins and breakfast cereals
- Candy
- Potato and corn chips
- Boxed or packaged food such as macaroni and cheese, frozen dinners (unless they are specialty organic brands)

If you stop eating all of the above, you will automatically be making a huge improvement in your diet and health. How hard was that?

## 68. EAT RIGHT, STARTING TODAY

Food is fuel for the body—you need it to operate at maximum efficiency. Junk food can weigh you down, literally and figuratively; is bad for your health; and will make you fat if you depend on it as a major source of sustenance and nutrition. Overdependence on junk and processed foods can also cause chronic health problems related to digestion. And, of course, the right foods can do amazing things for your body and your looks. Food is also an enjoyable part of life, and that aspect of eating shouldn't be overlooked. So how do you create an eating lifestyle that's good for you *and* enjoyable? It's not that difficult. Even small shifts in the way you eat can make big changes in your well-being. Cutting out processed and fast foods and replacing them with fresh foods (which can also be quick to prepare) will automatically make a difference to your health. Really significant changes in your diet will actually transform your health. Oz says eating the right foods can even prevent and reverse illness and increase longevity. And making the right choices isn't difficult, once you know what they are.

Oz says you don't have to be a gourmet cook, shop at out-of-the-way fancy specialty shops, or even spend a lot of time in the kitchen to reap the benefits of eating well, including weight loss. See **Tip 69** for Oz's simple eating plan.

There's much more to say about food, but this isn't a book about nutrition and eating. However, you will find some basics here to get you started. And I urge you to read Oz's books to jump-start your understanding of how fun and beneficial good nutrition can really be.

## 69. OZ GARCIA'S SIMPLE EATING LIFESTYLE PLAN

There's no need to buy your weight in diet books. The following plan is a very simplified version of Oz's Paleotech Diet found in his book *Look and Feel Fabulous Forever*. It's so easy to follow and so simple to shop for that there's no excuse *not* to follow it. The best part is that if you're on a date and he takes you to a fabulous Italian restaurant, you can enjoy a bowl of pasta without guilt. Eating Oz's way makes room for an occasional special meal. Another plus? You'll enjoy those special meals more if they are only once-in-a-while treats.

### Breakfast
Start the day with big glass of warm water and drink at least two quarts of water throughout the rest of the day, every day.

Choose from: eggs, berries, steel-cut oatmeal, yogurt, rice-based bread, peanut or other nut butters, and nuts.

**Lunch and Dinner**
Choose from: *all* vegetables, such as arugula, lettuce, mesclun, carrots, broccoli, green beans, beets, celery, onion, tomatoes, sprouts, mushrooms; tuna fish; chopped eggs; turkey; chicken; salmon; cottage cheese; cheese (feta, ricotta, goat); nuts; olive oil; and lemon juice. Don't forget herbs and spices to add great layers of flavor.

**Snacks and Desserts**
Choose from: all fruits, such as apples, pineapples, blueberries, blackberries, raspberries, melons; yogurt; honey; and sunflower seeds.
   *Note: Choose organic whenever you can. The less processed the food is, the better.*

Cooking or steaming food is important for releasing phytochemicals, which are plant-based chemicals such as antioxidants. They are DNA-repairing agents, and the only way you will get full their benefit is by steaming certain vegetables. For example, the lycopene in tomatoes only becomes viable when you cook them. So enjoy tomato sauce! Also consider gently steaming broccoli, leafy greens (spinach, kale, chard), and asparagus to enjoy these veggies' full nutritional benefit.

## 70. EAT POWERFUL FOODS

Maintaining your health is easy when you realize how much great food there is to choose from. Some foods even boost your energy, enhance your sexuality, increase your vigor, and help fight depression! According to Oz, these super-foods should be part of your regular diet:

- Fish such as farm-raised salmon, bass, and trout. Stay away from big predator fish, such as shark (which is endangered) and swordfish.
- Vegetables (the darker the color, the better).

- Multicolored fruit—the more colorful the better. Think blueberries, strawberries, and red grapes.
- Nuts—a great snack and very filling in small amounts.
- Low-glycemic carbs such as beans, legumes, brown rice, corn, barley, and lentils.
- Dark chocolate—70 percent dark chocolate is the best.
- Red wine—the redder the better—four ounces per day is good for your heart and immune system.
- Water.
- Green tea, which protects bones from arthritis.
- Organic chickens and turkey. Avoid eating red meat or meat from animals with hooves such as cows, deer, lamb, pigs, and sheep. If you do crave red meat, make it lamb.
- Vegetarian and soy-based proteins and soy-based products.
- Organic active yogurt and organic milk.
- Organic cheese—omit cream cheese or other commercial, highly processed cheeses.

## 71. WORK IT!

With the busy schedules women have, we don't always have the time to get to a gym. Yet, moving the body is linked very closely to your self-confidence, the way you choose food, an increased metabolism (which burns food more quickly), and the amount of energy you have. Your attitude toward health changes as you exercise. For example, after a workout you're more likely to order fresh fruit than a pastry. And exercise also lifts your mood and helps fight depression and stress.

Even if you don't have to lose weight, exercise and fitness are still important for your well-being. Vigorous or aerobic exercise (such as running or power walking) gets your heart rate up and helps you process food more easily—so that less of what you eat is stored as fat. Anaerobic exercise, such as weight training, uses up the energy stored in muscles very quickly.

Exercise that promotes flexibility and tone, such as yoga and Pilates, will keep you limber. A combination of all three will ensure that you are burning calories, strengthening muscle, and getting all the oxygen you need.

There are many ways to get your body moving. The trick is to find activities that you can enjoy (or at least tolerate) for at least forty-five minutes a day, three to four times a week. In Part 2 of the book I'll also discuss physical activities that are good for your health *and* that can help get you into new social situations. But right now, we're focusing on fitness. For aerobic fitness, Oz says vigorous walking, jogging or running, cycling, spinning, and skiing are all good choices. Calisthenics, yoga, Pilates, and stretching routines are good for tone, body sculpting, and stress reduction. Weight training develops muscles and helps burn calories very efficiently.

To maintain momentum and give *oomph* to your workout, consider hiring a personal trainer. He or she will focus on your individual needs and ensure you are performing exercises correctly. See **Tip 72** for the inside scoop on getting the most out of a personal trainer.

## 72. INVEST IN A PERSONAL TRAINER

You don't have to be an athlete, a celebrity, or a model to have a personal trainer. Most people hire a personal trainer to help them create an effective and efficient exercise program and to learn how to use exercise equipment efficiently. It's a worthwhile investment, especially if you're just starting out. A personal trainer will make sure you get the best results from your workout and eliminate the potential for injury. For about $500, you can hire a trainer to teach you, over several sessions, how to use everything in your gym in a way that will give you maximum results. Or you can hire a trainer to come to your house once every other week to teach you yoga or Pilates moves. In between sessions you can practice on your own. This is a *great* way of prolonging your limited funds while still maintaining a personal trainer.

My husband, a professional personal trainer *extraordinaire*, says that during the consultation the trainer should ask you questions about your goals and objectives. He should also demonstrate some exercises that he would actually be doing with you. "If you tell the trainer you want to focus on stretching and gentle movements, and he suggests you perform high-impact explosive-type movements, forget about it," cautions Allen. A trainer should create an individual program for you, instead of imposing his or her preferences. "That's how people get hurt," says Allen. "Just because the trainer likes to do those movements personally doesn't mean they're right for you."

Every town and city has good trainers. Talk to people you know and ask them if they have trainers or know anyone who does. It's ideal to find an instructor through the recommendation of someone who had positive results working with him or her. If that's not possible, meet with two to three trainers (they should give you a free consultation) and ask them about their methods. A physical education pro should have at least two years' experience working with clients one-on-one. He or she should also hold a nationally recognized certification in personal training and a four-year college degree in a fitness-related subject. The fees charged can range from $65 per session to $250 per session with the median at about $120 per session. Each session typically lasts at least forty-five minutes to an hour.

A trainer should perform two critical functions. The first is motivating you to exercise. However, the goal is to transform you from being externally motivated (because you hired him or her) to becoming intrinsically motivated. When you are intrinsically motivated, you *love* to work out because it feels good. Finally, he or she should teach you enough about your workout so that you can continue on your own. After that, every few months, or when you reach an exercise plateau, you can go back to your trainer for a refresher course, to jump-start a new workout, or just learn some new techniques.

## 73. LOOK YOUR BEST WHILE YOU'RE WORKING ON LOOKING YOUR BEST

There's no reason why you have to go into hiding while you're losing weight and getting in shape. If you *are* in the middle of that process, you can still be "out there." In fact, gyms, pools, tennis courts, running tracks, and yoga studios are all great places to meet new people, including men (some of them, like you, may still be on the way to looking their best). So don't be shy. You can look terrific while you're working out too: Throw out those old ugly sweats and baggy T-shirts. If you have great gear, you'll be more likely to feel good about going to the gym. So lose the crummy sneakers and the dirty running shoes. Invest in some up-to-date workout clothes that flatter your figure and feel comfortable. Pull your hair back with a pretty ribbon. Find a fabulous bag for your gym clothes. Carry water in a pretty and functional bottle. Have fun!

## 74. MUST-HAVE BEAUTY BOOSTS FOR WORKOUTS

Flattering yoga pants in slimming black, dark brown, or navy—the soft flare leg and slightly low-slung waist of yoga pants are both comfortable and neat looking.

- Tailored T-shirts that emphasize your curves without being too tight (oversized men's T-shirts aren't flattering).
- A top-quality fitness bra (see Chapter 2 for bra-buying how-to).
- A zipper sweatshirt cover-up to match your yoga pants.
- The right shoe for your chosen activity, in an up-to-date, flattering (not clunky) style.
- Absorbent, fine white cotton socks or sockettes (*no* thick tube socks allowed).
- An *outrageous* bag for your stuff—try leopard print, bright pink, or a retro or flower print. A fun bag will cheer you up *and* act as a "conversation starter" in lieu of the jewelry and other accessories that you won't be wearing in the gym. Please resist the temptation to don those chandelier earrings!

## 75. BE A SLEEPING BEAUTY

What's better than a good night's sleep? I can think of a couple of things, of course (snuggling with a sweetheart is one); but overall, a deep, comfortable, uninterrupted sleep ranks right up there with life's little and big pleasures. Sleep is also *great* for your health. Each of us has individual sleep requirements, and I have no doubt that you're aware of what yours are. Getting less than you need causes fatigue and lowers your ability to focus. I don't need to tell you how hard it is to get through a workday if you've haven't gotten the necessary shut-eye the night before. But when you do get a good night's sleep, it will provide you with the rest you need to conquer the world the following day. And that's not all. Deep sleep, including luxurious naps on the weekend, will give you lots of other benefits, ranging from optimum brain function to clear, smooth skin (instead of those disastrously puffy, sleep-deprived eyes!).

## 76. BEAT STRESS

Stress seems to be a fact of life. Professional obligations, family commitments, and demanding friends can add to your level of stress, anxiety, and

## UP CLOSE AND PERSONAL
### *Spinning Her Wheels*

**Debra, twenty-eight, is an adorable brunette with a knockout smile (dimples included). She needed to lose about twenty pounds, and I told her so. It's not impossible to be overweight and still meet a man—but it's a lot tougher. A man's initial attraction to a woman is *always* based on looks. Blame it on ancient biology—part of him is looking for someone who appears to be fertile even if the "modern" part of his brain isn't that interested in or ready for children. I wasn't telling Debra anything she hadn't heard before, but after I pointed out the connection between her weight, her love life, *and* her health, she had a breakthrough and got serious about her diet. But Debra didn't wait until she had lost every last pound to start meeting new men. Being out there and looking her best while she was in the process of dropping pounds helped keep Debra motivated to lose all twenty pounds. And yes, she met a great guy at her spinning class, after losing only half the weight. Now they work out together, and because of that, she looks forward to her trips to the gym.**

general crankiness. Just getting to and from work can drive you nuts. One "bad day" can lower your resistance and snowball into a cold, or it can lead to an unintended angry outburst toward someone who has nothing to do with your problems. That sort of thing can impede your readiness to search for and meet new men.

The best way to fight tension is to avoid situations that cause it. Easier said than done. Since it's unlikely that you can quit your job tomorrow, stop talking to your mother, or control traffic, you need alternative plans. Learn how to deal with potentially difficult situations instead (it will come in handy for dating later on, which can be *extremely* stressful). Exercise, as I mentioned above, can really help you beat stress. So can meditation. Deep or focused breathing will help (see **Tip 91**). Listening to beautiful music or watching a funny movie also will reduce anxiety and pressure—laughter really *is* one of the best medicines. I won't go into the science of music and laughter here, because you know very well how great you feel when you hear uplifting sounds or when you have a good chuckle. Put a lot of both in your life.

## 77. MEET A MASSEUSE

A great massage helps fight fatigue. It's also another wonderful way to get in touch with your body. *Après* workout, a massage can help tense muscles relax. As a finish to a tough day at work, a massage prepares you for a laid-back date or can simply help you forget the day's annoyances. There are a lot of theories about why we humans respond so positively to massages—human touch is therapeutic for many reasons. Ultimately, it's one of life's little luxuries and has health benefits, so indulge in one as often as possible. You deserve it.

## 78. GET A CHECKUP

I am always surprised at the number of women I meet who haven't had a checkup. If you're going to start any new exercise or eating regimen, it's best to check with your doctor, of course. But more than that, a thorough exam—done yearly or every six months, depending on your age—can give you a good picture of where you are and where you want to be. Your doctor can also identify any problems or concerns before they become irreversible. If you've put off your Pap test and mammogram, or haven't seen your doctor for six months or more, make an appointment now with both your OB/GYN and your internist or general practitioner. Either can discuss all the topics in this chapter. These docs can also give you good referrals to other specialists you might be thinking about seeing, including shrinks, plastic surgeons, and dermatologists.

*Being and feeling healthy are reflections of our engagement with life.*

## 79. DRINK WATER—LOTS OF IT

Water is the elixir of life and the ultimate cleanser. It's a great hydrator for every part of your body, inside and out. Water has a fantastic effect on your skin. It's essential to keep hydrated when working out! Oz recommends drinking two quarts of water per day. It seems like a lot, but if you replace a lot of other things you drink during the day (soda, juice, coffee) with water, you'll be on your way. Adding slices of lemon, lime, or ginger can pep up the taste of water. Always be sure you know the source of your water: Filtered or bottled water from a reliable spring is best. There are literally hundreds of brand-name waters available, both domestic and imported. Conduct a taste test to see which ones you like best. If buying a pretty or unusual bottle helps you meet your two-quart goal, go ahead and splurge. Or buy yourself a great-looking water bottle (be sure to wash it thoroughly with hot water each day). Fitness super stores sell lots of fun ones. For at-work guzzling, get yourself a pretty glass.

## 80. STOP COMPARING YOURSELF

If you don't look like Catherine Zeta-Jones right now, chances are slim that you'll look like her in the future. But who said you had to look like her or any other celebrity or supermodel or socialite, anyway? Stop looking at yourself in relation to famous people (their photographs are generally airbrushed, anyway). Also, please don't use your girlfriends or stunning women you see on the street as a mirror of what you should look like. Wasting time worrying that you don't measure up to other people is discouraging, depressing, and unproductive. Better to look at stylish, fit people for *inspiration*—what are they doing right that will work for you?

## 81. WALK IT OFF

I live in New York City so I walk *a lot.* I have friends who work and live in the 'burbs, and they spend an awful lot of time in their cars. And while it's not impossible to meet new people when you are sitting in a car, it's certainly harder. (I once met two guys stopped at a red light on the utility road of the Long Island Expressway. They were on their way to pick out a beach rental for the summer. But remember—I'm a pro.) Besides, walking has so many benefits, it's crazy *not* to do it as much as you can. In addition to being great low-impact exercise, a good, long walk can really clear your head. More than that, touring your town or neighborhood, or even a new city or town, gets you to see the world, and your surroundings, from a different, more personal perspective.

## 82. KEEP TRACK OF YOUR PROGRESS

It's essential to keep on top of the strides you make after embarking on a health program. Keeping tabs on your accomplishments (and setbacks) keeps things in perspective and shows you how you are doing. Time flies. Seeing what you've accomplished in a week, a month, or a year helps bolster your spirits and your commitment. And you will make headway! A progress chart also illustrates that your efforts are paying off and proves that it doesn't take as long as you think to make a visible difference in your appearance. Use the progress chart at the end of this chapter to get going, or create your own.

## 83. STRETCH LIKE A CAT

All of us sit too much. We sit in cars, at the office, and when we're at home. Sitting around diminishes flexibility, but you can maintain or even enhance your flexibility with a good stretch, which also provides an energetic boost. Stretching at the right moment can also be very sexy (more on that later). Get a head start and some health benefits by learning how and practice provocative stretching now.

## 84. REACH FOR THE STARS: STRETCHING 101

Professional personal trainer Allen Spindel (*my* Mr. Right!) has developed three basic stretches for you. Use them as a warm-up before a workout and to generally keep you limber and elastic. They are also great to do if you have been sitting at your desk for too long or in the evening before you go to bed.

**Dynamic stretch:** This is a high-energy stretch that mimics actual activities, such as golfing or kickboxing. It's rhythmic in nature and helps you limber up. Pretend you are swinging a golf club, arms out in front of you and slightly bent at the elbow. Clasp your hands together and swing them back as if you have a club in your hands and then bring them around in a swing all the way over to your opposite shoulder. Do this five to ten times on each side. Feel the stretch as you bring the arms into the swing. Now pretend you are kickboxing. Bend your leg up and then swing it straight out to the side. Feel the stretch as you bring it out. Do this five to ten times with each leg. Follow immediately with static active.

**Static active:** This stretch isolates a muscle for three to five seconds. Bring your arm across your chest and hold in a stretch with your opposite hand for three to five seconds. Do this five to ten times on each side. Then, bend your knee back and hold it by grasping your foot in your hands. You can use your other hand to balance against a wall or bar if necessary. Now you are ready to work out.

**Static passive:** This stretch is best done when you are finished with a workout. It is the same as **static active**, with one very significant difference, which really changes the stretch: You should hold your position for thirty to sixty seconds instead of only three to five seconds. You will notice the difference between this and the shorter version. This "long hold" ensures there is no lactic acid (a by-product of waste that accumulates after exercise) buildup in the muscles. It also allows the muscle to actually elongate. This is important to keep soreness at bay, as the muscles will actually hold this stretch for twenty-four hours, even after you're done and on to the next activities!

## 85. LEAVE YOUR WORK SELF IN THE OFFICE

It's unhealthy, not to mention boring, to be totally consumed with your work all the time. Break out of your rut—you are *not* defined 100 percent by what you do. You are so much more than sales reports, presentations, and client meetings. When you're not at work, don't work. Engage yourself with a hobby, sports, culture, and just in having *fun*. As I said earlier, a good laugh is a healthy elixir. So is being playful! All work and no play won't just make you a dull girl—it can lead to bad health. The stress, fatigue, and irritation of your job can invade your personal life if you let it. Going out at lunchtime to do something for yourself is one way to break away from office drudgery. Book a manicure or a facial. Make after-hours plans with people outside of work, and don't forget to change some aspect of your outfit before you meet up. A quick top change or shoe switch can really make you feel a little less tied to the job. Don't stay late in the office on Friday nights. In fact, if you don't have a date, make sure you have "early" plans (think 6 P.M.) with a friend so you're out the door by 5:30. And *please*, fight the temptation (if you actually have the urge) to go into the office on weekends! One more thing: Make conscious efforts to not talk about what you do when not at work—unless he asks. It's not that your work isn't important; it's just that I want you to break the habit of discussing *only* your job.

## 86. DON'T GET DISCOURAGED

There will be times when your diet and exercise program will not go as well as you like. You may miss some workout sessions or fall off the food wagon. When that happens, it's tempting to give up. But don't. Get right back on the horse and keep galloping forward. Just realize that there will be disappointments and hindrances along the way. If you prepare for them beforehand, you will be able to conquer them when they do come along.

## 87. START FEELING SEXY

Exercising and eating right will get you more in touch with your body. You may not have even *seen* your body in a while. Am I right? You'll start to be aware of your curves and your physicality. Take pleasure in the positive changes you see. Get in touch with your sexual side—this is *especially* important if you haven't been in a relationship for a while. Start wearing fitted clothes and fine lingerie. Treat yourself like the sensual lady you are.

## 88. REWARD YOURSELF (WITHOUT SABOTAGING YOUR DIET)

If you've reached a milestone (lost your first five pounds) or accomplished a goal in your fitness program (rode your bike ten miles, finally touched your toes), give yourself a gift. It can be as small as a new lipstick or as extravagant as a new pair of shoes. In fact, work three or four rewards into your overall Get Serious budget (page 11). A pat on the back lends incentive to the process.

## 89. ONLY THE BEST

If you want to reward yourself with a sinful food treat—or if you're celebrating a special occasion—make sure it's the very best you can afford and have only a small quantity. Life's too short for cheap champagne or

*What's hot:* **Silky, sexy panties, bras, stockings, and camisoles that make you feel good about your body**

*What's not:* **"Granny" underpants, thick knee socks, "armor" bras**

low-grade chocolate. Another plus? Rewarding yourself with something deliciously forbidden *once in a while* may help you maintain your new eating lifestyle the rest of the time.

## 90. STAND UP STRAIGHT

Good posture makes you look five to ten pounds thinner, gives you a confident aura, and benefits your back. Here's how to practice good posture: Stand against a wall and make sure your shoulders and butt touch the wall. Now, put your arm into the space between your lower back and the wall. Is your hand touching both the wall and your back? If it isn't, tilt your hips so that it does and hold this position for thirty seconds. Repeat. Walk away from the wall in position and practice holding yourself like this for the rest of the day. If you keep at it, good posture will become second nature.

## 91. CATCH YOUR BREATH

I won't get into the hocus pocus of what is known in New Age circles as focused breathing. I just know that controlled deep breathing reduces stress and promotes a feeling of well-being and serenity. It also brings a lot of necessary oxygen into your system! Here's a simple way to do it: Sit up straight in a comfortable chair. Place your right hand on your abdomen and your left on your chest. Breathe in deeply and slowly through your nose then exhale *slowly* through your mouth so that the right hand moves with your breath while the left hand stays still. Repeat this eight to ten times. While you are breathing, focus *only* on your breath. This exercise will relax your body and clear your mind.

## 92. LUXURIATE

Being good to yourself in small ways may not be a necessity, but it does help you feel good. Pamper yourself with visits to a spa. Indulge in fine soaps, creams, and other beauty products. Add thick, absorbent Turkish towels to your bathroom décor. Take bubble baths. Use a natural-bristle brush on your hair. Make your bed with high-thread-count cotton or linen sheets. You'll be surprised at how much these things count toward keeping you positive and happy.

## 93. DETOXIFY

At least one weekend day every other month or more frequently if you want, give your body a break and eliminate all the toxins you face every day, from processed food to environmental abuses. That means giving up coffee, tea, alcohol, candy, refined wheat products, meat or animal products, bad air and water, crowded and noisy streets, annoying people, and your cell phone. Eliminating external encumbrances and finding a change of scenery for even two days will both rev you up and calm you down, and it's pretty easy to accomplish. If you live in an urban area, you're probably just a car, bus, or train ride away from a bucolic spa or bed-and-breakfast in the country. No need to go very far. My husband and I traveled to a wonderful bed-and-breakfast on Long Island recently. It was less than two hours away from our apartment, but it seemed like a million miles from the honking horns and hordes of people we're used to in the city. And changing your surroundings, as we'll discuss later, may also present an opportunity to meet someone new.

## 94. TAKE YOUR VITAMINS!

Even if you're eating the right foods, you may not be getting all the nourishment you need. Women have complicated nutritional needs, and an all-purpose vitamin is often necessary to keep up with them. Oz Garcia says there are other "nutraceuticals" that can also be beneficial, especially for women. It's worth seeing a good nutritionist for advice about diet and vitamins. When your body has the vitamins and minerals it needs, the results can include extended longevity; fewer colds and "sick days"; and improved skin, eyes, teeth, and hair.

## 95. LET GO OF THE PAST

Everything that happened yesterday is over and done with. There's nothing you can do about it. But *today* you have a chance to change everything!

Take that opportunity and move on. Dwelling on past triumphs or tragedies keeps you from moving forward. Living in the moment and embracing the future enhances vitality.

## 96. CREATE A SUPPORT SYSTEM AND STAY CONNECTED TO IT

It's not easy to stick to a healthy eating plan or maintain a regular exercise schedule. Make sure you have a strong circle of friends and family that you can count on when you encounter difficulties. As I said in Chapter 1, "delete" anyone who *isn't* on board with your efforts. And don't underestimate the power of support groups focused on accomplishing certain goals (such as changing eating habits, quitting smoking, or running and walking together for fitness). They offer a sense of community that keeps you connected. That connection helps keep you committed and strong. Groups like these may also offer opportunities to make new friends, who may very well introduce you to your future husband!

## 97. FIND BALANCE AND NURTURE YOUR SPIRIT

Don't wear yourself out trying to meet unrealizable goals. Make sure you aren't doing one thing too much (toiling at the office, working out like *crazy*). Relax and take time to smell the roses. After all, "he" might be there amidst the flowers—and you wouldn't want to run past him on your way to the gym!

# CHARTING MY HEALTHY FUTURE

After you have discussed your current health picture with your doctor and have developed a course of action (including determining your ideal "fighting" weight), use this simple chart to track your progress. Most health professionals recommend weighing in at the same time of day just once a week. Use the same scale and wear the same amount of clothing each time. Be careful not to obsess over the results.

Other experts say that if you can do something for just eight weeks, it becomes a habit. Eight weeks! That's no time at all. So you have to chart your course only for a limited period of time. After that, your healthy habits will be second nature and part of your life. Congratulations!

**Current Weight**_____

**Goal Weight** _____

Week one_____

Week two_____

Week three_____

Week four_____

Week five_____

Week six_____

Week seven_____

Week eight_____

## Measure Up

Take your measurements now and at the end of four weeks and eight weeks (if you take them every week, the changes will not be very dramatic and you may become frustrated). Be sure to measure each part of your shape in the same place each time. Don't pull the tape measure too tight, but don't let it hang loose either.

**Starting measurements:**

Bust _____

Waist _____

Hips _____

Thighs _____

Upper arms _____

**Four-week measurements:**

Bust _____

Waist _____

Hips _____

Thighs _____

Upper arms _____

**Eight-week measurements:**

Bust _____

Waist _____

Hips _____

Thighs _____

Upper arms _____

**The Fitness Effect**

Try to exercise three days per week for forty-five minutes at a minimum. If you are committed to getting in shape and meeting Mr. Right, this is certainly a chunk of time you can make room for in your busy schedule. Use this section of the worksheet each week to note what activity you did and for how long. Make sure to write down anything new you tried or any physical goals you met. Seeing your accomplishments in writing makes a difference!

Week one _____

Week two _____

Week three _____

Week four _____

Week five _____

Week six _____

Week seven _____

Week eight _____

# *Four*

# Breaking Up Doesn't
# Have to Be Hard to Do

*P*art of cleaning house may involve the difficult task of leaving a dead-end, unsatisfying relationship. If your current boyfriend can't or won't commit, if you've fallen out of love, or if you know in your heart he's not "the one," it's best to make a clean break. Holding on prolongs the frustration and pain of breaking up.

Even trying to forget painful past associations can be difficult. For example, if you have been single for a while but your last relationship was intense, you may have residual feelings for your ex—his belongings and photos could even be a nagging presence in your home. You still have to "break up" with him (even if he's not physically underfoot).

It's not easy to end a relationship if you have shared your life with someone, be it for a few months or a few years. It's even more difficult, of course, if *he* walks away. That can be devastating no matter how you look at it.

There are a lot of things you can do to help ease the pain of a breakup, but the most important one is *not to put your life on hold*. To be "suddenly single" doesn't mean that you can't enjoy the sweet things in life. In fact, it's *most* important to savor and appreciate the things that make you happy when you are newly alone.

If you are unfettered by a past relationship or not in a situation that needs resolving before you get out in the dating scene, this is one chapter you can skip. However, you may want to come back to it if you end up meeting someone and things don't work out. For instance, you may find after three or six months of dating that the new man you've met after reading this book isn't for you.

What follows are some healthy, productive break-up strategies that will help you get back in the dating game. So please have the courage to end a relationship when things aren't working out. There *are* many men out there looking for serious relationships. Breaking up with someone who isn't right for you is much easier *before* you make the mistake of marrying the person—I have known all too many women who married men they didn't feel 100 percent confident about. Marriage is an awesome personal, social, and legal commitment, and divorce has serious economic and psychological implications. When you finally tie the knot, it should be in the form of a beautiful bow!

## 98. RESOLVE TO WALK AWAY

Knowing when to walk away from a relationship that isn't moving toward marriage really depends on your age and circumstances. If you're twenty-four there's no reason for you to have a three- or six-month cutoff point. If you want children and you're thirty-five, forty, or older, you really should follow the six-month rule. Single men and women over thirty-five are usually established or on their way to becoming financially and professionally stable. They know what they want. If you are at that point and in a relationship and he doesn't want to marry you—or you don't want to marry him—after six months, it's unlikely those feelings will change in the next six months or nine months or year.

Knowing that you have a date on Saturday night may make you feel comfortable, but just know that Comfortable Guy Road is a dead end! An ultimatum doesn't have to be handed down like a life sentence, but a point arises in a serious relationship when it's "now or never."

When I see a woman who is with a man for a year or two, knowing full well that he's never going to be marriage material, I have to ask her what she's doing. If marriage were your goal, why would you go out with someone for two years if you knew all along that he was not going to marry you or you him? Leave!

## 99. DO IT NICELY

It takes a lot of courage to break up with someone. That's why some people chicken out and either stop returning phone calls or carry on half-heartedly with dating. This makes me *nuts*. It's rude and cruel to ignore someone, especially if he has been kind to you. And it's just as bad to lead him on by continuing to see him.

It's okay to break up with a man on the telephone if you have gone on three to six dates and you haven't been intimate. What's *not* okay is to leave a message on his answering machine! You have to talk to him in person. Keep it simple and say something like, "I had a lot of fun with you and you're a great person, but I am looking for something different in a relationship right now." Or you can say, "I think you're a great guy, and I had a nice time with you, but I don't think that this will evolve into the kind of relationship I am looking for." The key is not to insult him or put him down. Why make him feel bad about himself? It's not his fault that you're not attracted to him.

If you're going to break up with someone whom you've been seriously dating and you know that marriage will not result, you must sit down face to face with him. It's going to be tough to let him go after investing so much time and emotion. But listen to me: It's not as brutal as staying in a relationship for six more months and *then* breaking up. If it's because you know he doesn't want to get married, you need to give that as the reason why you're leaving. It can be as simple as, "I really want to get married, and you don't. So I think it would be better for both of us if we called it quits." Reassure him that you have no hard feelings and you wish him only the best.

## 100. RECOGNIZE PROBLEMS FOR WHAT THEY ARE

If you and your partner are seeing a therapist while you're dating, quit while you're ahead. What's going to happen when you get married? Issues don't necessarily go away. Some women think, "I'll give it a couple more months." Uh-uh. It doesn't work that way. A friend of mine was with a guy for a year, even though she knew he was not for her. But there was always an excuse for her to stick around when she should have been out meeting new men. First, she was seeing him through career problems and she didn't want to leave him. When that was finished, it was something else. Ironically, as soon as his life was back in order, *he* ditched *her!* You're only fooling yourself and being self-destructive when you continue to work on unsolvable problems.

## 101. NINE SIGNS YOU SHOULD BREAK UP

Always be attuned to your inner voice when you're in a relationship. You should feel happy and confident in any relationship you're in. If you constantly feel annoyed, angry, depressed, put down, or mistreated, then it's time to move on. Here are nine signs it's time to get out:

1. You are six months into the relationship and he is unwilling to commit.

2. You argue with him more than you talk together.

3. You feel nervous and insecure around him and about the relationship.

4. You feel jealous and anxious when he's not around.

5. It's difficult to resolve disagreements with him, even though normally you don't have problems compromising with other people.

6. He doesn't make you feel pretty. If he doesn't make you feel like a lady or compliment you after the trouble you've taken to look fantastic, what are you doing?

7. You have few, if any, shared values.

8. You don't trust him.

9. You don't love him.

## 102. ACCEPT REJECTION GRACIOUSLY

If a man tells you he isn't interested in pursuing the relationship further, accept it with as few polite, civil words as possible and move on. It's hard to be rejected, even by a man you didn't particularly care for. Maintaining your dignity, composure, and good manners is very difficult at these moments, but it's absolutely essential. "Losing it" will make an unfavorable impression on him. His final memory of you shouldn't remind him of Lady Macbeth. More importantly, "scenes" leave you feeling really crummy. You can say, "I'm sorry to hear that," or "Thank you for letting me know—please keep me in mind for your single friends." The bottom line is that if he was a gentleman and a nice person and you liked him, you want to wish him well.

## 103. DON'T CONVINCE YOURSELF THAT TIME HAS BEEN WASTED

Just because a relationship doesn't lead to marriage doesn't mean the time you spent was squandered or lost. Every relationship provides you with insights into who you are and what you like and want in a man. (Make a note of them.) And there are many moments of fun and happiness in every relationship that are to be savored no matter what happens in the end. Time spent enjoying the company of another person is time well spent. Don't be hard on yourself—consider yourself lucky that you have learned something and have had the courage to move on from a situation that wasn't going in the right direction.

## 104. FORGIVE AND FORGET

The residual bad feelings and immobility that come from not forgiving someone can have devastating effects on your future dating life. So he was a bastard. Aren't you glad you're out of it? Forgive him for being a jerk (it's not necessary to tell him that—telling yourself is sufficient) and get on with your life! Obsessing over his shortcomings is a waste of precious time. It's also important to forgive yourself. If you were unkind to him, apologize, even in a written note. And then tell yourself you did the right thing (trust me, you did).

## 105. EIGHT THINGS TO DO AFTER A BREAKUP

Positive indulgences can go a long way in sustaining your heart and soul after a split. Here are some ideas:

1. Rent or go see a comedy—laughter is an important ingredient in the recipe for moving on.
2. Call a faraway friend you haven't seen or talked to in ages.
3. Schedule a vacation day from work.
4. Throw a cocktail party (in honor of your new cocktail dress!).
5. Buy the best bottle of champagne you can afford and share it with a friend.
6. Shop for fancy lingerie—and choose something daring!
7. Pamper yourself—get a facial, book time at a day spa.
8. Go out and meet new men!

## 106. FIND COMFORT WITH FRIENDS AND LOVED ONES— LOSE PEOPLE WHO TAKE PLEASURE IN YOUR PAIN

"There's nothing worse than a girlfriend who seems slightly pleased when you tell her that you've split from a boyfriend," says Elaine, forty-two, a tall, stylish member of JSSM. "It's almost as if they're happy that you're back in the same situation they are," she says. I could not agree more. Everyone has an agenda, and sometimes those agendas clash with our best

*Overheard:* "He didn't make me feel pretty, regardless of the effort I went to for him. But he would talk about other women in terms of their appearance," says Jana.

interests. If that's the case, think about reevaluating your friendships with people who aren't supportive of your goals or are a little bit giddy that you are feeling miserable after a breakup.

## 107. DON'T GO BACKWARD

Never break up with one man and then run back to a previous boyfriend for comfort. What's worse? Having sex with him, too. It makes you feel bad and it doesn't lead anywhere. I trust you enough to know that there's a reason why you broke up with your first ex—don't forget that after a recent breakup!

## 108. GET YOUR BEST SELF OUT THERE AGAIN!

You can mourn the loss of the relationship, of course. But don't let feelings of sorrow take over your life. *Now* is the time to reconnect with the single you—and that includes resurrecting activities, hobbies, and interests you explored before you were in what's now a defunct relationship. Maintain your self-esteem through work, developing talents, and engaging in social activity.

Don't throw yourself into your job as a way to compensate for being single. That may isolate you—and take you away from social opportunities and new men.

Don't accept too many invitations from couples unless they're asking you to an event where there will be single, available men. If you get in the groove of socializing only with married or paired-off people, you will soon feel like a fifth wheel. When you are with other single people you will be more open to meeting other single men. You won't feel like an outsider looking in. Of course, you should spend time with people you enjoy—just don't make a regular habit of hanging out with couple friends. Fight the urge to punish yourself. When we're sad we have a tendency to seek out comfort in various forms, such as eating too many of the wrong things or lying in bed instead of exercising. Sorrow can also lead to binge spending, which can get you in financial trouble. Have a game plan ready to combat these natural tendencies if you think you may succumb. Make sure you have nothing bad to eat in the house. Instead of indulging in too much chocolate, pasta, or other comfort foods, indulge in a new pair of athletic shoes or sexy heels. Instead of lying around in bed all weekend, make a plan for the weekend ahead of time, so that when Saturday comes you can get up and out of your house. Finally, don't go shopping alone. Make sure you go with a friend who has agreed beforehand to stop you from making any crazy purchases or spending over a certain amount.

## 109. FIGHT THE TEMPTATION TO GO BACK

If you have broken up with a man because you differ on the "big" life issues—such as marriage and children—*don't* go back to him because you're lonely! I have a client who's fifty-five and has never been married. She stayed with a man for twenty years—that's *twenty years,* ladies— essentially because she was afraid of the consequences of leaving him: being by herself. He did not want to get married or have children and she did. But at fifty-five, it was too late to have natural children and it was unlikely that she would even be able to adopt. The irony is *he* left *her* for another woman!

Tragically, she knew five years into the relationship that he was never going to marry her. He had been through a nasty divorce and he was simply through with matrimony. Occasionally, she'd make a break for it, but after a couple of months she'd find herself on his doorstep again. He accepted her back because it was convenient for him—he had someone to keep house, take care of him, cook, and clean without commitment on his part. Now, she is going to be a challenging, but not impossible, client to help because of her age and psychological baggage. A friend of mine, Sherry, thirty-nine, had a bad habit that she couldn't break: She kept talking to her ex—sometimes several times a week! What a mistake—she had

*Janis says:* If you gain weight, go into debt, or lose motivation, it can be extra difficult to get out there and meet someone new.

none of the benefits of a bona fide relationship, that is, dates, intimacy, and romance. But he was *never* going to get back together with her, and talking to him regularly filled her with false hope, which caused her difficulty connecting with new men. She would sit at my dinner parties and chat with the

> *If a man tells you he isn't interested in pursuing the relationship further, accept it with as few polite words as possible and move on. Keep it short, simple, and civil.*

person next to her but if he followed up with an offer of a date, she was reluctant to go! It wasn't until she got on a cold turkey program—which meant no phone calls, e-mails, or instant messages to her ex for eight weeks—that she was able to free herself from him forever!

## 110. GO SLOWLY IF FATE STEPS IN

If you are running into your ex in unexpected, odd, and random places, almost as if by "fate," you might want to pay attention to that. I am not an advocate of "magical thinking," but sometimes fate does intervene. If it's happening a lot, be conscious of your feelings when it does happen. Maybe the relationship is worth another try. But take it slowly. If you do start up where you left off and the same issues crop up, pack your bags. Sometimes people mature and change, and sometimes they don't.

## 111. DON'T SPEND TOO MUCH TIME WITH THE PEOPLE YOU SAW WHEN YOU WERE TOGETHER

It's not uncommon for couples to have friends together. When the relationship ends you may find yourself separating your friends like you separate your intermingled CD and book collections. While it is fine to remain cordial with people you knew as part of a couple, it's also important to focus on making new friends. Being around mutual friends will remind you that you are no longer a couple. And you run the risk of bumping into your ex—something you're probably not prepared for. My client Joyce, forty-four, said one of the best things she did after she broke up with her boyfriend of six months was to cultivate new people at a job she had started. For one thing, it helped her learn about the company. There was also little risk of her running into any part of her life with her ex when she socialized with them, and no need to explain "what happened" since they didn't know about him.

## 112. THINK ABOUT WHAT WENT WRONG, BUT *DON'T* OVERANALYZE

Learn from your dating experiences but don't obsess over them. Take note of the things you realized about yourself while in a serious relationship so that you can apply them the next time. But don't berate yourself for "failing" in the relationship. And *don't* put yourself down for not being good enough, pretty enough, thin enough, smart enough, sexy enough—whatever you are thinking, it's not true. If you saw something in your ex that you didn't like, keep it in mind when you meet the next guy.

## 113. DON'T THROW A PITY PARTY

One of the best ways to move past a breakup is to stop talking about it! Once you've told your friends that you've broken up and shared a few details with them, and had a good cry, you can stop. Believe me, your friends won't tell you this but I will: They don't want to spend all their time with you hearing about your ex. They may be nodding their heads but inside they are nodding off.

Lisa, thirty-six, a very successful photographer, did all the right things after a major breakup with a longtime boyfriend who was commitment-phobic. She finally walked away after way too long—five years, to be exact. She moved from Los Angeles to New York City, scored a phenomenal teaching job, started showing her work at galleries, and met a ton of new people, including a lot of eligible bachelors. However, she wouldn't shut up about Frank, her ex. She claimed she was heartbroken and still had "issues" about the relationship. In truth, she had moved on with her

life and was succeeding very nicely. But she had this need to be pitied—
Frank was the "great love of her life" and this "tragedy" offered her a
comfort zone. No one with a 2,400-square-foot loft in SoHo, a fantastic
career in the arts, a cute little figure, and money to spare should have anyone, anywhere feeling sorry for them at anytime! She was addicted to her
own misery. Lisa couldn't understand it when people drifted away from
her at social gatherings when she started in on Frank. Her carping was
unattractive to the opposite sex, to say the very least. Lisa had to get over
it. The funny thing, which she eventually realized, was that she actually
*was* over Frank—she just wasn't over the "romance" of the breakup.

## 114. DEVELOP NEW RITUALS AND SHIFT OLD ONES

If you spent Sundays with your ex reading the paper and sipping coffee at
a certain neighborhood café, stop doing it now. If you always went to the
same restaurant on Friday night, don't go there anymore. Replace little
habits, rituals, and routines you picked up from or created with your ex
with different activities and new rituals. Instead of going to the café to
drink coffee and read the paper, buy a paper and read it in the park or in a
different café at another time of day. You'll be surprised at how effective
changing your routine will be in forgetting the past. Use the worksheet at
the end of this chapter to sort out the routines you feel need changing.

## 115. DON'T DESTROY RELATIONSHIP MEMORIES—
## JUST PUT THEM AWAY

You have probably collected little mementos, photos, and souvenirs of
your relationship. Your first impulse may be to throw them away. Don't.
You may regret it later. Instead, pack all the little keepsakes in a box and
store it at the top of the closet or under your bed. Having little reminders
around is just as bad as going through the relationship rituals without
your ex. After a year you can reevaluate. If there are things that you find
you like that no longer hold potent memories of the relationship, keep
them and toss the rest.

## 116. DON'T MINE HIS BUDDIES FOR INFORMATION

If you're tempted to talk to his friends for news about what he's doing and who he's seeing, stop yourself. This is yet another damaging way of clinging to a relationship that didn't work out. It's also a guaranteed way to feel miserable and anxious. If you run into people you both knew together, especially his male buddies, be polite and say hello. But don't let the conversation drift into a rehash of your relationship with him or a discussion of his current state of affairs.

Let his friends see for themselves how great you are doing—make it obvious through actions, not words. If they ask what happened, say you parted ways amicably but you were both looking for different things in a relationship. Keep your answers brief and then change the subject.

## 117. OFFICE ROMANCE GONE WRONG?

Work-based relationships are always risky—for the very reason that you might break up. It's tougher than almost every kind of breakup I know because avoidance is almost out of the question. Keep your dignity—and your job—by being absolutely professional. If you are feeling emotional, go for a walk, visit the ladies' room, or call in sick. But don't let your performance falter or your work quality fall off. In fact, you both have to agree that you will not let the separation affect your respective jobs. If you respect each other's position in the company, chances are you will get through it.

## 118. RENEW OLD FRIENDSHIPS

When you're dating someone seriously, you may find yourself shifting time you would have spent with friends to your new boyfriend instead. Personally, I don't think you should ditch friends when you get a boyfriend—it's short sighted. Friends can last a lifetime, and they provide a unique type of comfort and companionship. But I am also a realist and I know that you will certainly have to make decisions about your time and that often you will make them in favor of your boyfriend.

Now is the time to go through your Palm or your address book and see who you've neglected or haven't spoken to in a while. If there are people you feel you have left behind because of the demands of the relationship, and you really shouldn't have, you are going to have to apologize when you contact them. Saying something simple and sincere such as, "I was in a relationship that made incredible demands on my time, and I am sorry about that. Those demands have been relaxed and I would really like to see you again," should be sufficient.

## 119. GET OUT OF TOWN

Post-breakup is the perfect time to take a weekend getaway! Here are a few suggestions:

- Spa—beauty treatments and pampering can make you beautiful and ready to face the world as a single girl again.
- Another city—a weekend in Denver, Dallas, New York, Chicago, or San Francisco may be just what you need to get your juices flowing.
- Beach or island—a sand-and-surf rest can be rejuvenating.
- Car trip—a leisurely drive through several states or along a coastline can be enriching, with surprises around every corner.
- Sports getaways—from hiking trips to bicycle rides, even a dude ranch, will get you moving with other people.

## 120. GO AHEAD AND HAVE A GOOD CRY

Don't bottle up your feelings. If you feel like crying, cry. It's okay to feel sad, frustrated, and even angry. If you feel a cry coming on when you're at work, go to the ladies' room. You may experience little crying jags for several months after an especially hard breakup. Crying can be good for you, but it should not become a habit. Excess crying can be a red flag. For example, if tears are flowing more than once a day, every day, it may be a sign that you are truly depressed. If that's the case, seek out professional help.

## 121. RECOGNIZE WHEN YOU ARE ON THE REBOUND AND WHEN YOU'RE NOT!

You've heard stories about women and men who hook up with the wrong people after a breakup. We're hurt and lonely and sometimes we pair up with someone we wouldn't ordinarily be attracted to. I've worked with quite a few men whose second marriage ended because they met their ex-wives on "the rebound" after being divorced or widowed. They want to find what they lost the first time around, or they simply don't want to be alone.

## UP CLOSE AND PERSONAL
### *Seeing What's in Front of You*

"When Jim broke up with me, it was really hard. I was so smitten with him and losing him felt like the end of the world," Anna, forty, said. She looked up to Jim, forty-seven, in a way that made their relationship unequal. He was prominent in the broadcasting world and had left her for someone who was equal to him in public fame. When one member of the relationship has a public profile, it can subconsciously weigh on the other person. Anna was in Jim's shadow. "I didn't realize it until he left me—I never felt like a whole person," she says. In fact, Anna is a successful executive at a large drug company. There is no reason why she has to be in anyone's shadow.

"There was a man in my neighborhood whom I always shared banter with. I felt comfortable talking to him because I had the protection of my relationship with Jim. He was a very good-looking guy, and I think I would have felt intimidated about chatting with him if I hadn't been with someone. By the time Jim had broken up with me, we were quite friendly so it seemed natural to keep up our rapport." Finally, Anna got the courage to ask the man to have coffee with her. "He thought I was still dating Jim, so he didn't dare ask me. The only way it was going to happen was if I did it myself." Fortunately, Anna didn't keep herself from enjoying the friendship of others, as sometimes happens when women are very consumed with their boyfriends. "I really like this man," says Anna, "and I am excited to see where it goes."

They rush into a second relationship before they've really had a chance to evaluate what they want and reflect on what they have been through.

Give yourself breathing space before rushing into another committed relationship. Instead, date several men and get to know yourself again. Rebound relationships generally don't work out, compounding the hurt you felt from the previous breakup.

## 122. DON'T MAKE DECISIONS ABOUT *ANYTHING* FOR AT LEAST A MONTH AFTER A BREAKUP

On a related note, it's very important not to make any major life or appearance decisions soon after a breakup. I had a client who cut off all her hair after a breakup. She may have been punishing herself, or perhaps she thought the change would do her good. It didn't. The haircut was unflattering and regrettable, and it took time to grow out. Other bad on-the-rebound decisions include quitting a job, moving, and engaging in risky behavior. While quitting a job or moving may ultimately be positive steps for you, you should take them only *after* careful consideration. Engaging in any kind of risky behavior, such as going to dangerous places (a stranger's apartment, an unsafe neighborhood); having unprotected sex; abusing alcohol; or, God forbid, taking drugs, never solves anything.

## 123. RECONNECT WITH MEN YOU LIKED BEFORE YOU WENT EXCLUSIVE

Seek out men you may have dated before you went exclusive with your ex. Drop a short note or an e-mail to men you dated in the past that you liked. It's a proactive step that will help get you back into the dating scene. "After my boyfriend left me for another woman, I reconnected with a guy I had dated in college," says Maria, forty-three, an acquaintance of mine. "A lot of the things I liked about him were still there, but he was more mature, as was I." That reconnection resulted in marriage. I can't guarantee that will happen to you, but it will help you ease back into the dating scene. A warning: Don't expect that old flames can always be rekindled.

## 124. IGNITE OLD PASSIONS

Now is the time to rediscover hobbies or social activities you stopped doing while you were dating. If you let your interest in arts and crafts slip because you were too busy with your boyfriend, go back to it. If volunteering at the animal clinic took a backseat, get back on their schedule. Igniting old passions is much healthier than a lonely routine of watching old movies, eating chocolates, and reading magazines. Getting in that sort of rut will also give you little to talk about when you *do* run into new men. For example:

"Hi Joann, it's nice to meet you. What did you did this weekend?"

"I watched five Audrey Hepburn movies and ate two pints of double chocolate Häagen Dazs."

A better reply would be: "I volunteer in a program that escorts tourists around town, so yesterday I showed a French family the local attractions. They invited me to stay with them in Paris! Then I tried this cute new Italian place, Eno's, with a friend. Have you been there?"

# REPLACE OLD RITUALS WITH NEW ONES

Make a note of things you used to do with your ex, and then right next to it, jot down something else you can do to replace it:

OLD                                   NEW

_____  _____

_____  _____

_____  _____

_____  _____

_____  _____

# Part 2

# WIDENING THE NET AND INCREASING YOUR CHANCES

Okay, you've nailed down what you want in a relationship and in a man. And you've gotten rid of Mr. Wrong. But you've also promised to keep an open mind. Now you have to get in the mood and develop the "certain something" that will make you irresistible. Start by using the tips and techniques in this chapter. You'll be bubbling over with magnetism in no time, and charming people make the world a better place—what could be bad?

I'll also review every great venue and situation where the potential to meet great guys is the highest. And since we've set your goal at one year or less, you'll want to rev up your meeting machine and stretch your net as widely as possible. So I'll give you the lowdown on professional dating and mating services you can use to enhance your romance while avoiding common mistakes others make. From matchmaking to Internet dating, you'll find it here.

# Five

## Get in the Mood and Become Date-able!

*D*isarming women seem to be born with a potent "gift of nature." When a woman can change the opinion of a prickly boss, make an elusive associate suddenly available, turn an enemy into an ally, or transform an awkward social situation into a pleasant one with a few words or actions, it seems magical. It's not. She's simply using an important tool to get what she wants. Charm. She and other women with the same *savoir-faire* know how to break down the barriers people often put up during initial encounters. Success in everything from selling real estate to getting asked on a second date can hinge on our ability to disarm others. The fact is, being charming and disarming can help you get things done faster and make your life more enjoyable. And with the positive reactions you'll get from the new beguiling, bewitching you, your self-esteem will soar.

If you don't have the right mindset and a bit of "magic" up your sleeve, it won't matter how white your teeth are or how fabulous your outfit is. Think about it—have you ever met a drop-dead gorgeous man or woman who, when they opened their mouth, was boring and vacant or snobby and mean? I have. Looks might get them through the door, but if they have no charm, empathy, or interest in other people, they won't get very far into the room. In other words, surface beauty can pique interest, but if there's nothing behind it, that appeal can be quickly lost.

On the other hand, think about the woman who isn't "model pretty," but who is attractive enough and very well put together. Thirty-three-year-old JSSM member Sarah is like that. She's not that different from 100 other women, except for one thing. Sarah simply *glows* from within. She looks a man in the eye when he talks to her, as if he were the *most* important person on earth (instead of half listening and scanning the room for someone more "important"). She's warm and funny and bright. She's a man magnet. That's why she is always at the top of the list for my intimate dinner parties. Male clients always ask if she will be there. The only reason she's not married yet is that she's having too much fun. But I expect her to be wearing an engagement ring by the time you read this.

You can be like Sarah, too. In fact, you pretty much have to be if you want to meet and marry a man in one year or less. It's all about opening yourself up, getting in the right mood, and developing qualities in yourself that others also want to find in someone else. If you practice the following tips whenever you're in any social situation, you will likely attract a person who is *at the very least* kind, happy, and open. That's a pretty good start, isn't it? Don't use these principles only on men you meet—implement them in all aspects of your life. That way they will become second nature—they will be sincere. Being open and charming to *everyone* you meet can result only in great things. Everyone is a human being. Even the nerdy guy down the street is a person—treat him like one! Besides, he might have an *adorable* friend, brother, cousin, or nephew!

You also have to learn to trick yourself into "working it" even when you don't feel like it. Not only will this skill get you through lots of situations, it will also make every social circumstance you find yourself in more fun! These same principles can be used at work, with friends and family, even when you're shopping or dealing with difficult salespeople. Why bother, you might ask. Because *every* situation you are in—from standing in line at the grocery store to sitting on an airplane—is a potential opportunity to meet your future husband or someone who will introduce you to your future husband. While it's sometimes difficult, being fabulous every second of the day is a proven way to increase your chances of meeting "the one"!

## 125. TEAR DOWN THAT WALL!

You may have been hurt badly in a past relationship and don't want it to happen again. So you build an impenetrable wall around yourself. It's a natural defense mechanism—who doesn't want some protection from emotional pain? But that wall is going to prevent potential mates from getting through to you. You *have* to open yourself up and break down barriers that are holding you back from being your best self. Listen, I'm not saying you will never be hurt again—you very well may be. Take setbacks and disappointments in stride and teach yourself to get back on the horse and keep riding into the future.

## 126. TAKE THE HELLO CHALLENGE

Okay, ladies! When you wake up tomorrow I want you to vow you will simply say "hello" to three men and see what happens. Do it *every single day* for a week. Saying hello is really easy, and it's so natural that no one will be put off. There's nothing more charming than a friendly woman. Just see how many men you can say hello to in one day. Challenge yourself to increase the number every day. The only way your friendliness will become natural is if you practice, practice, practice. If a man says hello back and seems interested, keep the ball rolling and go with it! Pull out a pickup line. If not, it doesn't matter. Just move on to the next guy. The point is to practice. There is nothing easier than saying "Hi." (To track your results, turn to the Hello Challenge worksheet on page 132.)

## 127. FIND COMMON GROUND AND PLAY OFF IT

Establish common ground with someone, and he'll lower his defenses. Ask questions of the man you're speaking to, or share information about yourself that will bring out something of his character, background, experience, or interests. When you hear something he says that you can relate to, use that as a jumping-off point. He'll feel more comfortable with you (and let down his guard) if you can establish that you enjoy hiking too or that Rome is your favorite city. Sharing common history is also a good way to forge a bond. For example, Joann, forty, met Marshall, forty-four, at one of my parties. She liked what she saw, and as they started chatting she asked him where he had grown up. That's a good, open-ended question that will usually be met with more than a one-word reply. They discovered they had both been army brats, which led them to a whole other host of mutual experiences, from moving frequently to seeing Europe. The next thing you know, they were continuing the conversation over dinner the following weekend.

## 128. LEARN A NEW LANGUAGE—BODY LANGUAGE!

A charming, disarming woman lets her body speak for her as well. The way you hold yourself sends a message to men about whether you are approachable or not. You know (or certainly should!) to avoid the obvious (sticking your breasts in a stranger's face is *not* the way to meet your mate!). Your stance should be open and welcoming. Women who stand with their arms folded or hold their body in a marine-like stance are sending a loud and clear "Go away, I'm not interested" signal. When you are at a social gathering, your arms should be relaxed at your sides. If you're talking, show some animation. If you're standing, both feet should be planted firmly on the ground, legs slightly separated. If you're sitting, your legs should be crossed at the ankles and your back should be straight. No hunching forward! If you're talking to a man, lean forward slightly from the waist. But don't get too close—no one likes it when his personal space is invaded. A few inches are a good buffer zone.

## 129. WHAT HIS BODY IS SAYING

Be aware of the signals his body language is sending you. If he's staying put but his arms are crossed or he's fidgety, he's probably just being kind and most likely not interested. If that's the case, give him an "out" (men can be notoriously bad at making a graceful exit) by excusing yourself politely. He'll be grateful—so grateful he may even change his opinion of you. If his arms are crossed and he's moving backward, again, he's not interested, so move on quickly. If he's getting close and responding in kind to your open body language, he's definitely interested! Don't lose the momentum—it may be time for you to give him a light touch on his forearm. If he's moving in for the kill and you're not interested, give him a polite, noncommittal nod and quickly excuse yourself—it's not nice to lead someone on if you're not interested.

## 130. PEP UP YOUR SENSE OF HUMOR

Humor and playfulness are enchanting. If you can make someone laugh, you're likely to put him at ease and make him remember you positively. No matter what temperament a person has, humor works. Everyone responds to it. I approach every encounter with a lighthearted spirit. It's not about comedy. In fact, telling jokes can be inappropriate in many situations (and *never* tell a joke that's cruel or nasty!). It's about laughter and fun.

## 131. MOOD BOOSTERS

There are lots of little tricks you can use to jump-start your attitude. I have found the following to be especially useful if you have a social gathering coming up and you need a little shot of happiness:

- Rent a comedy and have a good laugh.
- Take a one-hour yoga session—it's relaxing and invigorating at the same time.
- A brisk walk or bike ride will get endorphins going.
- Volunteer at the pound as a puppy-hugger (no kidding, you can really do this). An afternoon playing with adorable dogs should lighten anyone's load.
- Do a favor for a friend—sharing love lifts the spirit.
- Treat yourself to some pink polish or a new lipstick. Those little shots of color can perk you up without breaking the bank.

- Eat a small piece of the best chocolate you can find. Nutritionist Oz Garcia says chocolate has many healthy qualities (don't you just *love* this guy!) including as a mood booster. A little goes a long way, so don't indulge too much and buy the best you can afford!

## 132. SHOW GENUINE INTEREST

One of the best ways to get a man interested in you is to show interest in him. When you meet a new person, smile and introduce yourself and ask him a question. Then be an active listener. That means paying attention for clues to his personality so you can respond to his comments on a very specific, personal level. One of my clients, Audrey, forty-seven, is from Italy. Her ability to really focus on the person she is talking to—man, woman, or child—amazes me. Maybe it's her European upbringing, but when you talk with Audrey you feel as if you are the most important person in the room. Her trick? She really doesn't have one unless you consider sincerity as one, and I don't. Audrey really likes people and she is truly fascinated by them. People sense that from her, and it makes them want to be around her.

## 133. REACH OUT AND TOUCH SOMEONE

Making physical contact can be extremely effective in disarming a man and capturing his interest. The kind of contact I'm talking about doesn't have any obvious sexual overtones. When you're talking, softly touch (no grabbing) his arm. Your warmth will radiate and he'll be excited to be with you.

*If a man smiles at you, don't just stand there— do something!*

## 134. BE KIND

There's nothing more appealing than a considerate, generous woman. Gossip, negative talk, and the angry expression of opinion have no place in the charming woman's arsenal. Of course, you are entitled to your views, and engaging in a lively discussion with a partner can be exciting and even arousing. But never, ever embarrass him if you disagree and never belittle him (or anyone) because of their political or other views. You can share your views on a controversial subject without making the other person feel you're evaluating him in terms of the opinions he holds.

## UP CLOSE AND PERSONAL
### *The Red Shoes Theory*

"I was unapproachable," says Lana, forty-nine, a client and successful doctor in New Jersey. That's an understatement, to say the least. When I first met Lana, though very pretty and fit, she dressed in very conservative, almost matronly clothes. They were expensive and well made, but they were straight out of central casting for a librarian. Men just didn't notice her. Or if they did, it was only for a moment. She didn't hold anyone's gaze. Lana is also a serious person, and she found it difficult to break out of the shell of intellectualism. But even smart guys want a girl with a pulse.

"I knew I had to do something. I had to find a way to convey my charm quietly and in keeping with who I am," says Lana. She started small—instead of wearing the skirt and the jacket, she would just wear the skirt with a sweater and leave the jacket at home. That loosened up her look a little. And she did something else: added red high-heel shoes to her wardrobe. "It was very different for me, but every single time I put on those red shoes something happened to me and the little wild Lana came out a bit. And it was great because I didn't really want to approach a guy—I wasn't ready. I wanted to do something so they would approach me." And it worked.

When men saw Lana wearing her little blue suit or skirt and sweater with her red pumps, they were intrigued with the incongruous nature of her outfit. "Men started talking to me," Lana says. The red shoes gave her something to work off of in her own mind. And her newly created confident attitude was evident to others.

## 135. FOLLOW UP

Keeping a promise, getting back to someone quickly when they've asked a question, and saying yes to a favor and then doing it, are great ways to make a memorable impression. People will be pleasantly surprised and likely to remember you fondly if you follow up and follow through. People who send thank-you notes or the pertinent article mentioned over lunch always impress me. When you extend such courtesy, you are showing you've taken a few minutes out of a hectic day to think about him. If a special man made you a fantastic pasta dish the night before, drop a red rose and a short note off for him at the office the next day. He'll want to cook for you again! Or try this: One of my women likes to drop off a CD or book mentioned by her date the next day at his office. Accompanied by a simple note, "Hope you enjoy this, had a great time last night," the gift sends a lovely, generous message. If you go this route, be discreet—some men might be embarrassed to receive something like this at work. Although of the men I know, all said they'd be flattered, and indeed thrilled, to receive such gracious recognition.

## 136. BE YOURSELF

Present yourself sincerely and "as you are" and don't waste time trying to act like the personality *du jour*. It's hard to completely be yourself when you're meeting someone for the first time. But I find it works in my favor if I'm as close to behaving with new people as I behave with my friends. I don't mind going right up to a man and telling him he's stunning. My charm is part bawdy and part impudent and it works for me. What's yours? If you're not sure, start off slowly. Get a feel for the room or situation you're in. Talk to someone "easy" first to set yourself at ease, such as another woman or a younger person. When you feel relaxed and confident from the good vibes you get from them, move on to the men in the room.

## 137. BE INFORMED

Read the newspaper. Watch the nightly news. Know what's on the best-seller list and what's hot at the box office. Being smart and informed always gives you something to talk about when you're in a new situation. It also doesn't hurt to know how to cook one fantastic dish *and* how to open a bottle of champagne. Men do not want Barbie dolls, contrary to what some of you may think. They want a living, breathing woman who has opinions, thoughts, and passions.

Jerry, forty-three, a portfolio manager on Wall Street, came to me after a series of disastrous relationships with "perfect" women. Like most men, Jerry was initially attracted to these women's looks. But each one, after only a few dates, left him feeling disillusioned. Not one of them seemed interested in much aside from shopping and working out at the gym. And that really turned him off, despite his physical attraction to these ladies. Since he worked all the time, his only opportunity to meet women was at the gym—and the gym he went to attracted these kinds of women (men have to broaden their horizons too, but that's for another book). I was able to introduce him to three very pretty, vibrant, smart women. He fell hard for one of them—a Ph.D. in molecular biology!

## 138. BE DIRECT

There's something captivating about a woman who speaks plainly and doesn't beat around the bush. If you're friendly, cheerful, and soft-spoken, you can say just about anything you want to anyone you want. There's nothing wrong with saying what's on your mind to a man—from telling him you like his tie to asking him where he bought his fabulous briefcase (you want to buy one for your brother, right?). You can also tell a man he's handsome, has great eyes, or has wonderful taste in clothes. It's really as simple as that!

## 139. LADYLIKE MAKES A LADY LUCKY

Soft-spoken, gently flirtatious, sexy, and confident: Those are qualities men say they like best in a woman. Aggressiveness, talking in a loud voice, looking "cheap," and behaving in a cloying way are definitely *not* charming (see **Tip 143**). But expressing your femininity through your dress, manner, and speech is a turn-on. Men like women because they are feminine. The "girly" things about women—pretty clothes, soft hair, sweet voice, long lashes—are what turn men on initially. Being a lady means losing the trucker language. There is nothing more unappealing than a woman who swears or uses vulgar language to express herself. And as far as I'm concerned, there shouldn't be a double standard—it's unacceptable for men to talk that way, as well. If you're in a heavy-duty intimate relationship, there's nothing wrong with using "dirty" language if it's part of foreplay and you both enjoy it. But that's best left in the bedroom. Keep it to yourself.

## 140. MAKE EYE CONTACT, THEN LOWER YOUR LIDS

When you talk to a man, look into his eyes. Men are suckers for beautiful eyes. It's the best way to make an immediate connection with a man. Hold his gaze, but make sure to lower your lids occasionally when you're speaking. This demure little move lets him know his power is having an effect on you (and you *could* be persuaded to submit).

## 141. RADIATE WARMTH

It's a myth that men always fall for the tall, chilly blond. Okay, to be perfectly honest, tall and blond is pretty attractive to a lot of men—but not the chilly part. All women, especially pretty women, intimidate men. So if you're playing it too cool in a social situation, chances are a man is not going to feel comfortable approaching you. Most men I know say they are relieved when a woman approaches them in a friendly, warm, and nonthreatening manner. If a man smiles at you, don't just stand there—do something! Say hello. SMILE. And do it with warmth!

## 142. WORK IT!

There are some days when you simply don't feel your best. In those circumstances I suggest two things: Lay low or get yourself out of the funk you're in by *pretending* to be in a great mood. When you are in a social situation, including the dry cleaners, you really want to be working your assets because, as I have said 100 times, *you never know.* Mr. Right could be picking up his tux from the tailor. I am sure there is a scientific explanation for why feigning happiness helps create its reality, but don't ask me what it is. Just try it and you'll see. On the other hand, if you have a major pimple or you're physically under the weather or exhausted from a long week at work, get some rest and take care of yourself for a day or two. It's tough for even the most beguiling woman to be charming under any of those circumstances.

## 143. DON'T BE A DESPERADO

Charming, ladylike women who are engaged in life are never desperate. Men can spot a desperate woman a mile away. Don't behave in a pushy, aggressive, insistent, weepy, or depressed manner. All are signs of a desperate woman. Clothing can also scream desperation: Avoid anything too revealing (men actually don't like boobs sticking out for everyone else to see), tight, short, shiny, fussy, or obvious. That kind of dressing says "Look at me, I'm trying way too hard!"

I was in a very hot New York restaurant, Geisha, not long ago. Three gorgeous women were having dinner together at a nearby table. I mean, they were knockouts! It turned out that one of them had actually called me that day to get on the list for one of my intimate dinners. It didn't surprise me since those coincidences happen to me a lot (maybe because I talk to so many complete strangers throughout the day!). One of the women at the table was wearing a very low-cut top over a dramatic pushup bra. Two round melons poked up out of the shirt. I looked at her and thought, "Women watch too much television. Just because actresses wear revealing clothes on TV doesn't mean it's right for real life." Funny thing is, men were looking (of course) but they weren't stopping. And these three women were very laid-back and not intimidating in the least. And Geisha is the kind of restaurant where singles go to interact. There was no reason on earth that she had to try so hard.

## 144. MOVE ON

When you approach someone, or if your charm isn't working its usual magic on a man, don't push it—move on. He may be having a bad day or simply may not be in the mood to talk or flirt. Insinuating yourself into a situation where you're not wanted will only hurt you in the long run. An important lesson that I've had to teach many men and women is that when you are out there exploring your options, you are bound to come across people who are not going to respond to you for a million reasons that don't have anything to do with you personally. You have to find a balance between being sensitive to people so you can read the cues and having a thick enough skin that it doesn't bother you when you strike out.

## 145. MAKE EVERY SECOND COUNT

You may have noticed that I am going into a lot of seemingly minute detail about individual things you can do to attract men. Why? To help you learn to make every aspect of your life count toward fulfilling your goals and dreams! Life really is too short, so you have to make an effort to be fully conscious of your time and actions. Take, for example, the never-married women who come to me seeking help at age fifty or fifty-five. While they are not "beyond hope," they certainly would have been better off seeking my help or someone else's when they were forty or forty-five or even thirty-five. Why? Children are out of the question for these women under most circumstances. They have to accept the fact that in most cases the only men available to them are between sixty-five and seventy-five and that pool is very small. When I ask them why they have never been married, the majority of them say that they kept putting off the search. None of them actually worked at it. It's not impossible for these women, but it's very challenging. Don't wait. Get going. And appreciate all the moments and opportunities you have.

## 146. DO TWO THINGS AT ONCE (TALK AND SMILE)

Learning how to talk and smile at the same time is one of the most enchanting and effective skills you can acquire. The ability comes naturally for some women. But others have to practice so it looks natural. The one woman who really has smiling and talking simultaneously down pat is Marla Maples, the beautiful actress/model and Donald Trump's ex-wife. No joke, I have *never* seen anyone who looked so happy when she talked with people. The ultimate charm of smiling when you talk—it's infectious!

## 147. SHOW YOUR VULNERABILITY, BUT DON'T BE A HELPLESS FEMALE

If you're a professional with a lot of responsibilities at work, you're used to taking charge and delegating tasks. Or you may be a single mom juggling children, school, and work. You can handle it all and you're very self-sufficient. Good for you. Now ease up. My male clients tell me that even though they appreciate and are attracted to smart, successful women, they also like a woman who can be soft and ask for help, and isn't so self-sufficient she doesn't need a man. Think about it: If you are so good at running every aspect of your life, what do you need a man for? Let your guard down a bit, even if you have to start slowly at first. Ask a man his advice. Maybe you can homeschool three kids, change a tire, and run an international bank all at the same time, but do you really want to do that alone? Women who make men feel like mere accessories are intimidating. On the other hand, you don't want to behave like a quivering idiot. So find a balance that's natural. Often, it can be as simple as leaving your VP or managing director title in the office, where it belongs.

## 148. DO IT WITH OOMPH!

Use everything you've got when you greet or talk to people, especially new men. Your eyes, your smile, and your voice can be the tools of your charm trade. Wide eyes, a big smile, a genuine "Hello, how are you," will sweep men into your vortex, which is right where you want them. Living with oomph also means walking down the street with style and confidence, sharing your enthusiasm with others, and generally approaching everyday routines with gusto. You've got the power!

## 149. DEVELOP SCENT-SITIVITY

Perfume can be an important part of every woman's charm portfolio. But be careful not to let scent overwhelm you or the people you meet. The goal is to wear a light scent that people notice and are attracted to without being conscious of it. You want them to think, "She smells good," not "Her perfume smells . . ."

According to Jamie Ahn of New York City's Acqua Beauty Bar, the best way to find the right perfume is by testing the fragrance on your skin and living with it for a while to see how it reacts with your body oils. It's not good enough to buy a perfume or cologne because it smells nice on your friend. Fragrances smell differently on different people. Citrusy spice scents are very modern and light, whereas heavy floral and musk scents are a bit old-fashioned. Remember that after you've worn a fragrance for a while you become used to it and may not be able to smell it. That doesn't mean you should add more—other people can smell it, believe me!

Jamie says that a good rule of thumb is less is best. Your perfume should never dominate your surroundings. Apply scent with a very light touch to pulse points—inside the wrist, behind the ears, at the temples, behind the knees, the back of the neck, the cleavage area, between the toes, ankles, and thighs. Remember that perfume is the strongest of all scents, followed by cologne and then eau de toilette or after-bath sprays and splashes.

## 150. CAUTION, PLEASE

Finally, think safety first. You're about to enter or reenter the wonderful world of new men, freshly minted friends, and novel experiences. I believe that most people are nice. But there are others who are looking out for themselves and don't have your best interests in mind. And among the great men out there, predators lurk. I don't want to focus too much on this because I am positive by nature and I want you to get out there and have a good time. Part of finding a relationship is building on trust. But you do have to have rules for yourself: Never go anywhere or do anything you don't want to do. Don't give your number to anyone unless you want to. Never let a man or anyone pressure you into any activities you don't feel right about. In short, keep your antennae up and stay safe. That way, you'll stay charming for years to come.

# CHARM ALERT

Keep track of situations in which your charm paid off. Make a note of what you did and said. Keep a list of your most effective efforts for future use!

_____

_____

_____

_____

_____

_____

_____

_____

_____

_____

_____

_____

_____

_____

_____

_____

# HELLO CHALLENGE

**Number of men I said hello to in one day:**

_____
_____
_____
_____
_____
_____
_____

**What happened?**

_____
_____
_____
_____
_____
_____

**How did it feel?**

_____
_____
_____
_____
_____
_____

# Six

## Your Life as a Dating Venue— Where to Go to Find "Him"

Having loads of charm isn't going to help you if are sitting in your apartment hoping that "he" is going to get confused and think your place is his. Now that you know how to rev up your charm, you need to take your "It Girl" status public. Any one of the venues described in this chapter could be the place you will meet your mate. The big-picture message I want to convey is that every situation you're in presents an opportunity to meet someone new. Experience demonstrates to me again and again that a woman can meet her dream man just about anywhere—as long as she's actually *there*. I've known women who have met their mates in airports, at neighborhood coffee shops, and in hospital emergency rooms (that woman paired up with the doctor who fixed her dislocated shoulder!). The bottom line is, *don't sit at home*. Get out there and be proactive. If you're not "a joiner," become one! Any interest can be cultivated in a way that puts you in contact with other people. And if one crowd doesn't suit you, try another! Don't say, "There are lousy men in running clubs." The truth is, there may be unsuitable men for you in the running group you belong to. Find another one!

And stop negative thoughts, like, "joining clubs doesn't work" or "people don't make connections that way." You're right *only* if you maintain that pessimistic, closed-off attitude.

Some of the suggestions in this chapter require major changes in your lifestyle, and they may not necessarily be right for you at this time (then again, moving or changing jobs may be just what you need). But there are other ideas that are most definitely doable, no matter where you live. Terrific single, eligible men are *everywhere.* You can find them, but not if you spend all of your free time holed up in your apartment. Another fact to keep in mind as you embark on this exciting adventure: Great places attract great men. So wherever you go, make it the best of its class.

I hope your imagination is sparked by these suggestions. If and when you do meet someone in any of these places—or somewhere that I haven't mentioned—I want to hear from you. My contact information can be found in the back of the book.

## 151. TAKE STOCK AND THEN SHAKE IT UP!

What are you doing that's stopping you from meeting new people? What can you change that will allow you more access to social situations and new experiences? Take some quiet time to seriously think about these questions. The answers will give you clues to how you might be holding yourself back from meeting people. For example, something as simple as changing your route or mode of transportation to work can open you to new men. If you work outside a major city and drive in each day, consider taking the train. A lot of fantastic single men take the train because it gives them a chance to read the paper, have coffee, and talk to others. You really can't do that in a car. If you've been shopping at the same grocer for the last few years, go out of your way to try a new store. Use the worksheet at the end of this chapter to help you determine changes you can make.

## 152. HOW TO TELL IF HE'S SINGLE (AND WHAT TO DO IF HE'S NOT)

The first clue is the most obvious: Look at his left hand for a wedding band! If you don't see one (and there's no "tan line" to indicate he's taken his ring off), you can be fairly sure he's single. However, not all married men wear wedding rings. Once you have established he isn't wearing a ring and you strike up a conversation, you can simply work the subject into your talk. What I say usually depends on the situation. If I'm feeling playful, I will say something as straightforward as, "Are you a really cute single guy or a really cute married guy?" Even if he says he's a married guy, I don't let him get away so fast. You can ask him if he has any cute single brothers or friends. Alternatively, you can strike up a conversation, and if he's married, chances are he will mention his status pretty quickly, just so you know he's unavailable. It's something I have seen married men do a lot.

Be careful! If you do develop banter with a man who turns out to be married, don't let it go too far. You have to be very clear that you are not looking to have an affair—you are looking to him for friends. You have to know how to handle a married man or it could become an issue. I will say it once, but I will say it clearly: Don't go there. Despite advice you might have heard in the past, married men are not good "for practice."

## 153. NETWORK, NETWORK, NETWORK

It's all who you know! Tell everyone you know that you're interested in meeting someone. There are pitfalls involved with being set up on blind dates by friends and colleagues (they may not know your tastes as well as they think, for one thing). It's certainly not the most scientific way of meeting the right person. But it's possible to meet someone on a blind date, so why not go? Even if a blind date does not work out, you will have met another single person who is presumably looking for a serious rela-tionship. You can keep him in mind for your friends and he can do the same—that's networking, too. Attend as many social events as you can and make new female friends who will know single men. At the end of this chapter is a place for you to write down people you know whom you can start telling you would like to meet someone. Be expansive when you make your list. Remember, someone's ex could be your next!

## 154. BE A FRIENDLY NEIGHBOR

Neighbors can also be a resource for new men and enriching friendships. And getting to know your neighbors has other benefits—you can count on them in a crisis. Friendly neighborhoods mean safe neighborhoods.

In major cities it's not uncommon to be unfamiliar with your neighbors. Even in small cities and towns, people have a tendency to forget their surroundings because they're so busy. For example, I live in a towering high-rise on the Upper East Side of Manhattan, and loads of single men live in my building, along with lots of single women. I make an effort to say hello to the residents when I meet them in the elevator. I introduce myself to the people who live in the apartments on my floor. If you haven't met anyone in your building, start introducing yourself right now. It's as simple as knocking on your neighbor's door on a Saturday afternoon and saying, "I've lived in this building for _____ years (months, whatever) and I don't think we've ever formally introduced ourselves. I'm _____." If you live on an urban street full of attached or closely built houses, do the same thing. The same goes for the suburbs. There's no law against giving your neighbors a friendly hello and asking them over to your place for coffee.

When you're new in town it's essential to get to know others living nearby. It's the perfect excuse to meet everyone within a five-block radius! For example, when I rent a home for the summer, my first order of business (after unpacking and stocking the fridge) is knocking on the doors of all my neighbors and saying hello. That way, I know who's who and I can invite them for cocktails. Instant social life.

## 155. GOOD GREET!

Being a "greeter" in your town or city is a very unique way to volunteer, so I feel it's worth mentioning as an individual tip. In New York, an organization called Big Apple Greeters matches out-of-towners with unpaid staffers who take tourists and business visitors (men included, of course!) around the city. It's a wonderful organization. Other cities and towns have similar civic programs. They are often connected with the Chamber of Commerce. If your town doesn't have such a program, consider starting one. Becoming a greeter is a fantastic way to meet people from all over the world.

## 156. TALK TO STRANGERS

When you go anywhere, especially to the places I recommend here, you have to actually talk to people! Men may approach you, but chances are you will have to be the aggressor to a certain extent. Men say they *love* it when a woman "picks them up" or just says hello. Ask questions, seek opinions, and request advice when you're out and about.

## 157. CREATE A SUPPORT SYSTEM

A support system of understanding single friends means that you will always have a roster of people you can call to attend events with. The only requirement is that everyone has to agree that when attending singles events, parties, benefits, or even when you go to bars together, that you are there to offer encouragement and moral support—not to keep each other from approaching new people.

## 158. CHANGE JOBS

If you are serious about getting married, you may have to reevaluate what your job is contributing to your goal. I will discuss work as a venue for meeting a man (see **Tip 161**) and the pitfalls involved in that. However, your work and profession should provide outside-the-office opportunities that bring you in contact with new people. If they don't, you may want to give some thought to changing companies and even careers. A job that offers a chance to travel, attend conventions, be in close proximity to other people outside of your company (such as a large office building or downtown location) can really make a difference. Or transfer your skills to an aspect of your profession that brings you in contact with more people.

## 159. CONSIDER MOVING

Like changing jobs, a move to a new neighborhood, city, or state is a major step. I've done it myself and I know very well how daunting it can be. I've moved within the city and out of the city, from New York to New Jersey. And every summer I move from the city to the beach. Even moving across town can be a logistical nightmare. But it can also be exciting, invigorating, and fun! If you are stuck in the 'burbs (where it can be notoriously hard to meet single men) or if your city isn't contributing to your social life, you may have to look elsewhere.

I do not make this suggestion lightly. You have to consider the consequences and whether you will be able to find a job and a nice place to live. But I have also known women who have moved to a new part of the country for a "fresh start" and it paid off with a new beau. That's because when you're "new in town" you have a reason to approach people and ask advice ("How do I get downtown?" "Who's the best dry cleaner around here?" "Where's the best restaurant?" and so on). You've also left your "old self" behind, and it can be easier to reinvent yourself in a new place. This is particularly important for recently divorced women who live in small towns or cities. If people know you as "Bob's ex," it can be a tough label to lose. See **Up Close and Personal** in this chapter for a real-life look at why it may not be a good idea to hang around town after a breakup.

## 160. FAMILY FIX-UPS

Your family can make a contribution to your dating adventures—if you're straight with them. Sometimes the criterion a family member uses is "Well, she's single and he has a pulse, so let's introduce them." That's not enough, to say the least! So when you tell family members to keep you in mind, be specific about what you are looking for. Tell them about your non-negotiables. Give them an idea of what kind of person you would like to meet—and quiz them extensively if they do have someone in mind!

Finally, don't discourage family members from setting you up if one of their fix-ups doesn't work out. They may get it right the next go-round.

## 161. WATER COOLER COUPLES

Your office is an obvious place to look for love. It's not surprising that people who work in the same office develop feelings for each other. First of all, you probably spend more time at work than anywhere else. That means a lot of your social contacts are made at or through your job. And you will likely have a lot in common with your colleagues—after all, you were attracted to the same field and you have many points of reference in common. On the other hand, there are risks involved in looking for love at work. Your company probably has rules about dating and relationships, even though most businesspeople know it is impossible to manage love.

When it comes to the human heart, the bosses' bottom line counts for very little. Here are some things to think about when looking for love in the office: First and foremost, find out about your company's policies on office relationships. Some businesses do have policies directly dealing with interoffice romance. In fact, there are companies that require one person in a couple to resign if a serious relationship (or marriage) develops. Other companies have more liberal policies about office romances. But no company will tolerate a love affair that compromises productivity.

Second, men in positions of power tell me that they never date anyone at work. There are too many potential landmines they have to avoid (such as sexual harassment and discrimination lawsuits), so they say dating someone in their office is simply out of the question. Don't be offended if your boss or someone who is in a senior position to you in the office doesn't respond to your flirtatious advances. In fact, you may actually have to quit your job if you want to pursue someone like this. Is he worth leaving your job for? More importantly, do you think he will really be interested in *you*? If you are interested in a colleague who is on equal footing, you also have to observe some rules. Don't bring the relationship to your job. That means no fighting, cuddling, or smooching in the office! Be discreet. Most people say they feel uncomfortable and alienated when colleagues show open displays of affection.

Finally, are you willing to risk a breakup? Will you be able to continue to do your job in a professional manner and continue to work closely with that person? Can you promise yourself *and* your boss that a breakup with a colleague will not affect your performance? Would you be willing to give up your job if things turn sour?

## 162. BE A SPECTACULAR SPECTATOR

Large sporting events are *great* places to meet single men—especially basketball, baseball, and football games. It's worth learning the rudimentary rules of these sports so you can both follow what's going on and have something to talk about when you strike up a conversation with a guy at halftime or during a break (remember, that's why you're there!).

Sarah, thirty-three, the charmer with the great personality, is famous for meeting men at basketball games. She was not a New York Knicks fan until she figured out that a lot of men in New York were. So she started going to home games with a girlfriend and they made out like bandits! Since then, other women have had the same bright idea, so the competition is a little tougher, but men still outnumber women at these events.

Don't forget about the clubhouse of great horse-racing tracks, either. Most great tracks have upscale restaurants and bars where you can eat, have a cocktail, and watch the ponies. If you love horses and excitement, there's nothing better. Like gambling at casinos, men are attracted to racing. It's the sport of kings—and you may just meet one!

## 163. PICK HIM UP WITH AN IRRESISTIBLE LINE

Now that you've become used to saying hello to men, you are ready to move on to the fine art of the pickup line. Be creative with them—have fun and be playful. Men love it! And don't let the conversation slip away once you have his attention. Keep eye contact steady and start playing ball with the banter. The point is to say something that requires a response!

Spontaneity is probably the most important aspect of tossing out a great line. If something strikes you, go for it. Don't let the opportunity or the inspiration get away from you. Cautionary tale: On the first day of one of my workshops, one participant, Alyssa, forty, a spunky redhead, told the class she was walking down her street in the West Village and this really cute guy looked at her, smiled, and said hello. "I felt like saying, 'I hope I see you again sometime soon . . .'" "But that's *exactly* what you should have said!" I cried. The man was there, the moment was right, and the perfect line popped into her head. Yet, she said nothing.

One way to practice pickup lines is to respond to something he's doing or to the circumstances you find yourself in. Use the props around you. Play off the situation. That's the most natural and easiest way to go. And remember, men *love* compliments—even more than women do, I think. So you can never go wrong with pointing out something marvelous about a man.

Finally, don't cut off the conversation if you find he's married; he may have single friends or relatives who might be perfect for you. I cannot *tell* you how many guys I have picked up (as a matchmaker, Allen!) who have turned out to be married but had cute friends who were interested in meeting my women.

Here are some demure, sexy, and sassy lines that have worked wonders for my clients. Try them as is, or create versions of your own. These are perfect even for shy girls who want to draw him in gently:

- I couldn't help but notice that tie you're wearing. It really brings out the color of your eyes.

- The leather on your briefcase is really magnificent. You have great taste.

- Is that your cell phone ringing or mine?

- What kind of wine are you drinking? It looks luscious. (This line worked for my writer Karen. But she already has a fantastic husband! She was just doing research.)

- Have you ever been to a place this loud (quiet, crowded, slick, fancy, colorful . . .) before?

Sexy lines for when you are feeling hot, confident, and playful:

- I love your belt—especially the buckle.
- I have never seen more magnetic eyes in my life. I'm feeling a little shaky!
- I'm a sucker for cashmere, especially when it's covering such broad shoulders.
- If I didn't have to go to work tomorrow, I'd kidnap you and take you to Paris.
- You are an incredible specimen!

Sassy lines for when you want to go for it and make him sit up and take notice:

- You are *adorable!* How come there's no girl next to you?
- Okay, you are two really good-looking guys—where are the wives or the girlfriends?
- You're married? Do you have a single brother, cousin, father, or friend who's as good-looking as you are?
- Okay, tall, dark, and *really* handsome—you must have a girlfriend. Where is she?

## 164. TAKE A GAMBLE!

A lot of single men, whether they are in their twenties, thirties, forties, or fifties, love to get together for day and weekend trips to upscale casinos. So grab a couple of girlfriends and do the same. Nevada, New Jersey, and Connecticut are just a handful of the states that offer beautiful resort-like casinos with fabulous accommodations. If you are actually planning to gamble, however, set a limit. You are at a casino to make new friends, not to lose your house! And don't expect to pick anyone up at the blackjack table. When men are actually playing cards for money, they aren't that interested in chatting up their neighbor. Casino restaurants, lobbies (they are usually enormous and filled with people), slot machines, and bars are your best bets for meeting men after they've finished with their card games.

## 165. AVOID TRAVELING IN PACKS

Many of the suggestions in this chapter are appropriate to do on your own. But some of them, like attending a sporting event, eating in a great restaurant, and going to a bar, may be intimidating and not even much fun to do on your own. You may want to bring along other single girlfriends (or even married ones—they don't have the same agenda as you do). Fine. But don't travel in a pack! Seeing more than three women together can stop men dead in their tracks. Four women together looks like a "girls' night out," and most men will be reluctant to break up the party. Don't go out with other women if you feel insecure or inadequate around them. This defeats the whole purpose of going out in the first place. You want to feel great, so choose friends who boost your self-esteem.

## 166. INDULGE IN A GREAT MEAL

Single men eat out—a lot! Most don't want to bother with cooking, and they often combine their need to eat with business. But that doesn't mean they won't notice and talk to a pretty woman. I recommend trying new restaurants at least once a week with a girlfriend. Dining with a male friend may put off potential suitors. Dining with another woman who complements you is a good idea. By that I mean you should go out with a woman who enhances your appearance and does not distract or detract from it. If you feel like an ugly duckling next to a friend, do yourself a favor and don't go out with her if your aim is to meet men! It will spoil your evening. I guarantee it.

I have heard a theory that if you go out with a very beautiful woman friend, men will come over and talk to both of you. That might happen, but only if you exude confidence yourself. In my experience, if the woman you're with far outshines you in appearance—or even if you believe that she does—it can have a negative impact on your aura and demeanor. So just be cautious.

## 167. HAVE AN INTIMATE DINNER PARTY, *A LA* JANIS

Intimate dinners are something I hold all the time for my clients and web-site members. But it's something that you can easily do yourself with a group of between eight and twelve people. Here's how it works: To ensure an even ratio of men to women, ask each of your single friends to bring another single friend of the opposite sex to dinner. Make sure that your friends know it's a singles night, but don't put pressure on anyone. Make the party fun and casual. Serve food that people have to assemble or put together buffet-style. Create as many conversation areas in your house or apartment as you can so that guests feel comfortable mingling. This puts the focus on the food and requires guests to interact. Tacos, sushi, pasta, and pizza-topping parties are all great choices. I recommend

## UP CLOSE AND PERSONAL
### *A Moving Experience*

A client of mine, Marjorie, forty-three, lived in New Orleans with her hus-band, a prominent doctor in town. Everyone in New Orleans either knew them or knew who they were. They had attended many benefits, sporting events, and parties together. They were a high-profile couple in what is a small and close-knit city. When they split up, it didn't exactly go without notice. Marjorie is stunning, and she was a very popular guest and hostess in New Orleans society. Unfortunately, that very popularity was what put her at a disadvantage once she was divorced. No one wanted to invite her to a func-tion because they would inevitably see her husband there as well—and no man wants to be put in that position ("Hi Bob—meet my date Marjorie. You know her as your ex-wife!"). And frankly, Marjorie felt very uncomfortable meeting new men in a town where she was well known. Her only option, and one of the smartest things she ever did, was to move. She chose a city where she already had friends, to make the transition a bit easier. Once she was free of her "married city," she felt at liberty to meet new men—and she did!

holding intimate dinners once a month with a rotating group of friends so there are always new people in attendance.

## 168. LEARN SOMETHING NEW

Trying new things broadens your horizons, pushes your limits, and gets you thinking in new ways. Remember in Chapter 1 I asked you to make a list of things you have always wanted to learn how to do? Go back to it now. Over the next few months try three new things from that list. Obviously, it would be great if the three things also presented opportunities to meet new men. But you have to choose carefully. (See **Tip 169** for a list of places where you *won't* meet many men.) Journalism, business management, entrepreneurship, starting a new business, playing the stock market, and car repair are all activities that attract men. Sports such as skiing and golfing will also put you in contact with men.

## 169. DON'T GO THERE!

Here's a list of places where you are more likely to meet women or married couples than single straight men. Great for widening your circle of female friends (and they may indeed have the perfect man in mind for you) but not for making direct contact with eligible bachelors:

- Wine-tasting class (wine-tasting events at local upscale wine and spirits shops offer better odds for meeting men)

- Cooking classes

- Cruises (unless it is a cruise specifically designed for singles)

- Painting and drawing lessons

- Creative writing classes

- Jewelry-making class

- Interior design class

## 170. LIGHTS, CAMERA, ACTION!

Movie classes, either filmmaking or movie history/criticism courses, are particularly attractive to men. In New York there is a fantastic class called Movies 101 with Richard Brown. This is a very unique event that attracts a large number of people. Over the course of the class, several movies are shown before they are released to the general public. Then someone who worked on the film, either an actor or the director or other member of the crew, comes to discuss the picture. Lots of men attend this class, and from what I can see, a lot of them are single. I don't know if every city has a course exactly like this one, but most colleges and universities offer film classes as part of their adult education curriculum.

## 171. TAKE A HIGH-VOLUME VACATION

Meeting a man during a vacation does have some drawbacks. When you are on vacation you are not living your real life, and the fantasy of the setting may alter your perspective. You might be more prone to having a "fling" that doesn't result in a serious relationship. That's okay. In fact, when you get back to real life you might feel more open to talking to new people and making connections with others. And a vacation really can offer a viable way to meet a mate. It all depends on the kind of holiday you select. Resorts specifically designed for singles are an obvious choice. Club Med–style resorts offer singles all kinds of beach-y locales—from the Caribbean to Europe.

Cruises designed for singles allow you to get to know a particular group of people over a week or more. That can be great if the "floating resort" attracts people you're interested in meeting. On the flip side, cruising can be a bit risky. An onshore resort has turnover, so you're not stuck with the same group of people for your entire stay. You can take an island or Caribbean vacation on your own or with a friend. Warm climates, whether they're "planned" singles-only resorts or not, attract unmarried men. Be sure to avoid "spring break" week (because you are not seriously interested in meeting inebriated high school and college seniors). Most hotels and resorts can tell you the weeks that are optimal for meeting adults.

Big city vacations also offer top-notch opportunities to meet men. If you are thinking of moving, visiting a city is a good way to find out if you like the area. Finally, any sophisticated city has great museums, restaurants, clubs, galleries, and shopping. So you are bound to find yourself in many fun situations that offer a chance for you to start a conversation with others who are unmarried. (See **Tip 189** for a list of great singles' cities.) You can also spend a weekend taking a vacation and being a tourist in your own city. When was the last time you went to your local museum? Maybe it's time to check out what your own town has to offer.

## 172. TAKE IN A SHOW—A BOAT OR CAR SHOW, THAT IS

Car and boat shows are terrific places to meet single men simply because men seem to love these two "toys." The larger the city, the bigger the show. But even small cities host these events, and they are worth checking out. Shows to avoid: fashion, home, and gourmet shows seem to attract unavailable (think gay and married) men, women, and families.

## 173. RAISE THE BAR

Bars and pubs have always been natural meeting places so I have to include them. Conversation is easy because you are in such close proximity to people who are there to relax and unwind. But I do think bars have a few drawbacks. First, I believe bars are best for younger singles, those in their twenties and thirties, simply because bars are where people that age go to socialize. But bars can be part of your overall game plan, regardless of your age. Selection is key. Choose upscale bars in the best parts of town. If you have a neighborhood bar, you can certainly try it, but my feeling is that the same people frequent these haunts, and you may not

*What's hot:* **Being interested in where you are and what you are doing**

*What's not:* **Being somewhere *only* to meet a guy**

have a lot of choice from among the "regulars." Happy hour (5 P.M.–7 P.M.) is also a prime time in downtown areas for meeting men of all ages. The later it gets, the younger the crowd becomes. Avoid hotel bars: They tend to attract tourists and married men. Finally, please limit your alcohol intake or avoid it altogether: There's nothing wrong with ordering a club soda and lime. Making a dating decision when you're drunk is a serious no-no in my book!

## 174. BECOME A CHARITY CASE

Attending benefits, while potentially pricey, is a phenomenal way to meet men! One way of lowering the cost of attending benefits is by volunteering for the committees that organize them. That way, you can attend many events "for free" in exchange for working on organizing the event. And working behind the scenes at your favorite foundation or nonprofit will lead you to new people—and new friends means new men. But many benefit cocktail parties are affordable.

*Experience has demonstrated to me again and again that a woman can meet her dream man just about anywhere—as long as she's actually "there."*

You can learn about them by checking the websites of charities or causes you care about.

Men attend benefits either because their company supports the charity or in order to network for personal professional growth, or simply because they support the cause. I am so convinced that attending benefits is a terrific way to meet great men, I offer a service called "Attend a Benefit with Janis," where I take a single man or woman to a benefit and teach him or her how to work the room. It's really not that difficult—everyone is at the event for the same reasons, so that gives you something in common with everyone in the room. That's reason enough for you to say hello and introduce yourself to a man.

## 175. DO YOUR CIVIC DUTY

If you get called for jury duty, go! Because of tighter restrictions on who can and can't "get out of" serving on a jury, just about everyone has to do their duty and show up. Aside from other single male citizens who get called, courthouses are filled with lawyers, judges, and other professionals who are part of the legal system. Do I have to tell you to please avoid defendants, even if they *are* innocent until proven guilty? Seriously, jury pools can be a great place to meet others. Be willing to strike up a conversation with the men around you. Lunch breaks also offer an opportunity to explore local restaurants where lawyers, jurors, and businessmen often eat.

## 176. GET RELIGION

Churches, synagogues, and other spiritual centers offer many social functions for singles, but even attending weekly services offers you a chance to connect with people who have similar values. The church or synagogue across town might offer more events or a population that is closer in age or interests to your own, so explore your community for a house of worship that suits you.

## 177. YES, IT *CAN* HAPPEN!

Here are just a few of the other places women have met their husbands:

- Doctor's waiting room
- Elevator
- Gym
- Apartment building or complex
- Coffee shop
- Dry cleaners
- Newsstand
- Hailing a cab

- By a hotel pool

- Museum

- Marina

- Art gallery

- Shoe store

- Intermission at the opera

- On a street corner, waiting for the light to change

## 178. JOIN THE CLUB

There are all kinds of clubs you can join. First are country clubs, especially if you find yourself in suburbia. Not all country clubs attract families. Check out your local club scene to see which one seems to attract single people or has singles' events. Country clubs with golf courses and tennis courts are especially good choices—you can learn and practice your sport, and mingle with others while you play. And afterward, you can grab a salad and iced tea at the bar or "nineteenth hole."

Private clubs, especially in big cities, are another comfortable way to meet men. Many clubs expect you to be nominated for membership, but your networking efforts can help you find out who is a member of what club. Colleagues and friends may also nominate you for memberships. If you went to an Ivy League school, it is obviously worth becoming a member of your school's association. Such organizations usually have reciprocal relationships with other private clubs, and you will be able to create an entire network of places you can visit in your own or another city.

Finally, clubs that reflect your interests can bring you in contact with men with whom you will find immediate common ground. For example, a client of mine loves bridge and she joined a bridge league. She discovered quite a few male members and has since gone out on several dates with some of them. Plus, she's doing something she really enjoys. Since she is focused on the cards, it's easier and more comfortable for her to strike up conversations with fellow players.

## 179. TAKE A CUE (A POOL CUE)

Upscale billiard halls (not poolrooms) attract single men of all ages. Most often found in classy bars and private clubs, billiard halls often offer dartboards, backgammon, chess, and other games in a comfy, "clubby" setting, which makes relaxing and socializing very easy. Ask someone not involved in a serious game to teach you some basics.

## 180. HOW TO WORK A ROOM

When attending any kind of large social event, pause and survey the room. Take some time to get the lay of the land when you enter. Pick out a few men you think you'd like to approach. Don't rush up to the first person you see whom you know. If you immediately gravitate to the familiar, you will find it difficult to approach a stranger. Approach a new man first and then go toward someone familiar. Bounce back and forth like this during the evening. Ask the people you know if there is anyone you should meet and ask them to make introductions.

If you don't know anyone, go up to the first friendly person you see and say hello, even if it's another woman or a younger person. Keep circulating and get comfortable with talking to strangers. Head for the bar or the canapé table and start talking to the person next to you. This is very natural and accepted—in fact, it's expected.

## 181. WALK THE DOG

Cats are low maintenance, but it's hard to take them out for a walk. Dogs require a different kind of commitment, but they also happen to be a great tool for meeting men. I cannot *tell* you how many women I know who met their husbands through a puppy or a dog! It's a walking conversation starter. And most men love dogs. In fact, when I was single, I met many men when I was walking my dog each morning before work. Dog runs are great meeting places in cities—but you can go only if you actually have a dog. Even in small towns, walking a dog makes you approachable. So if you don't have a dog, buy, borrow, or rent one!

## 182. PLAY POLITICS

Every political party has associations or clubs you can join. Men are very drawn to politics and political work. Some see it as a way to raise their profile in the community; others are simply committed to certain ideals that can be expressed politically. If you feel strongly about public policy or specific social issues, joining a political group is a great way to work toward goals *and* meet like-minded single men at the same time. Working on a political campaign, for example, is very energizing and puts you in contact with a large group of people. I realize that in this age of skepticism it might be hard to picture yourself really liking a politician. But there is a good chance that a particular congressperson or local representative stands for the things you believe in, so find out who that person is and volunteer at his or her headquarters. You can bring any professional expertise to the table, which they will appreciate, and you will meet a whole new group of people with similar interests. As an added plus, you may receive invitations to loads of social events.

## 183. READ UP ON IT

Join a book club and regularly visit the bookstores in your neighborhood. Super bookstores that offer tables and chairs and attached cafés are great places to meet people who share common interests. The expansive magazine section seems to be the most active part of these large stores. They are usually located on the street level with in-store cafés nearby. Small neighborhood bookstores that encourage browsing also present a cozy atmosphere to chat with other customers.

## 184. BOOKWORM BEAUTY

Saturday afternoon in a bookstore means casual and laid back. The perfect look? Natural hair, blown out or softly pulled back with a simple ribbon. Simple makeup means blush or light bronzer, sheer lipstick, and a bit of eye-widening shadow. A winter/fall outfit that's both very sexy to men and appropriate for the occasion consists of a neatly pressed, soft sweater or a tailored shirt and tight (well-fitting) jeans and boots. In warmer weather try jeans with a crisp white shirt or T-shirt and sexy sandals with a low princess heel.

## 185. EAT SUSHI

Single men eat at sushi bars. It's as simple as that. I have met more great men at them than I can count. Why? Busy single men like the idea of sitting at a barlike place to eat dinner. A sushi bar is meant for single diners to grab a quick, delicious meal. An added bonus: People are expected to sit down and eat by themselves, so there is no reason for you to feel uncomfortable about it. Scope out the best sushi bars in your area and try them once or twice a week. Sit next to a man and talk to him!

## 186. SHOP FOR YOUR DAD, BROTHER, COUSIN, OR BEST MALE FRIEND

Another great place to meet men? In the men's section of upscale department stores. Places like Bergdorf's for Men, Barneys, and Saks Fifth Avenue sell beautiful men's clothing. Next time you owe a male friend or relative a gift, make it a point to shop at an upscale men's store, and ask for advice from male shoppers!

## 187. GET LOST (AND ASK DIRECTIONS)

Even if you know where you're going, ask directions anyway! Being lost is the perfect excuse to start a conversation with any man, especially if you're otherwise shy. What gentleman isn't going to help a lady in distress?! I've met men driving out to Long Island, in my car. I am not kidding. I can count on my hand—and that's five if you're keeping track— the number of times I have picked up guys just by asking where the *heck* the local Y or community college is (usually I am running late for a speaking engagement). Five guys picked up on the service road off the Long Island Expressway, in less than a year. That's *got* to be some kind of record.

## 188. BECOME AN ACTIVE ALUM!

Attend events held by your college or university. Most schools have alumni events, and you undoubtedly receive invitations and mailings about them. If you think you're missing out on postgraduate functions, call your alma mater and make sure they have your correct mailing and electronic address. All schools have websites where past grads can reconnect. Check yours out. I know several men and women who have met old classmates and either rekindled old flames or started new fires burning hot, hot, hot!

## 189. JANIS'S CITIES FOR SINGLES

Many magazines and websites publish lists of great places to live if you're single. Check them out by using the key words "great cities for singles." I see fantastic people almost anywhere I go, with my highly developed "single sensor." But for those of you without the gift, here is my list of cities where you can find a lot great single, straight men:

1. Manhattan—hands down, I believe New York has the most incredible single people in the world

2. Miami

3. Denver

4. Washington, D.C.

5. Los Angeles (great if you like actors and people in show biz)

6. Dallas

7. Houston

8. Chicago

## 190. SHARE A BEACH- OR SUMMERHOUSE

The "summer share" has been the classic New York City single's way of escaping the city heat and hooking up with new people *forever*. If you don't live near a beach that you can get to every June, July, and August weekend, think lake or mountain resorts. Or consider taking your two weeks in summer at a beach community and take a house with a couple of single friends. Amazing things can happen in two weeks at the beach! I've seen it with my own eyes. Every community has vacation spots that attract singles. I guess that, because I live on the East Coast, I'm partial to beach houses. I think the beach and resort environment breaks down barriers between people who might normally be less inclined to reach out to strangers.

## 191. CHANGE YOUR ROUTE TO WORK

If you commute to work on a train or bus, change the time you go as often as you can (as long as it doesn't make you late for work). Even a few minutes can mean a complete change of "scenery," meaning a 7:30 train will have different people on it than the 7:40 train. If you walk to work along city streets, change the way you go—even if it means going out of your way. And if you drive, think about switching to a park-and-ride system, which will put you on a commuter bus. Change as often as you can. See who's going where when.

## 192. TAKE YOUR EXERCISE ROUTINE OUTSIDE

Long winter months spent at the gym may have kept your waistline in check (bravo!), but the same old workout in the same old place may have stifled your social life. As soon as the weather gets warm, take your routine outside. Running tracks are man magnets (cities large and small have them), as are tennis and racquetball courts and walking paths. Safety first, however: Don't walk or run anyplace that feels uncomfortable or desolate (hey, you want to meet people, not avoid them!).

## 193. DON'T SING THE SUBURBAN BLUES

I do have clients who live in the suburbs, and I admit it's tough to meet single men in a small town. They're there—they are just harder to find. But believe it or not, many single men who work in a city prefer to live outside of it. I know a fantastic single international lawyer, Jacob, who lives in one of those quaint small towns along the Hudson River, just outside of New York City. He says it's hard to meet women in the supermarket or mall because they often come with kids, "so you don't know that they are single." His advice for *you*? If you're a single mom, try to find some shopping time without your kids. The grocery store on the weekend can be a good place to ram your cart into Mr. Right! Jacob says he's met suburban singles through the Internet and at local parties given by neighbors. Get involved in local politics or town projects. Think *outside* the confines of your town—look to larger towns or nearby cities for things to do. Get in your car and drive to another town for shopping, the movies, or just walking around.

## 194. DON'T DO TAKEOUT

Cancel your subscription to the paper right now, today. Start buying it yourself, along with your morning coffee. Try a different newsstand or coffee shop every week. See who goes where. Buy the guy in front or in back of you in line his morning *Times* and latte. Men really do love a "woman who pays." Plus, all men are suckers for gifts, and coffee and the paper qualify. End takeout service too. Instead of dialing up unhealthy Chinese food or pizza, visit the best gourmet food shop in town and get delicious, healthy carryout. Remember, many single men don't like to cook and they don't always want to eat in restaurants. You'll meet them at the takeout counter.

## 195. TAKE A BUSINESS TRIP

Volunteer to attend every conference, out-of-town presentation, and convention you can! It's easy to meet people when you share common ground (work and profession). It gives you a perfect excuse to introduce yourself, and a business trip puts you in a new place, and in a (typically) good business hotel. Sandra, thirty-two, a buyer for a large cosmetics company, says if she's going to a function where she doesn't know a lot of people, she knows exactly what to do. "I head for the bar. Not because I'm nervous and need a drink! I usually get a club soda with lime. The bar's the best place to start talking to people. I make contact right away with the person next to me. I introduce myself, look them in the eye, and ask them something specific or compliment them on something they're wearing—anything to establish the fact that I'm interested in *them*. There's usually a domino effect from that first conversation, I get introduced to other people . . . and end up with several new acquaintances."

## 196. GO FIRST CLASS (OR AT THE VERY LEAST, BUSINESS CLASS)

It's not that you can't meet a cute guy in coach, it's just more likely that you'll meet others and feel more comfortable (literally—have you ridden in coach lately?) talking to your neighbors in first or business class. Both are smaller than the big coach sections of airplanes. And the seats are larger so you're not contorted into a pretzel. (Physical discomfort can make flirting extremely awkward.) When you and your fellow passengers are comfortable, you are more accessible to each other. Some very interesting people fly first class, and the level of service and extra room in the front of the plane can make your trip feel more romantic. It's an opportunity that shouldn't be passed up.

## 197. BE A PROFESSIONAL

If you are a professional of any kind, become a member of an affiliated professional organization or association. Almost every profession has related advocacy groups, foundations, and educational groups. Those groups hold conventions and conferences. Even attending a professional association's meeting once a year can put you in contact with all sorts of people. Interest groups have organizations you can join, and they also have events and meetings. For example, there are horticulture, food, and wine groups that attract men (the ones who are *not* going to cooking or wine-tasting classes).

## 198. MAKE HIM NOTEWORTHY!

Someone in your apartment building or office complex intrigues you? Leave him a note on his car. One of my clients told me a woman in his apartment building left him a message every week for about a month—a "secret admirer" note tucked under his windshield. "It was very intriguing, and when she finally revealed herself to me I liked what I saw," says Larry, thirty. "But the notes helped a lot. And that meeting blossomed into a long-term relationship." Writing a note to any prominent single man can be an effective way to attract his attention. Keep it simple and short to avoid appearing pushy or, heaven forbid, like a stalker.

## 199. GO SUPER SHOPPING

Large pet and sporting goods "super" stores are *phenomenal* places to meet single men. These stores are everywhere—from big cities to small towns and everything in between. This kind of retailing is considered "destination shopping," and it's really true. Many people go just for the sake of going. Don't hesitate to ask advice from other (male) customers. Large home centers may also attract single men, but these kinds of stores are more of a draw for families.

## 200. ATTEND OPENING NIGHTS

Opening nights or the beginning of anything in the arts—gallery shows, opera, plays, concerts, or the ballet—attract a lot of people, including single men, and not just gay men, if that's what you're thinking. Many men attend openings as part of their jobs, to impress the boss, or simply because they enjoy culture. Opening nights are fun because they offer the perfect excuse to get dressed up and look your very best. These occasions are also festive, and during intermission, people are often giddy and excited—and often feeling friendly and talkative. Work your magic!

## 201. *DON'T* READ A BOOK (ON THE SUBWAY, TRAIN, BUS, PLANE, ETC.)—BE AWARE OF YOUR SURROUNDINGS

It drives me absolutely *nuts* when women tell me they read a book while riding the subway, bus, or train! If you have your nose in a book he can't see you, and you certainly can't see him. Jump-start your commute by looking around at who's on board. Mr. Right might very well be sitting across from you, but you will never know that if you're buried in the morning paper or the latest bestseller. I meet more cute guys on city buses than I can count. They're there, and they might be sitting next to you. But you can see them only if you look up.

## 202. TURN OFF YOUR CELL PHONE!

When I see women walking down the street talking on a cell phone, it makes me nuts. And I see a lot of women chattering on their cells. I use a cell phone myself so I understand the temptation to use it, especially if you're a multitasker. But you can't make eye contact, pull off a great pickup line, or catch someone's eye if you are gabbing on your telephone. When you are walking down the street or out in public anywhere, break the habit of making calls and catching up on conversations. If you aren't paying attention to what's going on, your potential future mate won't pay any attention to you!

## 203. TAKE A WALK—A GALLERY WALK

It's become very popular for galleries that are clustered in a single area of town to have Thursday or Friday night gallery walks once a month and sometimes more frequently. A friend of mine in Hollywood makes a point of going on gallery walks every Thursday night in her area of town. Wine is served, the artists are nearby to take questions and chat with visitors, and there's a general festive feeling in the air. It's become a great way for her to meet neighbors. She has talked to lots of guys and become friendly with many.

## 204. SAIL AWAY!

Sailing, yachting, and fishing are activities that specifically attract a lot of male interest. Many marinas and yachting clubs offer sailing lessons. You don't have to live near the shoreline to partake—many landlocked states with large lakes have docks and boat clubs. Sign up for sailing lessons, or go on a chartered fishing trip with a friend or by yourself (if you're brave). The community atmosphere of sailing makes it easy to start up conversations with the other participants. Another plus? The wind and the surf add to the excitement and beauty of watercraft activities.

# IT'S WHO YOU KNOW

Make a list of *everyone* you know who could possibly introduce you to someone new. After you have made the list, start calling! What are you waiting for?

NAME                              NUMBER

_____        _____

_____        _____

_____        _____

_____        _____

_____        _____

_____        _____

_____        _____

_____        _____

_____        _____

_____        _____

# LIFE CHANGES

Take time to think about the ways you can change your routine, lifestyle, and everyday habits. Small changes can result in a big payoff.

_____

_____

_____

_____

_____

_____

_____

_____

# PICKUP LINE HOMEWORK!

When you wake up tomorrow you have to promise me and yourself that you are going to try a pickup line on at least three men—that's right, tomorrow, *in one day*! Then do it again the next day, until you've thrown a line out to three men for five days—fifteen men in all. How did you do? Write down what happened and how each man responded. And don't forget to make a note of the lines that really seemed to work.

Every situation is different, of course, and you are going to tailor your pickup lines to each situation, each guy, and your mood. But sometimes you say something that works, well, like a charm! Don't think you'll remember it two weeks from now? You won't. Jot down your favorite lines, line you've heard other people say, or ones that strike your fancy from a book or movie. Even if you don't use them verbatim, they can inspire your own pickup line creativity. *(continued)*

**Response to my pickup lines**

_____
_____
_____
_____
_____
_____
_____
_____
_____
_____

**Pickup lines to remember**

_____
_____
_____
_____
_____
_____
_____
_____
_____
_____
_____
_____

# Seven

## Going to the Pros

*P*rofessional matchmakers and organized singles' events and other services *can* be helpful, if you choose among them wisely. Using established singles' services and events to supplement your activities helps to widen your net, but never *replace* your own efforts with them or depend on them to fill up your social calendar. Sitting home scanning Internet dates is not going to be enough to meet and marry the man of your dreams—you have to be out there and visible, because real chemistry happens only in person. And you may feel undue pressure to "perform" when you attend singles' events.

There are so many options available that it can be confusing to know where to begin and what to watch out for. Not all singles' services are reputable or worthwhile. And some may not attract the kind of men you want to meet. You also have to know how to use dating and matchmaking services to your advantage. The first part of this chapter outlines the major professional services for singles. The second part includes tips on how best to use them.

While there are cheats and liars everywhere in "real life," those kinds of people seem to have found a very comfortable home online. Nefarious men find the Internet a convenient, anonymous, easy place to "trawl" for unsuspecting women. Be aware and careful!

## 205. MATCHMAKER, MATCHMAKER, MAKE ME A MATCH

I love what I do and I am in love with love. I have been a professional matchmaker for ten years—*I get people married*. I practice primarily in New York City, Connecticut, New Jersey, Miami, and Canada. I am highly selective, so I screen clients carefully before I take them on and spend a good deal of time with them before I start introducing them to people with whom I think they would be compatible. I have been right about 1,200 times in ten years—more than 500 marriages and 700 serious, committed relationships have resulted from my introductions. So I know I'm good. And I also know that there are a lot of other great matchmakers across the country who do help people meet and marry. Don't be afraid to seek out professional dating help.

The first thing you have to do is get over the stigma of going to a matchmaker for help. A common misconception is that there's something "wrong" with people who have to hire a matchmaker. Nothing could be further from the truth. Good matchmakers take on only people who are physically, psychologically, and emotionally "together." Men come to me because they are very busy and have a hard time meeting women at work or in their daily lives. Most of them work all day long on Wall Street or in banks and law firms. They simply don't have time to go out and meet a lot of women. I help facilitate introductions they would not otherwise have made on their own. My male clients are motivated because they want to get married and possibly start a family. The same is true of the women I work with. They are busy professional people who have limited time. They are doing everything they can to meet new people, but they want the extra edge a matchmaker can give them. And they know that a good matchmaker will introduce them to people who have been carefully screened and scrutinized.

A good matchmaker will have a proven track record and a solid reputation. He or she will ask you a lot of questions and get to know you before any introductions are made. Before you go on any dates, he or she will coach you on image (and perhaps send you to an image consultant) and dating etiquette (even the most sophisticated people need a refresher course in manners now and then). After a date the matchmaker will have a postmortem discussion with you and discuss any feedback he or she has gotten from your date. I am so excited and usually can't wait, so I call my clients as soon as I think they have gotten home to find out how it went. Afterward, I tell each person what the other thought, always keeping sensitivity and kindness in mind. But I am *always* honest.

Unfortunately, some people who call themselves matchmakers aren't highly skilled. Right now anyone can hang out a shingle and call herself a matchmaker. So checking references *carefully* is important. It's worth checking the Better Business Bureau to make sure no serious complaints against the matchmaker have been filed. But you also have to remember that a matchmaker can bring a horse to water but cannot make it drink. That means that a good matchmaker will introduce you to people who should be compatible with your goals and dreams, but chemistry is elusive and that's something even the best matchmaker can't guarantee. I can boast a 91 percent success rate—which is pretty darn good. But I screen my clients very carefully and I work only with people who want to get married. *I do not run a dating service.* There's a big difference.

When you hire a matchmaker you should make sure that his or her business philosophy matches what you are looking for. My company, Janis Spindel Serious Matchmaking, Inc. is a one-on-one personal matchmaking service for people who want to get married. If you hire a matchmaker because you want to get married, make sure that's the kind of matchmaking the person you hire does. Some matchmakers are dating services in disguise, and all of their clients may not be marriage-minded.

Prices for pros can run into five figures for one-on-one services. But often matchmakers have less costly services that will put you in contact with other like-minded singles. For example, I offer a whole host of events, dinners, cocktail parties, and outings that prescreened members can attend. I know other matchmakers in other parts of the country do the same thing.

## 206. INTERNET AT YOUR SERVICE

There are three kinds of Internet dating services. The first are basically online classifieds that allow you to post yourself and browse and search the site for compatible men who have also registered. They offer a fairly safe way to contact the people you select, without having to give away your personal e-mail address until you feel comfortable with your correspondent. Some are very general and attract a wide range of people and ages, such as Match.com. Others are oriented to particular kinds of people, such as J-Date, which is for Jewish singles.

All Internet dating sites have search capabilities that allow you to locate people in your area who meet physical, age, and professional characteristics that you've determined are important. If you haven't tried these sites, think hard before you spend your money. Most charge a listing and membership fee but make no guarantees. If you do sign up and register your profile and photo on one or more dating sites, I'm certain that you will be asked on dates. Don't be disappointed if Internet dates *don't* lead you to a meaningful relationship or marriage.

If you have signed up for Internet dating, you know what I'm talking about. Many men who join singles' websites are actually married—estimates of married men who trawl online dating sites can reach 30 percent, in fact. Second, and most important, is that men are like kids in a candy store when they go online to find dates. They know that it's a "buyer's market," and they enjoy going on date after date. As one man I know put it, "I am not interested in the vast majority of women I meet online." Once men have gotten a taste of the possibilities—that they can go out with a lot of women by signing up on an Internet service—they are going to enjoy themselves! I believe women are beginning to move away from mega-sized Internet dating because they find it more satisfying and less disheartening to make connections in person.

The second type of online matchmaking requires you to fill out an extensive questionnaire that the provider runs through their database to find men who have questionnaires that seem compatible with your own. The site then sends you matches, and it's up to you to follow through. Internet services, no matter how comprehensive their questionnaires might be, are still matching you by a list of attributes. What looks good on paper doesn't always translate into real-life excitement. Even the most sophisticated set of "algorithms" can't replace a face-to-face meeting with someone, nor can it guarantee chemistry and physical attraction.

The third type, known as online dating, is a bit different from Internet matching sites. Online dating means you actually "go out" with the person online for a while before you meet him. Honestly, I don't see the point in this, but I have certainly heard stories about people who "dated" online and then met in real life and married. Some women may feel more comfortable meeting men in singles' chat rooms and then talking online or on the phone for some time before they meet. It's one way a relationship can develop without the pressures of personal meetings—and it certainly gives people a little breathing room before they have to deal with issues of sex. Ultimately, I'm old-fashioned. I understand why online dating is appealing, but I still think that nothing beats meeting someone in person and getting to know him in real time.

Finally, a matchmaker's online dating site, like mine, is more selective about members and is very intimate and boutique-y. Such smaller matchmaking sites feel more comfortable to people who may be intimidated by massive online dating services. Luckily, you actually have options now: You can select a huge site with lots of members and big volume (and turnover), or you can select a smaller site with people who have gone through a slightly more rigorous screening process. Or both!

## 207. FINDING SOMEONE UNDER CHALLENGING CIRCUMSTANCES

The Internet is particularly effective for those women who have unusual attributes. Dr. Richard A. Levine, Ph.D., a sex therapist in Brooklyn, New York, says that women who are very short, tall, overweight, or physically impaired in some way may find it easier to meet a man over the Internet than in ordinary day-to-day life. "The Internet is especially important for people with special qualities," he says. "If you're honest about yourself, you are drawing on a pool of thousands and thousands of people, and you can meet people who will find your characteristics acceptable. That's a wonderful thing."

## 208. OUT OF BOUNDS

Check out online singles in other cities. If you find there seem to be a lot of prospects, well, I can think of worse reasons for making a move!

## 209. PUT IT IN WRITING

Before there was Internet dating, there were personal ads. And they are still an affordable meeting option for some people. Most major cities have newspapers or magazines that accept singles or personal ads. City-specific magazines such as *New York, Boston, Miami, Dallas, Chicago, Los Angeles, Palm Beach,* and local or regional *Time Out* magazines (not every city has a version) are known as good places to run a personal ad. However, ads are *very* public statements, and you may not feel comfortable about placing one. They aren't for everyone. You will also get a lot of mixed responses since replies will not be prescreened. And you may be disappointed with some or all of the replies you receive.

## 210. FAST FORWARD TO SPEED DATING

Speed dating swept the country a few years ago. Speed dating events are held at various restaurants, bars, or cafés. The people who sponsor them will sign up an equal number of men and women in a particular age range (or at least this is what they should do). When you arrive at the café or bar, you sign in and get paired off with a man. The sponsor then gives you a fixed amount of time, generally under ten minutes. When the time is up, you switch partners again and again throughout the evening. (It's kind of a boot camp cocktail party.) At the end of the night, you have met many people for a brief period of time and given them your card or contact information if they asked for it. Then you wait to hear from them. You may not. Joan, thirty-seven, a woman who came to a dating workshop I teach after a negative experience with speed dating, said of the adventure, "The speed dating event I attended was like a little clique. All the people knew each other and weren't really that interested in meeting a newcomer. I found it strange and left without connecting with anyone." You may not have the same experience Joan did if you try speed dating. But if you do try it, keep an open mind and go with low expectations. That way, you won't be disappointed if the evening doesn't pan out.

# UP CLOSE AND PERSONAL
## Crossed Lines

Lisa, forty-four, and Harold, forty-eight, met online, but not in the usual way. Lisa began going online about a year after her divorce, and had been at it for about two years. She was living in the suburbs with her two teenage boys and they were a handful. That meant Lisa could not realistically get out that much to explore "real-life" dating opportunities. She wasn't meeting any men in her neighborhood, so the Internet was her best bet. Lisa signed up on two sites, Match.com and American Singles. "I really didn't know what to do so I just started writing, but mainly about my situation and my interests. I didn't get into any deep feelings or fears. I would just write that I was a mom, and I loved walking and swimming and running. I wanted to convey that while I have the responsibilities of two boys, as well as a job at a university, I also love to be active and am fit and energetic." Lisa got a few nibbles and went out on a couple of dates. But nothing clicked for her.

Flash forward two years. Harold had just gotten divorced after a long separation. He went online to see who was "out there," and he came across Lisa's listing on American Singles. He sent her a note; meanwhile, at about the same time (the same day, in fact), Lisa noticed Harold's listing on Match.com. He called himself WALKERMAN. One of Harold's prime interests was walking and hiking. Lisa was attracted to that, so she sent him a note to Match.com! They met and started going out. "As soon as I saw Lisa, that was it for me. I was done," says Harold, a tall, very handsome executive for a transportation company. Lisa felt the same way. They are now in a committed relationship and are buying a house together.

The moral of the story is that Lisa never gave up. She put herself out there and was willing to wait. "I don't think there is any stigma in getting online to meet people," she says. "For someone like me, it's the only alternative." Dr. Levine agrees that online dating sometimes provides a means of contact for people like Lisa, whose particular circumstances make in-person access to other people difficult.

## 211. THE CREAM IN YOUR COFFEE—CAFÉ DATING

Upscale, comfortable coffee shops have always been great places to meet other people, whether they cater intentionally to singles or not. Not every single person who goes to a singles café goes there to meet someone (some go just because they like the coffee), but primarily they are like singles bars without the alcohol. Café dating takes this idea a bit further. It's a unique concept, and not every city will have this kind of opportunity. Usually, you go to the café and fill out a form. The café will give you an anonymous code and keep your first name, phone number, and e-mail address on file. They will not give out your contact number, but the café singles' director will call you to set up a date if someone picks you out of their book. Café dating primarily seems to appeal to younger singles who hang around coffee shops anyway.

Coffee shops and bars also have regular dating nights. They often come complete with gimmicks to get people talking. For example, all the women get a little lock that they wear around their necks and all the men get keys. If a man is interested in a woman, he approaches and unlocks her lock. Or she can approach a man and ask him to unlock her. If you're in a good mood, and you can talk a few girlfriends into going with you, it might be fun.

## 212. SINGLES CLUBS AND EVENTS

Every city has singles' clubs and holds events specifically for single people. If you have an avid interest, you can find a singles club or event, from bird watching and ballroom dancing to golf and skiing. While café dating is geared mainly to people in their twenties and thirties, singles clubs often attract older singles, in their forties and fifties. Look for singles clubs and events in your local newspaper and online.

## 213. PICTURE PERFECT

The number one complaint I hear when men meet women through an Internet ad is "She didn't look like her picture"—and they don't mean "she looked better than her picture." They mean that her picture was dramatically deceiving. He will not be dating your photograph; he'll be dating you *if* he likes what he sees when he sees *you*. A story that illustrates what I mean perfectly was told to me by one of my clients, Jim, fifty-one. He had answered an ad on a popular Internet dating site. "The woman looks beautiful. She said she was forty-five, which is okay with me, but she looked fantastic in her picture. We made a date to meet at a nice local bar." Jim arrived at the bar and looked around. None of the women there looked liked the person he had made a date with. He waited fifteen minutes, but no one arrived who looked remotely like his date. There was a woman who had been sitting at the bar alone since he arrived. She did not look like the picture he had seen, but he took a chance and asked her if she was Shirley. "Yes," she said, "I'm Shirley." "I was dumbfounded," said Jim, "She did not look a bit like her picture so I told her that I just had not recognized her. She laughed and said that she did not have a recent picture of herself and she was in a hurry to put herself up on the website. She had simply used her daughter's picture because, as she explained it, everyone told her that her daughter looked exactly like her!" Needless to say, she did not look exactly like her daughter—she looked like her daughter in the way mothers and daughters can often resemble each other. Jim was put off. They had a drink together but the meeting ended there. The moral of the story: Use a picture of yourself!

"Glamour shots" are also a no-no. These pictures are often characterized by an air brushed and soft-focused woman with big hair wearing too much makeup and holding a red rose. This is appropriate only if you are a flamenco dancer, and even then it's questionable. Your portrait should be recent and natural. Yes, you should have your makeup and hair done before you have your picture taken. But both should be casual and flattering, not overdone or too stiff and formal looking. Air brushing, if done at all, should be subtle. A good photographer should be able to clean up a picture and enhance it without making you look like someone else. And don't forget to smile!

Don't even think about *not* including a photograph! Men will automatically believe you have something to hide—your face. It is a rare man indeed who will contact a woman on a dating site if he cannot see what she looks like, especially since men don't spend a lot of time reading ads, as you will learn in the next tip.

## 214. PRESENTATION IS EVERYTHING— AND SPELLING COUNTS

Here's a news flash—writing a great ad is easier than you think. Every man I have talked to about Internet Web ads say *that they do not read really long ads*, and, in fact, they say that ads that go on too long or divulge too much personal information *turn them off*. Men tell me that they look at a woman's picture, her vital statistics (including physical stats as well as profession, religion, and major interests and hobbies), the headline, and that's about it. If they like what they see, they will respond to the ad. It doesn't matter how poetic you are; you will not get a reply if you write a long ad. And therein lies the truth about many men: They say they care about values, personality, and intelligence. And they do. But the initial attraction comes from appearance and simple facts, even on a PC. So do not waste your time writing a brilliant essay about your innermost feelings, hopes, and dreams. Keep it simple, keep it honest, and keep it *short*.

Consider hiring a professional personal ad scribe—yes, such people *do* exist. For a moderate fee they will either edit and punch up an ad you have written or they will help you compose an ad from scratch. Some online dating services offer this service, and independent copywriters can also be found by searching the Internet with key words such as "personal coach" or "personal ad professional."

## 215. DO'S (AND ONE DON'T) OF INTERNET AND PRINT PERSONALS

- Do follow all the rules of the site or magazine when writing your classified ad.
- Do be honest about all of your claims, photographs, and "vitals." Lying will be uncovered very quickly.
- Do use simple, clear, and direct language—this is not the place to show off your amazing vocabulary!
- Do run a few ads in different places, worded differently, and keep records of which site or publication produced the best results.

- Don't give up. If your ad doesn't pull great responses after a couple of weeks, try rewriting it. One or two different words or a better-quality picture may do the trick.

## 216. MAKE YOUR HEADLINES HOT

Men may not pay attention to the body of an ad (they're more interested in *your* body), but they will notice a headline. It's worth putting some thought into a catchy banner. Headlines in print personals are even more important, since photos don't generally accompany them. That means your heading should be as sharp, provocative, and witty as you can make it. By provocative I mean it should pique a man's interest, not make him think you're for hire! I have read advice columns about ad writing that suggest using very sexually provocative headlines like "Do me instead," or "I'm hot and available," and I am completely against that. If they see a headline that says "My place or yours," or "I'm easy," men will assume—and frankly, I can't blame them—that you are available for sex and that's about it. Instead, you can be playful and sexy without being obvious and cheap. Headlines that will grab his attention might include:

- "My fabulous smile is just the beginning"
- "My big _____ (blue, brown, green) eyes want to gaze into yours"
- "Curvaceous and happy" (Note that men really love happy women, so anything you can do to convey your happiness in an ad is a plus.)

If you are very interested in meeting someone who shares a particular interest or hobby, make that clear in the headline:

- Bicycle rider who craves the outdoors
- Cooking expert is ready to start simmering
- Hiker girl looking for a mountain-loving man!

You get the idea—headlines should be concise, sassy, funny, and sexy, not raunchy! Remember that your goal is to meet men for a serious relationship and dating. You're not starting a 1-900 number business.

## 217. WRITE AN AD THAT WILL ATTRACT WITHOUT DISAPPOINTING

That means:

- A picture that really looks like you at your best.

- Stats that reflect your actual appearance and personal profile (religion, marital status, etc.).

- A description that's short, to the point, and intriguing. List interests you would like to share with a man instead of exploring your dreams and feelings.

## 218. "READ" MEN'S ADS AND ONLINE DESCRIPTIONS

If you sign on to a dating website and you get responses from men (and I believe that you will), you're going to have to assess their postings before you respond. In my experience, men tend to lie about two things in ads (aside from the thirty percent who are married and claim to be single): their age and their height. Men care desperately about the hair on their head, but it's harder for them to lie about it when they have to post a picture of themselves (of course, they may not be posting an accurate photo). But you will usually be able to tell from their picture whether they are bald, have a giant comb-over, or are wearing a toupee. Men think that women care about these things, but women actually don't care about them as much as men think they do. Here are some general rules of thumb: Add at least five years to their stated age and subtract two inches from their stated height. For example, if a man says he is six feet tall, he's probably 5'10". If he says he is forty-five, think fifty. And so on.

*What looks good on paper doesn't always translate into real-life excitement.*

Basically, you have to go with your gut. When you look at ads, look at his photograph, and then look past it to what he's saying about himself and about the statistics you care about: what he does, where he lives, and the few things that he says matter to him. If your initial impression is positive, then respond and chat online for a bit before you agree to meet. You will get an additional "feel" for him this way, and you will know if you want to "consummate" your e-mailing with an in-person get-together.

## 219. SHARING INFORMATION SAFELY

If you do start to hear from men and strike up e-mail conversations with them, don't give away too many facts about where you live and work until after you have gotten to know them better. Guard your anonymity. Create an e-mail account only for dating. There are many free services on the Internet that will provide you with mailboxes that you can keep separate from your usual personal and business e-mail accounts. Never, *ever* e-mail someone your home address, phone number, or place of business until you are comfortable. If anything makes you feel awkward or "creepy," stop e-mailing them immediately, and block the person from your mailbox. If you do decide to meet for coffee or a drink, play it safe and meet in a public place. And meet only when you are ready! In general, I believe that a man should pick a woman up and then ensure she gets home safely either by getting her a car or taking her home himself, and we'll talk about that in the next chapter. But with Internet dating, I feel that setting up a meeting in a well-known place that's convenient for both of you to get to makes safety sense. And tell a friend where you are going and when you expect to be home.

## 220. PLAY IT SAFE

Watch for signs in e-mails or other communications that a man may not be who or what he appears to be. You should be concerned, obviously, if a potential date seems passive-aggressive, is too pushy, or makes jokes that are demeaning or nasty. You should also use caution (and put an end to your communication) if a man provides inconsistent information about himself, his profession, his marital status, interests, or appearance. If he does not answer questions directly, watch out. If he refuses to speak to you or call you on the telephone after you have chatted for a while online, this could be a sign he is married (or is in some other restrictive situation). Finally, if you do meet him and he behaves or seems very (unpleasantly) different from his online persona, end the meeting as quickly as you can and steer clear of him in the future.

## 221. USE E-MAIL ETIQUETTE

If you have met someone or talked to him on the telephone and you feel comfortable communicating with him via e-mail, it's important to maintain the same level of civility and charm that you would use if you were talking to him in person. Sometimes we have a tendency to forget that e-mail is a real form of communication that has an effect on people. We tend to be more casual or sloppy in e-mail. Don't. Following are some important things to keep in mind about chatting with a date online.

## 222. BE CAREFUL WITH ADDRESSES AND PERSONAL NAMES

- Always provide a personal name if your mail system allows it—a personal name attached to your address identifies you better than your address can on its own.

- Use a sensible personal name. "Guess who" or other such phrases are annoying as personal names and hinder the recipient's quick identification of you and your message.

- If your mail system lets you use personal names in the addresses to which you send mail, try to use them. This will often help a postmaster recognize the real recipient of the message if the address is invalid.

## 223. SUBJECT LINE SENSITIVITY

- Always include a subject line in your message. Almost all mailers present you with the subject line when you browse your mailbox, and it's often the only clue the recipient has about the contents when filing and searching for messages.

- Make the subject line meaningful.
- If you are replying to a message but are changing the subject of the conversation, change the subject, too—or, better still, start a new message altogether. The subject is usually the easiest way to follow the thread of a conversation, so changing the conversation without changing the subject can be confusing.

## 224. LENGTH AND CONTENT COUNT

- Always begin the e-mail with a greeting using the person's name, as in "Hi Bob" or "Dear James."
- Don't type your message in uppercase letters—it's extremely difficult to read and it generally denotes anger or yelling (something you want to avoid!).
- Use correct grammar and spelling. If your words are important enough to write, then they're also important enough to write properly.
- Keep it short and conversational—like ads, e-mails are not the place to convey deep thoughts or heavy emotions.

## 225. REPLY STYLE

- Include enough of the original message to provide a context to your answer.
- Answer as soon as you can (don't leave him hanging for more than forty-eight hours; it's rude, much like not returning a phone call).

## 226. SIGNATURE SAVVY

Always sign your e-mail in a way that identifies you. Include alternative means of contacting you *if* you want to be contacted—such as your office phone number. See **Tip 151** for a safety reminder.

## 227. COURTESY MATTERS

Electronic mail is all about communication with other people, and basic courtesy is always welcome.

- If you're asking for something, don't forget to say "please." Similarly, if someone does something for you, it never hurts to say "thank you." While this might sound trivial, or even insulting, it's astonishing how many people who are perfectly polite in everyday life seem to forget their manners in their e-mail. An e-mail can appear to be very rude if it does not include these simple niceties.

- Always remember that there is no such thing as a secure mail system. It is unwise to send very personal or sensitive information by e-mail. Remember the recipient—you are not the only person who could be embarrassed if a delicate message falls into the wrong hands, especially if you are replying to someone at his or her business e-mail address.

## 228. ADD HIGH-TECH "EMOTICONS" TO YOUR MISSIVES

E-mail has the immediacy of a conversation, but is totally devoid of "body language." Creative Internet writers have had an answer to this problem for years—"smiley faces," characters that are meant to look like a face turned on its side. Used sparingly, they can add a playful "wink" to your e-mail and can assure someone that your message is friendly. Just don't overuse them.

There are now many emoticons available for free downloading on the Internet, and some are very elaborate and even animated. But you can still "build" your own. Here are some examples:

:-) or :)
A smiling face seen side-on; generally used to indicate amusement, or that a comment is intended to be funny or ironic.

;-)

A winking smily face usually indicates that you're being playful and mean something in an ironic way.

;->

A mischievous smiley face usually indicates that a comment is intended to be provocative or racy.

## 229. MANAGE YOUR EXPECTATIONS

Finally, keep your emotions and hopes in check. Don't build up the Internet or any dating device into something it's not. Internet dating sites, singles cafés, speed dating, and even matchmakers are all tools you can use as part of your *entire* repertoire. If you don't meet anyone online the first time, try again. If you meet someone and he doesn't spark your interest, go out with someone else. Don't expect every meeting, e-mail, or phone call from a man to be terrific or perfect or exactly what you're looking for. Keep a light and open mind. If something doesn't work out, you have to pick yourself up and get right back out there.

# AD WORKSHEET

Before you put an ad on an Internet matchmaking site or in a newspaper, practice!

_____

_____

_____

_____

_____

_____

The same is true for headlines—try some first, before you post them.

# *Part 3*
# DATING TOWARD MARRIAGE

You look hot, you've met loads of men, and now you're on your way. If your goal is marriage, dating takes on a whole new purpose. Before you made the decision to meet someone and get married you might have been stuck in endless dating cycles that led nowhere. Or you were just having a good time, dating around, keeping commitment in the background. There's nothing wrong with that, but now you feel differently. That means you have to approach dating differently.

While I stress that you should not get uptight about dates or push too hard, I recognize that you are on a mission. So the following chapters are devoted to showing you how to prepare for a date. Here's a clue: You want to do your best to blow him away with your beauty and charm. Then we'll move on to how relationships develop and what you can do to make great dates turn into a fantastic relationship leading to marriage. It's important not to stop trying when you think you've met Mr. Right. I also think this chapter is very useful for those of you who might be coming out of a relationship and starting over. And just so you're not left hanging when you have met the man of your dreams, I'll talk about commitment and marriage. After all, this is a full-service guide and it doesn't end when you get the ring on your finger. In fact, it's only just beginning.

# *Eight*

# The Big Date: Ready, Set, *Go!*

*Y*ou've laid the groundwork, put yourself out there, and made major changes in your life, appearance, and attitude. And now it's finally happened. A man (or even two or three) has asked you for a date. Congratulations! Anticipating a first date can be very exciting. It can also raise a lot of emotions such as fear, anxiety, and overwhelming joy—*especially* if you are hoping that one date will evolve into a lifetime spent with Mr. Right. But focusing on that idea alone, to the exclusion of everything else, can sabotage a perfectly nice evening. If you indulge the fantasy that your entire future hinges on this one meeting, you will be a nervous wreck. And *he* will be able to spot your desperation the second you meet. The idea that intelligent, sophisticated women could put that much pressure on a first date seems preposterous, but I have seen many women fall into this trap to no good end. First thing to remember: It's only a date! Lighten up.

I am absolutely not saying that the date could not turn into a serious relationship—quite the opposite, in fact. As I said earlier, your future husband can be found just about anywhere, and that's why you always have to be prepared. But your life and your future are not held in the balance by a single date, encounter, meeting, or event. While you should treat any date as if you could be meeting your future husband, you should not put pressure on yourself or him for the date to "succeed" on the grounds of "This date must turn into a marriage; otherwise I am a complete failure." Your attitude should be "This could be my future husband, how exciting," not "If this date doesn't turn out to be my future husband, I am going to stop breathing."

In this chapter, we'll carefully review all the preparatory steps you can take that will help you to exude an air of confidence and happiness when you meet someone for the first time. A man will appreciate the effort you put into making yourself look pretty and relaxed, even if he's not conscious of it (although there's a good chance he will be). Presenting yourself with charm and grace is also essential, and even though you may know that intellectually, it can be difficult to put into practice when you're feeling a bit edgy and fluttery. So we'll go over first-date do's and don'ts, too. This refresher course will help calm your nerves and prepare you for what lies ahead.

I'll also address potentially awkward moments during the date—from the initial hello (Do I shake his hand or kiss him on the cheek?) to that parting moment (Should I tell him I'd like to see him again or wait for him to say something?). Good manners are always in style, of course, but there are certain guidelines that, if followed, will put your date at ease and leave a favorable perception of you in his mind. And you'll have a better time if you are courteous and caring. Knowing how to handle date one is a major jitters-buster!

Finally, *every* first date should be treated with the same care and time. Never skimp or think, "I don't think this guy is really that great so I won't get my hair blown out; I won't wear that new leather skirt." Wrong! Practice makes perfect, so even if he doesn't turn out to be the one, it's still worth making the effort. He's a person, after all, and he deserves to be treated with dignity. Think about it this way: Would you ever go on a job interview or to an important business meeting looking like you just got out of bed? Of course you wouldn't. So why isn't someone who has taken an interest in you and offered to take you out just as important as a work engagement?

## 230. IT'S A DATE!

The circumstances in which you meet a particular man will help you determine how you respond to him when he asks you on a date. If you met him online, you obviously want to chat with him via e-mail and on the telephone before you decide to meet. Once you do agree on an in-person encounter, it's a good idea to plan something that isn't too open-ended and that takes place around other people. That's why I am against "a walk in the park" for a first date. See what he has in mind first, of course. If he asks you for dinner, suggest lunch or drinks instead. You're doing him a favor, for one, because both of those alternatives are less costly than dinner out. Second, it's more awkward, though not impossible, to put an end to a dinner date as soon as coffee is served and the check arrives.

If you meet for lunch or cocktails and your initial "electronic impression" of him turns out to be quite wrong, you know the date has a defined end and you can relax, be polite, and then get out when it's over. A weekday lunch meeting gives you a perfect "out" (i.e., you need to get back to the office) if things don't work out. Even a Saturday lunch date gives you a chance to say, "I promised my Aunt Sophie that I'd take her shopping at 3 P.M." In other words, you can make plans for later in the day. Either way, if you have a great time, he'll want more and you can make another, different kind of date for next time. A drink date is another alternative. You can always say you have dinner plans (and you might even consider making dinner or movie plans with friends for later in the evening). The same advice goes for men you may have met on your own, at a function, or just in a chance meeting.

If a date comes out of a personal introduction from someone you know well, you can be a bit more open about when and where you meet, especially if you trust the person who has made the introduction. If your date is someone you have known for a while and you've suddenly "discovered" each other, then by all means, have fun and have dinner, go for a walk, or go to a museum together. It's really up to you.

Just remember to let him ask you on the date, and if his suggestion doesn't sit right with you for any reason, politely offer another suggestion that is fair to him and still makes him feel as if he's in control. For example, if he asks you to dinner on a particular night, you can say, "I have another obligation that evening, but I am free for drinks or lunch on that day."

Give yourself plenty of time, too: Don't accept a date for the next day. If the date blossoms into a relationship, you can certainly accept spur-of-the-moment and spontaneous invitations (life should be filled with excitement, shouldn't it?). But early on, you should only accept a date at least one week in advance. Why? Because you don't want to appear too anxious, and more importantly, you need time to prepare!

## 231. DON'T DISGUISE YOURSELF!

When you arrange to meet a blind date at an appointed time, you will likely have to tell him what you will be wearing. Even someone who has seen your picture on the Internet and has a general idea of what you look like may not find you to be immediately recognizable in person. So when you tell someone what you will be wearing, wear that outfit. Don't think you can show up in another, completely different outfit to "spy" on him and then leave if you don't like what you see. It's rude, it's mean, and it's dishonest.

## 232. "MEETING" YOUR EXPECTATIONS

The old-fashioned part of me feels that men should pick women up for a date—any date—whether he's meeting you for lunch, dinner, or a softball game. But the modern part of me says that on a first date with someone you don't know, it's better to meet at the agreed-upon location. My male clients say that when they go on blind dates, 98 percent of women prefer to meet somewhere (at the restaurant or bar) the first time instead of being picked up at home. That's because women may feel some trepidation about a man's knowing exactly where they live or work. As I've said, if you met online or "on the street," meet him at the appointed location. If you know each other or if you have been introduced by a reliable friend or family member, I think it's absolutely appropriate for the man to pick you up and take you home or back to work at the end of the date.

## 233. GET YOUR HAIR BLOWN OUT

I tell every one of my female clients to get their hair washed and blown out before a big date. A blow-out should enhance your natural style and make your hair shiny and full of movement. If you need a trim or root touch-up, get it done at this time as well. This is *not* the time to try something new! No short haircuts, funny colors, or weird hair ornaments. Meeting for lunch during the week? Make the time—take time off in the morning. A blow-out should take no more than half an hour.

## 234. HAVE YOUR MAKEUP DONE

As far as I am concerned, great makeup is another first-date must. Do not—I repeat, *do not*—"touch up" your makeup after work (if it's a drink or dinner date) or do it yourself that morning. Those kinds of slap-dash lipstick-and-blush jobs simply do not cut it on a first date. Make an appointment with the best makeup artist (the one I helped you find in Chapter 2) and have your face "done" professionally and naturally (a great makeup artist won't pile it on). It should take no more than half an hour, but it's *so* worth it—you will look and feel spectacular. When I see a woman who has had her hair blown out and her makeup done, she radiates confidence, beauty, and sex appeal. Having your makeup professionally applied before a big date will help you become a super version of yourself!

# JANIS FACT

### FIVE QUESTIONS WOMEN ASK ME THE MOST BEFORE I SEND THEM ON DATE 1:

1. Is he smart?
2. Is he funny?
3. How many kids does he have?
4. How long was he married?
5. He's a really nice guy . . . not crazy, right?

## 235. DATE MAKEUP, VINCENT LONGO STYLE

After twenty-two years in the fashion business as an image consultant, makeup innovator, and stylist for people like Cindy, Vendela, Naomi, and others, Vincent Longo knows whereof he speaks. Vincent says that first-date makeup has to be fabulous but natural. He advises keeping skin as clear as possible, so its texture and fineness is visible. "I either leave the skin fresh from a beauty regime or simply spot it with a light foundation," he says. That's because, according to Vincent—and I could not agree more—men like to see the transparency of the skin.

"If you have problem skin, first spot the offending area," advises Vincent. "Depending on how problematic it is, you may need a heavier product. If it's just a blemish, a dot of concealer and some powder should do the trick." Whatever you choose, Vincent cautions to use it with a light touch.

"A lot of women have this idea that shine is appealing and it's *not,* especially on a date," says Vincent. He says it doesn't register as polished or stylish. "It's not as clean as if you just had a light dusting of powder on. Within a few hours your own glow will start coming through," he says.

Vincent prefers powders that are highly refined. One way to check out the fine quality of a powder is to apply it to your inner wrist. Then close your other hand over it. Remove and blow on the wrist. If the powder is stuck in the lines don't use it. If it blows away, it's a good product. There are a lot of powders that will stick, and those are the ones that will cake on your face.

Vincent suggests using lash tips on outer corner of your eyes or individual lashes. But if you have a nice lash line you don't necessarily need the extra help. A curling mascara and a lash curler can do the trick. "I like mascara, men in general like mascara," says Vincent. The two things they don't like to see too much of: lipstick and heavy foundation.

For blush, Vincent suggests a cream. "They are softer and more approachable. If he kisses you or there's smooching going on, it won't streak and stick to him, and if a little does get on his cheeks, he won't notice it," says Vincent.

As for lips, Vincent says gel stains are long-lasting. "You can use them for cheeks as well, and the color will not transfer onto him," he says. Finally, sweep a light eyeshadow across the lash line. Then take a darker shadow, whatever works for your outfit, and place the brush on the outer corner or lash line and sweep color inward. They should then meet halfway and blend into each other. Blending in this way is easier and looks more natural, so remember that light shadow *always* goes on first.

## 236. WHAT MEN SAY ABOUT THEIR "IDEAL WOMAN"

When I ask my male clients what they are looking for in an "ideal" woman, these are the things I hear over and over again:

- Attractive
- Nice figure
- Sweet
- Intelligent
- "Up" personality and naturally happy
- Sense of humor
- Shared values
- Bright and educated
- Sincere
- No "daily catharsis" to deal with

## 237. MANICURE AND PEDICURE PERFECTION

Don't forget your nails and toes. We've talked about how chipped polish is a major no-no. Make sure your manicure and pedicure are perfect and subtle (no purple polish please!). Do it the day before, to save time. Make sure you have the same color in your bag for little fix-ups.

## 238. THE CLOTHES HAVE IT!

Be beautifully dressed for a first date—and all dates for that matter. That doesn't necessarily mean "fancy," unless the occasion calls for it. Even if you are meeting for a casual Saturday lunch, you should look groomed, fashionable, subtle, and sexy. A seductive outfit isn't about cleavage or skin—it's about showing off your figure to its best advantage. Sexy is about looking like a lady. Men love skirts and heels. If you don't wear something fitted, they will assume something is wrong with your figure. The same thing goes for wearing pants. If you wear pants on the first date, he will think you don't have nice legs. Sounds crazy, but it's unfortunately true. If you *don't* have great legs and you feel more comfortable wearing pants, make sure they flatter your figure. Your top should show off your great neck, arms, and breasts (without actually showing your breasts). Think fitted knit top or tailored shirt or blouse. Don't do loose and flowing tops with pants or wear any outfit that doesn't accentuate your curves and best features. Even chronically casual guys (you know the ones I mean—the ones who think khakis and a white shirt is dressed up) like to see a woman well put together.

If your first date is after work, be sure to take along alternate high heels and a camisole top or something lacy to stick under your suit—anything to make your work outfit look sensual, feminine, and fresh.

## 239. AFTER-WORK DATE COUNTDOWN (FOR 7 P.M. DATE)

Follow this countdown schedule to ensure you're picture perfect for an after-work first date (or any date). Be sure to make all appointments well in advance so you get the times you want.

### One week before date:

- ☐ Dry clean, mend, or press any clothes you are planning on wearing
- ☐ Make sure all accessories are in order
- ☐ Make sure you have the right shoes and that they are polished and in excellent condition
- ☐ Purchase pantyhose, stockings, or other lingerie, if necessary

### One to two days before date:

- ☐ Manicure and pedicure
- ☐ Touch up roots, if necessary
- ☐ Facial and any other spa treatments

**Day of date:**

☐ 5:00: Change top, shoes, hose, etc.

☐ 5:30: Get makeup done

☐ 6:30: Hair blow-out

☐ 7:30: Meet your date!

## 240. REMOVE THE WORD "LATE" FROM YOUR VOCABULARY

When you make a date with a man (or anyone for that matter), show up for it on time. There is *nothing* that drives me crazier than people who are perpetually late for dates and meetings. A man will appreciate your promptness but will feel slighted if you're late. And justifiably so. My client George, thirty-six, said about a recent date, "I loved that she was early; it really made an impression on me." Bottom line, it's just plain rude to keep someone waiting. Lateness says, "I don't care about you or your time. My time is more important." If you've kept men waiting, you shouldn't wonder why you're single. They hate it, and it really is unacceptable behavior. Give yourself enough time to get where you are going. If you're early, walk around the block or go to the powder room to freshen up.

## JANIS FACT

### FIVE QUESTIONS MEN ASK ME THE MOST BEFORE I SEND THEM ON DATE 1:

1. What does she look like?
2. How old is she?
3. Is she thin?
4. Tell me again what she looks like.
5. What's her hair like?

## 241. IF YOU *ARE* GOING TO BE LATE, CALL HIM

Some events are out of our control—to a certain extent. Traffic is bad and even though you thought you gave yourself enough time to get across town or down the highway, you're at a standstill. Or your boss just walked into your office and asked you to make a call, pull together a report, or one of a million other annoying last-minute requests. We both know that life can get in the way of the best laid plans. If that happens, *call him* and tell him you will be late for unavoidable reasons and let him know as close to exactly when you *will* be appearing. There is nothing more wrong than assuming that the person will "understand" why you are late or know by magic that some unavoidable circumstance has prevented you from showing up. Even Houdini would have a hard time figuring that one out.

## 242. MAKING YOUR MARK

It can be sexy to leave a little lipstick on your wine glass. It's even better to avoid leaving any marks, if possible. Vincent Longo says to sip from the same spot and discreetly lick the glass before sipping to help prevent lipstick marks.

## 243. MAKE AN ENTRANCE

You have only about five seconds to make an impression, so make it a positive and lasting one. When you enter a restaurant, pause at the entry and scan the room. Be sure to stand up straight with your head held high. If you don't see your date or he does not approach you, you can approach the maitre d' to inquire whether your date has arrived and has been seated. I don't think men should seat themselves before their date arrives, but many do it. For example, a man I know, Bob, says, "I like to arrive early and sit at the table—it gives me a panoramic view so I can see my date's body and what she looks like in clothes." If Bob were a client of mine, I would insist that he meet dates in the entry or lobby of the establishment. If your date *is* sitting at the table when you arrive, you can also pause in the doorway of the dining room and then continue following the hostess or maitre d' to the table. My attitude is, if he wants to take in how gorgeous you look, let him!

## 244. BAR MEETS GIRL

Meeting at a bar presents problems because you don't make reservations to sit at a bar, and consequently, the restaurant personnel may not know who you are or with whom you are meeting. So you are on your own. When you arrive at the bar, make your entrance (see above) by pausing and scanning the room. If you don't recognize your date, once you have your bearings you can go ahead and sit down. But there's a real upside to meeting a blind date in a bar: It gives you the perfect excuse to approach any cute guy who might be sitting there and ask, "Are you Joe Jones, by any chance?" If he says yes, you've met your date. If he says no, you can introduce yourself and make a new friend while you wait for your real date to show up. There is nothing wrong with this—bars are social places and as soon as your date arrives you are going to excuse yourself from your new friend's company. Another plus? If your date sees you talking to another guy, he'll be more intrigued by you and you can bet he will not show up late the next time!

## 245. SAY HELLO

When you're finally face-to-face with your date, what do you do? First and foremost, SMILE. But you know that already, don't you? Should you shake his hand? Peck him on the cheek? Hug him? Women ask this all the time, and I think you should determine that by your gut reaction to seeing him and how you naturally express yourself with people you know. If you see him and melt, by all means, a quick peck on the cheek is utterly acceptable. "If a woman kisses me on the cheek the first time, I think she likes me," says my client George, thirty-eight. Other men I know concur. "I really like it when a woman is spontaneous and affectionate in a lady-like way," says my client Jay, fifty. Shaking hands might feel too formal, but if you don't want to kiss him on the cheek you can take his hand (rather than shake it), and touch his forearm with your other hand as you say hello and look into his eyes.

## 246. LET HIM TAKE CHARGE!

Competent, successful women who are used to taking care of themselves sometimes forget to let a man open the door for them, or they approach the maitre d' in a restaurant or in general take control of the evening. Men tell me there's nothing that turns them off more than a woman who charges ahead of them through a door, advances to the reservation desk

## UP CLOSE AND PERSONAL
### *Three's a Crowd*

Marty, forty-nine, met a woman, Ella, forty-six, online and they arranged to meet for a dinner date. Marty arrived early, so when Ella entered the restaurant, he was waiting for her with flowers (Marty's a great guy). She looked fantastic. The only odd feature of her outfit was an oversized bag. Soon after they were seated, Marty discovered what was inside the bag. The maitre d' told Ella and Marty they could not eat in the dining room if Ella insisted on bringing her little dog, Charly, inside. That's right, inside the mega-bag was a little dog. "Ella told me that she never goes anywhere without her dog, so we had to leave the restaurant to find one that allowed pets," explains Marty. It was a long evening. "We went to about six restaurants until we found one with an outdoor café that allowed Ella to eat with her dog," says Marty. And Ella wasn't kidding about wanting to eat with her dog. "The first thing she did was order soup. As soon as it arrived, she took Charly out of the bag and placed the soup bowl on the floor so he could eat," says Marty. It was embarrassing for Marty, and all he could think about was the dog licking all of the dishes in Ella's apartment. The moral of the story: Leave your pets at home for dinner dates (save it for walks in the park). If you have any quirks, the first date is the time to let up on them a bit.

before him to ask for a table, or orders a bottle of wine without consulting him. Let him open doors for you (you've been opening doors all day, it's time to take a break), and let him get the table in the restaurant and order the wine. Is it going to kill you? No. Is it going to make him feel like a man? Yes. I know that you often have to forget you're a woman in the office (although there's a good argument against doing that, which I won't get into now), but when you're on a date, let your femininity glow.

## 247. MAKE A DATE, NOT AN ARGUMENT

A first date should be light, fun, and uncontroversial. I know, I know. You're opinionated, dynamic, and intelligent. Congratulations, that's wonderful. But really, the majority of men *do not* want to spar over politics, social issues, feminism, or gun control on the first date. Even social justice lawyers I know don't want to discuss public policy and case law with a woman they've just met. If you're thinking, "But I don't want to suppress my intelligence just to catch a man," get over it now. No one is asking you to act like the proverbial dumb blond—and men say that they do want to be with a woman who knows what's going on in the world and understands current issues. On the other hand, they want to feel as if they are *on* a date, not *in* a debate. Men appreciate clever banter, humor, and interesting discussion—which means you should be up on current events, but don't present a position paper on global warming during the main course. And don't crowd him out with your own chatter and opinions.

## 248. LISTEN AND PAY ATTENTION

Show an interest in what he's saying. Even if you disagree with an idea he expressed or you aren't curious about March Madness basketball or fly fishing, if he's talking about it, it means he *is* interested and he is sharing his enthusiasm with you. Take that as a compliment and listen to what he has to say and respond accordingly. This is how you would like to be treated, and it is how you would treat any other person you met.

## 249. PAY PALS

In the early stages of dating (the first few dates) I believe that if a man invites you on a date, he should pay for it. If you invite *him*, you should treat. In other words, don't expect him to pick up the tab if you have planned an elaborate outing or you made reservations at a chic new restaurant. However, I do think it's a bad sign when, on a first or second date where *you* are the invited guest, he wants to "go Dutch," or worse, expects you to cover the entire evening. If a man has treated you to a wonderful time three or four times, it is time for you to treat him to a wonderful meal, a show, or a hot new flick. See the following chapter (**Tip 277**) for more about who pays for what in a more serious relationship.

## 250. LEAVE THE SKELETONS IN THE CLOSET

Inevitably, you are going to discuss some personal subjects—hobbies, favorite vacation spots, memories of an adventure you took, or a funny anecdote about something that happened at work. All those topics are great and they give your date some insight into who you are and what you like. But there are topics you should steer clear of completely on a first date. They are: your ex(es), problems with your kids, your pets, past bad breakups or relationships, money, illness, bad habits, or other peccadilloes that are better left at home. This is a date, not a therapy session. And if a man suspects you come with a lot of baggage (and I am not talking about the Louis Vuitton variety!), he is not going to stick around. Whining about the bad deal you've been handed, complaining about your lot in life, and trashing friends or ex-husbands are also big-time no-nos.

*While you should treat any date as if you could be meeting your future husband, you should not put pressure on yourself or him for the date to "succeed" on the grounds of "This date must turn into a marriage; otherwise I am a complete failure."*

The only thing really personal you should make him aware of on the first date is whether or not you *have* children. All parents know that children come first, and they can make unexpected demands on our time. So it's only fair to your date to let him know you have little (or big) ones at home who may need you, even if you're on a date. But as I mentioned in the paragraph above, avoid discussing fights you have with your teen or other issues that could be perceived as a troubled relationship with your offspring. It's a turnoff.

## 251. DON'T GIVE HIM THE THIRD DEGREE

Along the same lines, don't interrogate him as if you were an FBI agent. Don't push him for the details about his divorce or why he's never been married. Nathan, a fifty-something single and never-married man, says that women, when learning of his lack of marital experience, will often ask, "What's wrong with you?" That line of questioning will only put him on the defensive, which will not result in a pleasant evening. Don't grill him about what kind of job he has, how much money he makes, what his net worth is, or how many women he's slept with. Ask questions that bring out his interests and try to find a topic that you can both enjoy discussing.

## 252. TURN THE CONVERSATION AROUND

The number one complaint I hear from women is that a man can spend an entire evening talking about himself. I have asked dozens of men about this tendency and many of them reason it out in the following ways:

- The woman wasn't saying anything and he felt the need to fill in the conversational gap.
- The woman really wanted him to do the talking.
- He was nervous, and when he's nervous he talks.

Some other men I know believe that "if a woman likes you, it doesn't matter how much you talk. If she doesn't like you, she will focus on your conversation and everything else she has decided she doesn't like about you."

Those are harsh words, but they make a good point. Ask yourself, is it irritating you that he is talking so much because you simply don't have any chemistry? And if you really liked him, would it matter how much he talked about himself? Is he responding to your behavior?

The good news is, you can turn the conversation around. Interject something about the *topic* he is discussing, not something about you. The object is to turn the conversation around to a topic that is not "about" either of you. If you are an active listener, you will be able to pick up on ideas or subjects in his conversation that can act as jumping-off points for another conversation. For example, if a man is talking about his work, wait for a natural gap (when he takes a breath) and pick up on something he said that has a general application to a broader topic or to something you're interested in:

HIM: "I just finished a big auditing project."

YOU: "Those accounting firms that were messed up in the corporate scandals are really in trouble. Every auditor in the country must be feeling the heat. . . ."

And perhaps you can get into a conversation about business in general and then move that along to other topics.

If he's still simply not letting you get a word in edgewise, you might try excusing yourself for a moment. Go to the powder room, and when you return you can come back with a topic in mind and start anew.

If nothing works, he may very well be self-absorbed and completely oblivious to you or anyone else when he's pontificating. For example, if he asks you a question and you've said only a few words and he gets a glazed look in his eyes—or worse, stares off into the distance—you may be in trouble. You'll really have to wait until date number two to find out for sure.

## 253. CALL HIM BY HIS NAME

Use his name when you talk to him or ask him a question. There is a real connection that is formed when you use someone's name. It may be subconscious, but it's powerful.

### *Manspeak*

**"There's nothing sexier than a leather skirt worn with boots or high heels,"**
**declares my client Richard, thirty-nine.**

## 254. DRINK DATE DECORUM

Many men and women say meeting for a cocktail is their favorite first date. As I discussed earlier, it doesn't have to last too long and it provides a comfortable and somewhat festive setting. But a drink date isn't an automatic invitation to dinner, even if the date goes well. He may have another engagement (as might you). On the other hand, he may ask you to dinner if the date goes well, and you have the option of saying yes and continuing the date or saying no because you have other plans for the evening.

If a man asks you to meet him for a drink and *you* suggest dinner and also take it upon yourself to make a restaurant suggestion, and he agrees, keep in mind that you have now asked *him* on a date and you should pick up the tab for dinner. Bottom line, it goes back to control. If a man asks you on a particular kind of date, say yes if you are interested in seeing him. Don't force him to take you to dinner if that's not what he had in mind.

## 255. AFTERNOON DELIGHTS

An afternoon lunch or museum date can be a nice way to meet someone without the pressure that Saturday night can often put on people. A lunch date is a more defined period of time, so if things don't go well, you know it will be over in less than two hours. Logistics may be challenging for a lunch date: You still have to get hair and makeup done if it's a first date. Get your blow-out and makeup done any time in the morning if it's a weekend lunch and before work if it's during the week. Many hair and beauty spas open early, before traditional 9 A.M. work hours, precisely because they cater to working people. It's worth finding and cultivating these kinds of salons in your area.

## 256. OH, THOSE DRINKABLE LIPS!

Makeup expert Vincent Longo says it's very sexy and elegant to reapply a little lipstick after dinner, and I agree. The trick is in doing it properly. Don't open your mouth too much, and just do a light application of lipstick while looking into a compact. It shouldn't take long—the whole movement should last no more than fifteen seconds. It's one way of putting on a little show. Smile demurely. Practice at home first if you don't feel confident you can pull it off!

## 257. DINNER DATE SEATING

Restaurant seating can present some awkward moments. A maitre d' may offer you and your date a choice of seating situations—side-by-side, across, and corner. Let your date take charge but if he defers to you, go for corner seating, if it's available. It allows you to look at each other in an intimate way. Side-by-side seating is a little too intimate for a first date and doesn't allow you to look at each other, which you really should do. A center table that puts you across from each other is a bit formal and may not be as relaxing. The soft seats of a corner banquette are ideal. If that's not available, try to encourage your date to sit at a forty-five degree-angle to you, not across from you. It's the next best thing to a corner booth. One way of doing this is to sit down and then gently pat the place where you would like him to sit. Or turn in the direction of where you would like him to sit. I think he'll get the hint.

## 258. DON'T BE A PICKY EATER

For heaven's sake, this is *one* night of your life. Can you leave the vitamin pills, supplements, powders, and crazy diet restrictions at home? Don't make a big deal of food phobias or allergies. Most menus offer something you can order easily without making your food preferences the center of attention. Be discreet and keep it simple. Try not to give the waiter the third degree. Men always mention that it's a big turnoff for them if a woman is neurotic about her food. A client who recently married related a story to me about a woman he dated once who ordered a salad before each meal. No problem with that. But in her large purse she kept a bag of red onions, black olives, "special" oil, and vitamin E pills. She would "dress" the salad with these items, squirting the contents of the vitamin E pills on top. She said her nutritional counselor told her that eating such a salad before each meal would ensure her longevity and health. It was both embarrassing and somewhat gross to watch her perform this ritual—for him and the diners around them. It certainly didn't add to the longevity of their relationship! My advice is, if you have an odd dietary requirement, fulfill it *before* you meet your date.

## UP CLOSE AND PERSONAL
### *Rude and Crude Doesn't Cut It*

My client Gavin, forty-six, told me about a date he didn't have, which illustrates that there's a reason why some women aren't married. Gavin met a woman on an Internet dating site. They exchanged e-mails and pictures and then decided to meet for a drink one evening after work, at 6:30, at a very posh Manhattan bar. Gavin, who happens to be a very busy and distinguished international lawyer—arrived at 6:25. He found a nice, comfortable table and chairs and sat down with great anticipation. At 6:40 he started to worry a bit. Maybe rush hour traffic is bad, he thought, and she's stuck in a cab. But wouldn't she call and say so?

At 7:00, he began to wonder if he'd been stood up. But since his e-mail and telephone exchanges with the woman had been quite pleasant, Gavin naturally assumed that something unavoidable had happened to his date and he decided to try her cell phone. "When she answered, she told me, very angrily, that an afternoon meeting was running late," said Gavin. "When I asked her when she thought she might be getting to the bar, she snapped, 'Maybe in forty minutes!'" Gavin was astonished, but since he is a curious and confident guy, he asked her very nicely if she had been planning on calling him to tell him any of this. "She said no, she wasn't! It was unbelievable to me that she could be angry at me because she was late and had no intention of telling me," said Gavin. Needless to say, he finished his drink and left. Luckily, he had a dinner engagement. But that woman missed out on a terrific, smart, funny, good-looking guy. And I'm sure she's still single and wondering why.

## 259. IF YOU ARE NOT FEELING WELL, IT'S BETTER TO CANCEL—AND RESCHEDULE

If you are feeling sick, had a very bad day at the office, or have a huge pimple that doesn't seem to be going anywhere, you are often better off canceling and rescheduling the date than going. That's because you will not make a good impression if you don't feel your best. I generally don't believe in canceling, but I do think it's the right thing to do in one of these cases. However, make sure he knows you are canceling because you don't feel well, and do reschedule for a specific alternate date before you hang up to reassure him again that it's you, not him. Reiterate that you are looking forward to it. And send him a note or e-mail as a follow-up saying you appreciate his understanding.

## 260. TURN YOUR CELL PHONE OFF—AGAIN!

Do I have to explain this one? Do not spend your first date taking calls from your friends!

## 261. WHAT NOT TO EAT

Avoid messy or potentially messy, noisy, or hard-to-eat foods on a first date. You really want to choose a meal that doesn't require a lot of thought on how to maneuver it into your mouth. Play it safe, and don't order:

- Spaghetti
- Salad (hard to eat gracefully, dressing can splatter on you—or him)
- Oysters (see above—they require you to make noise and they drip—wait until you're naked and in bed before you eat these with a date!)
- Soup or stews
- Potato chips or anything extremely crunchy that makes a noise when you eat it
- Lobster or crab in the shell (wait until the third date before you go to a lobster bar!)

## 262. IF YOU ARE DISAPPOINTED, BE A LADY ANYWAY

What if there's no chemistry on your end? He's perfectly nice but there's no spark? It happens, but that's what dating is all about. You really don't know until you actually spend time with someone whether you will have a connection with him. That's precisely why you have to go on a lot of dates and meet as many people as possible. If you don't feel like there's any magic, don't cut the date short or behave rudely toward your companion. The date represents a couple of hours of your life, so it's not the end of the world to finish the evening or afternoon with grace and good manners.

When the meal or drink is over, you can fill in that awkward gap by telling him you're tired and have to get up early the next day. There's nothing wrong with telling your date that you have to get home. But do it nicely and do thank him and show appreciation for the date. If he asks to see you again, you really can't lie and say yes if you don't want to go. Tell him you'd like to think about it, and if and when he calls, you can tell him that you are really looking for a committed relationship and that you are not sure he's the right person *even though he is a lovely person*. This is the perfect time to tell him that you think he's so nice that you will keep him in mind for your single friends and you hope he does the same—and then follow through! This is the way people meet each other!

## 263. GOING HOME

If a man asks you out on a date, I think he should be a gentleman and see you home or at least make sure you get home safely. Jenna, twenty-eight, told me about a date she had with a man who hailed a cab at the end of the night and *got in it himself,* leaving Jenna on the street to fend for herself. And this was after a successful date! I do not know what planet this guy came from, but that is simply rude. I am an optimist and don't believe this is a common occurrence. However, if you don't feel comfortable having a first date take you to your door (letting him know where you live), you need strategies for making sure he sees you safely on your way. If you have both driven to the location, make sure he walks you to your car and watches while you drive away. If he doesn't "get it" on his own, it's perfectly acceptable to ask him to see you to your car. The same thing goes for hailing cabs on city streets. See what he does at the end of the evening.

If it looks as if he doesn't understand that it is a gentleman's obligation (*not* his prerogative) to ensure that you get home safely, you can tell him nicely that you would like him to see you to a cab. That's a minimum courtesy—he should also hail the cab for you and open the door. When it comes to your safety, there is no such thing as being too cautious. This has nothing to do with following rules or playing games. If he doesn't understand that, you may have to think twice about going out with him again.

## 264. A KISS GOODNIGHT?

Whether or not you kiss someone goodnight really depends on the date. If it's gone well and there's a spark, your feelings will tell you if it's okay to kiss lightly or passionately. I think any kind of kissing after a first date is fine as long as you feel good about it. Don't be pressured to do anything, including kissing, unless you want to. I think that even if a date wasn't as successful or as exciting as you hoped, a chaste peck on the cheek at the end of the evening is acceptable—but even that is up to you. A gentleman will not force his face on yours.

## 265. "I'LL CALL YOU"

I tell all of my clients and JSSM members not to say, "I'll call you," unless they are planning on actually calling. But I also know that a lot of men say this without really meaning it. Men who have no intention of calling you again think they are being kind when they say they will, but they aren't. They are lying to you, and that is extremely unkind. Unfortunately, there's nothing you can do if a man says he will call you but doesn't. My advice: *Do not* call him. And don't panic if two days go by and you don't hear from him. Men often wait a few days, even a week before calling again (news flash: men play games, too). You need to follow the I'll Call You "rule" too—if you are not planning on calling him, do not tell him you will. If you say you will call him, call him. It's not "okay" to lie to someone if he lies to you. Why stoop to his level? At any rate, you are on a serious mission (to get married), so you really don't have time to lead people on and give them false hope.

## 266. SAY NO OR GIVE HIM ANOTHER CHANCE— I SAY GIVE HIM THREE DATES

I say, if a man wants to go out with you again, give him two more chances before you make up your mind about him. You really can't tell if you like someone until you have gone out on three dates. I tell my male clients that, too. But if you don't have me telling the guy to go out with you one or two mores time, you are going to leave that decision up to him. I do not believe in asking men on dates. I just don't think it works. You can "pick them up," or initiate a hello, but as far as dates go, it's his call as to whether he'll ask you on a second date. If that happens, you decide whether to accept. The second date can be so much better than the first— or worse! Which is why you have to go!

## 267. IF HE CALLS YOU, *CALL HIM BACK!*

Here's a rule for you: If a man calls, leaves you a message, and asks you to call him back, *please return his phone call.* It's simply rude not to. Men are human beings, and not returning the call of a man who took you out is treating him like a "nonperson." Men are not "intrigued" by rude women. You can remain a "challenge" to a man and still return his call. If you are both sophisticated, intelligent people, playing games like not returning phone calls just doesn't wash. Every man I know says it turns them off when women don't return phone calls: They know exactly what you're up to and they are not impressed.

## 268. JUST SAY NO . . . TO SEX

Men don't expect to have sex on the first date. I'm not saying it doesn't happen. But in this day and age, I don't think any man assumes that he will sleep with a woman the first time they go out. Even if everything goes well and you feel a very strong attraction, I would hold off until you know each other better. You've had a big night and it's been a very long day—you should go to bed alone and give yourself a chance to take in the date and your thoughts about him before you get physically intimate. It's not so much that the man will think you're "easy" (some will and some say it doesn't affect their opinion of a woman one bit), but it's not good for you to put yourself on that emotional rollercoaster so soon.

## 269. SEND HIM A THANK YOU

There's nothing wrong with thanking someone in a note or e-mail for a lovely evening. If you had a great time, tell him so in writing, and be sure to add a detail from the evening so he knows you are sincere. Keep it short and sweet. "Dear John, I had a really great time with you last night. The Twilight Lounge was really the most unique nightclub I've ever been to. Thank you! Fondly, Joann."

## 270. DO-IT-YOURSELF POSTMORTEM

When I introduce two people I always have a very detailed postmortem with both of them after the date is over, often the same evening (I'm impatient). Every first date I send two people on is like a first date for me, too. I am anxious to hear if I have matched people correctly and how the evening went and what they thought of each other. If you meet someone through your own means, you are not going to have the benefit of a third party to help you think about the date. But you can do a critique on your own by considering what you thought his negatives and positives were. A negative could be that he had bad table manners (wolfed down his food, elbows on the table) and a positive could be that he was a fantastic listener and had a great sense of humor.

Once you see these lists side by side you can think more clearly about whether you should give him another chance. A postmortem should also include some thinking about how you behaved on the date. Are there things you wish you had done differently (worn something else, asked him more questions)? Was his body language telling you anything about yourself? This may help you make changes for the next date and so on. Keeping a log of postmortems is a reality check of both how great (or not so great) the man was and how you carried yourself throughout the evening. Use the worksheet at the end of this chapter to get you started.

If your date was the result of a fix-up, ask the person who introduced you if he or she would be willing to give you feedback from the date. If the person says no, don't make a big deal of it—he or she may feel awkward about betraying a confidence. On the other hand, people who are set up by a mutual acquaintance often convey information about their feelings on the date via the person who orchestrated it. However, you have to commit to this person and to yourself that you will not hold any criticism against him or her. Beware: This is difficult with friends and much easier with a third-party professional who is not your friend.

# FIRST-DATE POSTMORTEM

Write down your thoughts about the date and about him specifically. Write down both negatives and positives. Then, look hard at the negatives and cross out the ones that don't really matter. For example, if you didn't like his hair (or lack of it), ask yourself if that is *really* a stumbling block to a beautiful relationship. (See your non-negotiables. Is well-styled hair one of them? I doubt it!) Once you have crossed off superficial negatives, how does that list compare to the positives list? If it's longer than the negatives list, you should really give the guy another chance if he calls. On the other hand, some negatives (he smoked, he was rude or used vulgar language, he was aggressive or pushy, he was inconsiderate) may be deal breakers.

The second part of the worksheet is reserved for a critique of your own behavior. Would you dress differently next time? Were you a good listener? Did his body language give you any clues as to how he was responding to you?

Use a copy of this worksheet for all your first dates. (*continued*)

## HIM

| Positives | Negatives |
| --- | --- |
| _____ | _____ |
| _____ | _____ |
| _____ | _____ |
| _____ | _____ |
| _____ | _____ |
| _____ | _____ |

## YOU

Fill in what you thought you did well (conversation, use of humor, dressed sexy but appropriately) and things you think you could do better next time that will have an impact on his impression of you.

_____

_____

_____

_____

_____

_____

_____

## OTHER THOUGHTS

_____

_____

_____

_____

_____

_____

# Nine

# Relationship Building and the Three Stages of Dating

ow that you're sitting pretty on the other side of date one, what's next? First and foremost, keep it up! Maintaining a wide net wide means continually dating and meeting men. That's the way you find "the one."

If a date went well the first time, meaning you liked him and had a good time, and he calls you for another date, *go!* It is unlikely that you will fall head over heels in love on the first date (it happens, of course, but don't count on it). You have to give nice guys a chance. Use my three-date rule: After three meetings you will know whether there's a chance for the relationship to go further. And don't stop dating other men—exclusivity can come later, when you're really sure.

If, after three dates, you just don't see any chemistry developing, you can cut your losses knowing that you gave the guy a fair shake. Still, don't lose him completely. If you have gotten along (and he obviously likes you, otherwise he wouldn't keep asking you out), make sure you tell him how much you like him and enjoyed spending time with him. If you don't feel he's right for you, learn how to let him down gracefully. In fact, use some of the tips from Chapter 4 to help you.

If you do meet someone you'd like to keep seeing and he shares your feelings, you will likely go through what I term the three stages of dating: the dance, the power struggle, and the comfort zone. It's important to understand these stages and what to expect from each: You'll be better at gauging the right time to bring up serious issues, and it will help you determine what you really want. All the groundwork you have worked so hard to lay in the previous chapters will really come in handy as the stages develop.

In this chapter I'll give you plenty of tips on how to keep a relationship growing toward marriage. It astonishes me how many men and women I meet have either forgotten or don't know the basics of relationship building. And it really begins with old-fashioned manners, consideration, and sensitivity. The good news is that once a relationship has started, you have a lot of control over how it goes. *One* person can make or break a relationship depending on how she behaves (that means you, honey!).

These tips and nuggets of wisdom are based on the ways couples I've introduced have made their relationships work and on my own twenty-one-year marriage. There is still so much more to do once you think you have met *him*.

Much of the dating advice I have read focuses on getting you paired off but then leaves you hanging. But what comes next is just as important in getting you married—from treating him well to learning how to discuss big issues to staying sexy and having a snazzy home in which to entertain him. Although having a well-stocked pantry may seem trivial next to discussing big issues of money and children, that too is part of showing that you are a well-rounded woman who values herself and her future partner. These big and little details are the nuts and bolts of making him fall head over heels for you while still building the foundation of a lasting relationship and protecting yourself from toxic or noncommital men. Read on!

## 271. STAGE ONE: THE DANCE BEGINS

Getting to know each other on the second date can be so much better (or worse) than the first. As I've said, the only way you'll find out is by going. Men tell me that they start looking at the traits that are important to them in a woman after the second date. That's the point when you'll start learning more about him, too. Questions such as "Does he like me as much as I like him?" "Will he be The One?" "Is he really who he seems to be?" will no doubt run through your mind. All of these thoughts are natural. This is the time to start sharing more of yourself with him to see if you have similar values and goals. This is not the time to bring up marriage or your desire to have children, however.

## 272. IF YOU KNOW HE'S NOT FOR YOU

You are definitely holding all the cards if he is pursuing you and you're not interested in him. You have to learn how to be firm but kind when that happens: "I'm flattered that you're interested in me, but I am looking for something different." Make it clear that you aren't interested in pursuing a romantic relationship with him. You can avoid hurting his feelings further by telling him that he's so terrific you will keep him in mind for your female friends. And then do it. Give it some time and then call or e-mail to ask him if he would like to take one of your friends or acquaintances out (check with her first, of course, to see if she's willing). If you've handled it correctly, he may even do the same for you with one of his friends. The point is, if he's a nice person, find a way to keep the lines of communication open. There's another reason not to count him out completely—you may change your mind. I can't tell you how many couples I have introduced who didn't fall for each other at first but got together months or years later! That's one reason why it is *never* a waste of time to

### *Manspeak*

"I wasn't feeling a lot of chemistry with the women I had been dating, and I don't think they were feeling it with me. So in order to add a spark to my next date, I went to a toy store and bought a children's chemistry set, then brought it along to give to the woman. It made her laugh, and the date got off to a great start. The gesture did set off a little spark between us," says Marcus, forty-two.

go out with someone who doesn't turn out to be "the one." And of course, you don't know who's right for you until you meet him!

## 273. WHEN HE DOESN'T THINK YOU'RE FOR HIM

If you had a good time on a couple of dates, but after that he doesn't call, you really have to chalk it up to experience and move on. Men call the shots in the early stages of dating. To avoid disappointment, it is *essential* to go out with as many men as possible. Getting stuck on someone early on can be disastrous for your mental health if you have cut off all other options and mate-finding activities. Don't let that happen! Ultimately, men are much less prone to give women a second chance if they didn't feel any attraction the first time out—even if they had a good time. This drives me crazy, and I insist that my male clients take a woman out two more times if they had a good time on the first date (even if they say there was no chemistry), before they make up their minds completely. Unfortunately, you won't have me around to tell them this, so you will have to learn to handle your frustration if he doesn't call. Distracting yourself with other dates is a good way to start.

## 274. STAGE TWO: COMMITMENT AND INTIMACY

As the relationship develops, you are going to have to define when the first "conversation" is going to come about whether the relationship is headed toward commitment—and possibly marriage. Ideally, the talk should coincide with the decision to sleep together. One of my women went out with a guy and slept with him the first time. What planet was she on? That's her. It felt natural and she went for it. There is not a right or wrong answer about when to become physically intimate; it really depends on the situation. You do, however, have to be really careful about sex.

Women have a tendency to think that sleeping together means they are exclusive. Men generally don't think along those lines. A man I know said to me about a woman he was dating, "I don't know if it's going to go anywhere, but she's fun," and that sums up a lot of men's attitudes about sex and women. Men think about sex before they think about the relationship. That's why, if you are considering taking the plunge to be intimate, you should ask him the question, "What does sleeping together mean to you?" If he answers, "Sex is just sex," or something equally noncommittal, you may want to think twice before you sleep with him.

Knowing when to have the conversation is very individual. A couple I introduced at one of my intimate dinners will be getting married soon. They clicked right off the bat, and seeing a lot of each other right away felt right to both of them. They are on a very accelerated path—they had about ten dates in two weeks after they first met. They've been moving at that rate ever since—about three months. How many dates have you had over what period of time? If you are having three dates in the first week, that will certainly bring you to a closer level than three dates over a month. Six dates in three weeks, you can say, "Hey, I like this person and he obviously likes me." And you can take sex and intimacy from there very easily. If you are seeing each other that steadily and three months have passed, I think you can safely bring up commitment and marriage. If you are seeing each other once a week or once every other week, I think it's safe to broach the subject after four or five months.

## 275. KEEP DATING UNTIL HE'S COMMITTED

Until you get to stage two in dating, intimacy and commitment, don't cut off all social contact with other men. A commitment happens when you *both* agree to it, and if it has not been made or agreed upon by both of you, then you should keep dating. *He is,* believe me. In other words, if he is not ready to commit, don't get stuck in a trap of being confined to a "relationship" that doesn't really exist. Dating other men gives you something to compare him to. It also keeps you from pinning all your hopes on one person. If there's no ring on your finger, you're not committed.

You can certainly be in a serious relationship without being engaged, but for many women, especially those of you who want to get married, the symbolic meaning and tradition behind an engagement ring should be important to you. That's not to say you should date other men as a way of getting a ring from the man you want to marry. What I am saying is that commitment to marry, usually implied by words and deeds (such as the offering of a ring, whether modest or extravagant), is an important threshold to cross before you make the decision to cut off any other potential mates. This may be a traditional view, and some may think it old-fashioned, but experience tells me that an engagement ring and the words "Will you marry me?" are as potent for the man as they are for the woman. Until you are at that point, you are not on your way to marriage.

## 276. STAGE THREE: THE COMFORT ZONE

The ultimate stage of dating is when you have committed to exclusivity and you are comfortably intimate with each other. In other words, you're in love and you're letting it develop. At this point you really start to know his quirks and personality in a deeper way. You should think about getting engaged and making it official. If you are over thirty-five, or in your forties and fifties you should really put a three- to six-month limit on this stage—especially if you want to have children. Under those circumstances you should have a ring and a wedding date, and it should be less than twelve months away. Three months may sounds drastically fast to many of you, but when you are a certain age you need to find out sooner rather than later what he's thinking. It really depends on how you feel about the relationship. Many of you may feel more comfortable waiting until the six-month mark.

## 277. AVOID SERIAL DATERS—AT ALL COSTS

Serial daters—also known as confirmed bachelors—can be fun, charming, witty, and exciting. These are men who often have interesting careers and dynamic social lives. There are thousands and thousands of

*Manspeak*

**"If we have nothing in common, I would still sleep with her, but a relationship? No," says Brian, thirty-eight.**

these men in New York City and other major cities across the country (and the world). They love going out with beautiful, fascinating women. They know a lot about food, wine, travel, and politics. But marriage material? I doubt it. These men are fun to go out with, but they are never going to get married, despite their protestations otherwise. I know several serial daters (and I do not fix them up with women), and they often say that they haven't met the right woman yet, one who "shares their values." Hello? If you can't find a partner who shares your values in a great city that is *filled* to the brim with extraordinary women, excuse me, but there's a problem. Why are these men so committed to being single? Because they have become accustomed to their life alone, they are set in their ways, and they really enjoy the excitement of dating (and sleeping with) a lot of women. You can certainly hone your dating skills by going out with one of these men, but don't fall for one. You'll be setting yourself up for a lot of heartache. See **Tip 279** for clues to identify a serial dater.

## 278. DON'T EXPECT HIM TO BANKROLL EVERY MEAL

One of the biggest complaints I hear from men is that women expect to be taken out to a fancy, expensive restaurant on every date. While I am old-fashioned enough to believe that if a man invites you to dinner he should offer to pay, I am not of the mind that he is responsible for making sure you have a four-star dinner every Saturday night. "I am not attracted to a woman who wants to be taken out all the time to expensive restaurants. I feel used," says one JSSM member. And I have to agree. A man will lose interest if he feels his only value to you is his Amex card. If that's all you are interested in, then you really aren't interested in building a real relationship. If you are going out on a third date, offer to pay for something. A third date usually entails a meal and a movie, so the woman should make an effort to buy the film tickets and an after-show drink or coffee. I suggest arranging to meet the man at the theater and getting there early so you can buy the tickets before he shows up. That way, there's no question about who will pay.

## 279. EIGHT SIGNS YOU MAY HAVE A SERIAL DATER ON YOUR HANDS

If two or more of the following are true of your date, you may have a chronic problem on your hands:

1. You met him on an Internet dating site (these men think of the Internet as the Costco of dating).

2. He's over forty-five, professional, and has never been married.

3. He claims to want to settle down and get married but has not been in a committed relationship in over two years.

4. After the first few dates, which were fantastic, he simply stops calling and doesn't formally break up.

5. He's charming but can never achieve psychological intimacy (although he has no problem trying to bed you down).

6. He loves to talk about his work to the exclusion of other topics (many serial daters are married to their jobs, which is why they aren't married to a person).

7. He's up on trendy restaurants and bars—often even before they are open (part of the excitement for a serial dater is more about being seen at hot spots and less about spending time with someone he could potentially share his life with).

8. He's content to spend weekends by himself or with male buddies and has no interest in seeing you.

## 280. LOSE THE PLAYBOOK

"I don't like women who have a lot of rules. I'm an adult and I hope she is, too. I have enough rules in my life; do I really need them in my relationship?" says my client Mark, thiry-seven. Men don't like women who have hard-and-fast dating rules. Grown-up men like grown-up women who are flexible, understanding, self-respecting, and happy. And men see right through rules very quickly. You aren't fooling him by not returning phone calls, ignoring him, behaving disinterestedly and aloof when you do talk to him, and generally expecting him to be at your beck and call twenty-four hours a day. He *knows* what you're up to. And it turns him off.

Why would you like someone who responded favorably to that kind of shoddy treatment anyway? Marriages that are built on that kind of behavior will eventually end in divorce. Yes, it's true that men like a challenge—but being a challenge simply does not include being rude.

## 281. DON'T LOSE SIGHT OF THE VALUE OF YOUR OWN TIME

Sometimes when a woman meets a man she's crazy about, she has a tendency to let all other parts of her social life fall by the wayside. The urge for many of us is to center our lives around being with him. Big mistake. Take command of your social calendar! Don't drop friends, eliminate social activities that don't include him, or put an end to exploring new interests and hobbies. Include him in your life, but don't rearrange it to meet his needs. Making time for all the things you enjoyed before you met him makes sense. Those interests and your engagement with life are the reasons he was attracted to you. Take those things away and he may feel you're not the person you seemed to be.

"When I first met Susan I was really attracted to her independent spirit and her love for photography and animals. I liked that she had this corner of her life that was different from mine. But when we started dating, she began to drop those interests and focus on me to the point of suffocation," says John of a woman he met at a humane society benefit. "The things I liked about her disappeared. I am not sure why she thought I would like her to become my personal sycophant. I didn't, and we broke up," he says.

Not only is losing yourself completely in him a turnoff for most self-confident, healthy men—it's also bad for you. Drifting away from those activities and interests that make you happy and fulfill your creative impulses can lead to unhappiness and depression.

## 282. GET YOUR HOUSE IN ORDER

Whenever I take on a client I do a "home visit." I want to make sure that he or she has a neat, clean, comfortable, and presentable place to live. First of all, the way people live says a lot about them. If they are messy and disorganized, that tells me they may not be reliable or considerate. If they are too neat (i.e., books *and* canned food are shelved alphabetically), that may mean they are rigid and stuffy. Beyond that, a person's taste in décor and colors tells me if they are casual or formal, cutting edge or traditional.

*Make sure he sees you in situations that demonstrate your great qualities, such as your generosity, creativity, resourcefulness, grace, and wit.*

If you are dating someone and it's getting serious, there's no question that he will see your home. Whether it's for a drink before dinner, at a cocktail party, or at a romantic dinner for two, your home will take center stage at some point in the relationship. It should be spotless, tidy, and softly feminine, no matter what your style. A sloppy pad that's crying out for help will not instill a lot of confidence in a guy. Men also say a woman's home that is masculine, hard-edged, and coldly modern is a turnoff. On the other hand, a profusion of pillows, ruffles, and pastel doilies can be off-putting, too. A few strategically placed down pillows, a cozy throw, flattering lighting, fresh flowers, and a well-stocked bar and refrigerator are sufficient to allow any man to make himself at home.

## 283. RECOGNIZE THE POWER OF BIOLOGY

He likes you because you're female. Use your femininity and his natural animal attraction to it to build a successful relationship by dressing, acting, and responding like a lady *throughout* the courtship. Simply being a woman is a currency that has potent value. If you think I am telling you to become a helpless female or a "dizzy blond," you are missing the point. Your femininity, the physical and psychological things that make you different from a man, gives you power. Being able to beat a man at golf or chess or basketball doesn't.

## 284. GIVE HIM AN OUT (IF HE'S OUT OF IT)

Have you ever been on a date or even out with a friend and sense that your companion is tired? If his energy seems low, give him an out. Say something such as: "You're obviously not yourself. Do you want to go home and we'll do this another time?" He'll appreciate it and he may not even take you up on your offer to end the date. Your concern may energize him. It will also most definitely demonstrate that you are sensitive to his needs (and not just your own) and that you care about his well-being.

## 285. DON'T APPLY "MANAGEMENT TECHNIQUES" TO THE RELATIONSHIP

Men do not want to be reminded of the women that they work with when they are on a date or involved in a romance. Managing a man or the relationship with him as if it were an assignment from your boss is a losing proposition. First, a man doesn't like to be told what to do. He doesn't want to think of Barbara in HR, who's always biting his head off about one thing or another, whenever he hears your voice. Management techniques and business school strategies work in business, but they don't necessarily translate to love. If he feels you are making demands or handing him too many ultimatums with deadlines attached, he's out the door. He can get that at work—he doesn't need it at home. Simply put, a man doesn't want a woman to have power *at his expense.* It's all in the presentation. When discussing important issues, making requests, or planning activities, keep it light and nonconfrontational.

## 286. SHOW OFF YOUR GREAT QUALITIES

Make sure he sees you in situations that demonstrate your great qualities, such as generosity, creativity, resourcefulness, grace, and wit. Pay attention to how you speak to other women, for example. Show him you are

considerate and gracious. Men also watch how women interact with waiters, service people, clerks, and secretaries. Your treatment of the people in
your life gives men clues to your personality and temperament. "After
going out on some dates where the women were nice to me but treated the
waiters like personal slaves, I really thought about giving up," says
Bernard, sixty, an international lawyer. "Christine was different. She was
a lady to me and to everyone she came in contact with, which made a
good impression on me. My feeling was, if someone is going to order a
waiter around like a serf I'll probably get treated like that too at some
point in the relationship." Bernard is not alone. All the men I talk to say
that if a woman talks down to service people and subordinates, they
assume she will do the same to them or their children.

## 287. MAKE DINNER

Stage a dinner party—for the two of you. The way to a man's heart is still
through his stomach. The good news is you don't have to be a gourmet
cook. A home-cooked meal can be simple and delicious or it can be
ordered from your local prepared food shop.

All the ingredients should be "best of class"—that means even if you're
making a simple roast chicken it should be the very freshest free-range bird
you can find. The salad should be crisp and the dressing should be made
with the best Italian extra virgin olive oil available. The vegetables should be
fresh, organic, and cooked to tender perfection. The wine doesn't have to be
expensive, but it should be delicious and complement the meal. Make friends
with your wine merchant and ask for advice. And don't forget dessert:
Whether it's apple pie or chocolate cake, buy it from the best bakery in
town. Almost every city and suburb has fantastic food shops, so there's no
excuse for not serving a meal that's delicious and beautifully presented.

## 288. NOW YOU'RE COOKING!

Many of you probably love to cook. If that's the case, you can skip over
this section. But for those of you who don't know the difference between
a spatula and a cake knife, you might consider learning how to make a few

basic dishes that most men love. Luckily, the recipes and instructions can be found in any good basic cookbook, such as *How to Cook Everything* by Mark Bittman or the classic *Joy of Cooking*. Here are some man-tested dishes that will come in handy on a late Saturday night or Sunday afternoon at home:

- Omelet (with cheese and fresh vegetables and herbs added for extra punch)
- Roast chicken
- Filet of beef
- Lobster (You can do it!)
- Beef stew
- Pasta carbonara
- Turkey pot pie
- Creamy macaroni and cheese (homemade, with at least three cheeses!)

## UP CLOSE AND PERSONAL
## *"The Mashed Potatoes Made Me Do It"*

**Elliot is one of my favorite people. He's a fantastic guy who recently married a beautiful lady he met at one of my large cocktail parties. "It was all about her cooking," he told me. I had to laugh because both of them are pretty high-powered attorneys and I thought, cooking? Don't these people eat out every night? As it turns out, they don't. "Alicia made me the best mashed potatoes one night—garlic, chicken broth—I don't know what was in those things but by the time I finished eating them I was eating out of her hands!" Cute, but when it came right down to it, it meant a lot to Elliot that Alicia took the time to make him something special that she knew he would love. It also showed her ability to provide a warm and cozy environment for someone she cared about.**

- Roasted potatoes
- Mashed potatoes
- Perfect, fluffy rice
- Green salad with vinaigrette
- Apple pie
- Brownies
- Chocolate chip cookies

## 289. BE PASSIONATE ABOUT WHAT YOU DO

As I said earlier, I don't believe you should manage your relationship the way you manage your job. I know that many of you work really hard and have fascinating careers. Let your passion for what you do come through to him. For example, I sent three men out on a date with a gorgeous, bright, and funny woman. None of them liked her, and each man said it was because she wasn't focused and seemed not to care about the job she was spending most of her day doing. "She's obviously smarter than the job she does, so why did she choose that line of work?" one of the men asked me. The idea is that men don't really care what your career is, and they are not looking for a mirror image of themselves. But coming off "like a flake," to use the words of one of the other men, isn't attractive either. "I love a woman who has a passion and a focus," says the third man. I talked to the woman about this problem, and she knew that her job did not reflect her talents or abilities. But she was more interested in meeting a man to marry—and see how it backfired. As I have recommended in other parts of the book, she'd be better off finding something she's really excited about and pursuing it.

## 290. UNDERSTAND THE DIFFERENCE BETWEEN INFATUATION AND LOVE

If your passion for him is making you dizzy and confused, slow down and step back. It might be infatuation and not true love. A good way to know the difference is to examine how you feel. Dr. Richard A. Levine says that a feeling of insecurity marks infatuation. "You are excited and eager, but not genuinely happy. It's a bond or attachment that is not entirely based upon reasonable perspectives. It is often accompanied by the suspension of rational decision making," he says. If the relationship keeps you off-balance and everything about the man is unpredictable, you may be headed for trouble.

## 291. WHEN HE STOPS CALLING

If you thought there was chemistry and he stops calling after several dates, e-mail him and ask why. Tell him it's for your own personal well-being and knowledge. Don't come off as angry—you're just curious. And

## *Defining Commitment*

One of the issues you have to discuss when you have "the conversation" about common values and your future together is how you each define commitment. What does it mean to him? If it doesn't mesh with your definition, you need to think hard about whether he's the right man for you. For example, one of my women, Samantha, thirty, is in a serious relationship. I recently ran into her at the beach and she told me she was moving in with her boyfriend, Justin, thirty-two. Inevitably, I asked, "Why aren't you getting married?" She told me that Justin had given her and her parents a four-month time frame. After living together for four months, he told them, if all went well they would get married. That's his definition of commitment and Samantha is willing to go along with it. The problem is that if he doesn't think it worked during that period, she'll have to pack her bags and move on. Since they will have been living together it will be more difficult for her than if they had just kept dating exclusively. But she's willing to take the chance. I don't think it's a risk worth taking, but I hope for her sake things turn out well for her and they get married.

you deserve to know, too, since you have spent some real time together. He may not respond, but if he does (and he should) you may learn something. You have nothing to lose, especially if it looks like the relationship has hit a dead end. If and when he does respond, use the information as food for thought as to what might be hindering you. Don't take his comments, whatever they are, as marching orders for you to change. His reply, if it's unkind or perfunctory, might also give you insights into the kind of men to avoid in the future (men like him).

## 292. KEEP EXPECTATIONS IN CHECK

Don't let fantasies about a relationship or its possibilities get in the way of real life. This can lead to disappointment and heartbreak and prevent you from living in the moment of the relationship. Pressuring yourself about big expectations can lead to behavior that's destructive, such as making demands or indulging in angry or other emotional outbursts. That sort of behavior will drive him away.

## 293. TAKE MAJOR WEAKNESSES SERIOUSLY

If a man has a problem with drugs, alcohol, aggression, or promiscuity, you're headed for trouble if you stick around. The same goes for men who are in constant financial trouble (here's a clue: He wants to borrow money from you) or who quit jobs frequently. Character flaws like these can lead to misery for both of you. Even simple incivilities, such as bad table manners, rudeness in social situations, and lack of consideration, can be clues to larger anger-related problems. You may think this advice is a no-brainer, but I know many women who have fallen into relationships with toxic men because they didn't listen to what that little voice in the back of their heads was telling them: He's trouble! That's why I go out on simulated dates with men *before* I introduce them to any women. I like to see how they treat me, the waiters, and others we interact with during the session. Observing how a man treats those he comes in contact with, including his colleagues, friends, and family, will give you clues to his personality.

## 294. TALK SOFTLY AND WITHOUT ANGER WHEN DISCUSSING IMPORTANT ISSUES

Keep your emotions in check. If you don't think you can discuss big issues without getting upset, wait until you are feeling more composed. If you discuss highly charged topics, such as marriage, kids, money, and jobs, when you are feeling panicky or depressed, you may find yourself saying things you don't mean or saying them in a way that is unintended and off-putting. Discuss difficult topics softly and calmly. If you don't think you can, put off the conversation until you've collected your thoughts and emotions.

## 295. CAN I GET YOU A DRINK?

If you ask your date to come up for a drink before dinner, impress him with your stunning array of first-rate spirits and bar ware. Stock up with:

**Bar**
Scotch
Light and dark rum
Vodka
Gin
Cognac
Seltzer
Club soda or quinine water
Cola
Ginger ale
Champagne (chilled, of course)
White wine
Red wine
7–Up
Limes
Lemons
Cocktail onions

Olives
Maraschino cherries

**Pantry**
*Have plenty of little nibbles on hand for predate cocktails.*

Nuts
Olives (a variety of green and black, cured and marinated, are nice)
Crackers
Capers
Cheese
Fruit
Mints

## 296. VALIDATE HIM

Everyone needs to be loved and understood—including men. If he's proud of an accomplishment, enjoy the moment with him! Don't obscure or ignore it by turning the conversation around to yourself or by dismissing an achievement with a verbal brush-off. Some fun ideas: Give him a standing ovation, buy him an incredible dinner, or treat him to a back rub (the kind you do yourself). Little things that make him feel needed and important go a long way in building a strong bond.

## 297. APPRECIATE YOUR OWN WORTH

The old-fashioned exhortation of "respect yourself" works wonders, especially in what has become a very disposable society. Recognizing your own value as a person will help you avoid getting into a master/slave relationship with a man. That means you should do only what feels comfortable for you. Don't accept shabby treatment as natural, and don't let him take advantage of your time or good nature. No self-respecting man wants a relationship with a doormat, anyway. If he doesn't make you feel special, reevaluate the situation.

## 298. PAST + FUTURE = PRESENT

Discuss important topics such as careers, children, and money only when you both feel calm, happy, and ready. If you're getting serious, start to learn everything you can about his "emotional baggage" as well as his ambitions, goals, and dreams. You should share your point of view on these issues with him. It's the only reliable way of identifying his past "residuals" and dreams for the future and how they both might be reenacted in the present. For example, a man who has issues with his mother may have very marked opinions on child rearing. Or a Wall Street type might yearn for a different kind of life as a rancher or a writer. And your issues and dreams will also have an impact on the relationship in the long term. Better to get them out in the open before marriage.

## 299. KEEP OBLIGATIONS TO OTHERS IN CHECK

I realize that many of you have complicated professional lives and lots of other responsibilities. Don't allow these demands to elbow your relationship into a corner. I am not suggesting you quit your job to work on your engagement plans or ditch your family until after you've tied the knot. But do put a priority on your relationship by asking yourself "Is this really important?" whenever something comes up that may interfere with a previous commitment with your mate. If work gets in the way of your love life, try to find a way to curb those demands on your time without shirking the job at hand. It's possible to negotiate work deadlines and be more efficient and delegate whatever you can. Neglecting a relationship is like neglecting a plant: It will eventually die.

## 300. BE YOURSELF

A love relationship should be the safest place to be "you." You are unique and distinct from everyone else. Don't try to be someone you aren't just because you think it will please a man. If he likes you, it's because of the individual qualities he sees in you. For example, turning from a successful, independent thinker into a simpering female catering to his every whim will embarrass him in social situations and turn him off when you're one-on-one. Having a strong sense of self will also enable you to handle the inevitable ups and downs of a love relationship.

## 301. KISS AND TELL

Don't *love* the way he kisses? Give him kissing lessons! Tell him your lips would like to show his tongue some new moves (this will excite him—it will not hurt his feelings!). And don't forget to practice, practice, practice!

## 302. BRING YOUR CREATIVITY TO THE DATING PROCESS

The best way to learn about how you are with each other is to engage in a variety of activities together. Your man's not creative about planning and thinking about date diversions? Bring your creative juices to the process and suggest and plan fun things to do that require different ways of thinking, problem solving, and physical interaction. You'll get to know each other in deeper ways and have fun at the same time. See **Tip 305** for simple, fun activity date ideas.

## 303. THROW A PARTY

A dinner party is a *great* way to show him you can entertain. It's also a wonderful way to introduce him to your friends, your sense of style, your knowledge of food, and how you manage a social event. Most men want to see how you handle yourself in such situations, especially Wall Street and other businessmen who will want to entertain associates at home with your help and good taste. This is the time to pull out your best linens, china, and silver. Worried your cooking skills won't survive the stress of an important gathering? Have the main course catered (and dropped off or picked up before your guests arrive).

## 304. LEARN TO APPRECIATE HIS TASTE

If you are going to be in a relationship with a man, you should know about what makes him happy. It's not necessary to love football, only to understand it when he wants to spend Sunday afternoon watching the game with his friends. In the process, you may also develop a fondness for the things he likes and you can share them with him—how great is that?

## 305. DATING MAGIC: PLAN THE UNEXPECTED

Here are some magical moments you can plan that will surely sweep him off his feet:

- Hot air ballooning
- A ride on a ferry or riverboat
- Tango lessons
- Rent a luxury sports car and take a ride in the country
- Attend a high-end or celebrity auction
- Fly-fishing
- Miniature golf
- Bowling
- Horseback riding lessons in the park or at a local horse farm
- An outdoor summer music festival or concert
- Tour a winery (many states have wineries, from Massachusetts to Oregon!)

## 306. ANTICIPATE TO AVOID DISAPPOINTMENT

Moments of closeness with your man may be followed by periods of distance. This is natural for men, especially when they begin to feel close to a woman. He may feel his autonomy is being threatened or he is beginning to realize that he wants to spend the rest of his life with you—and that can be scary. Anticipate his reaction and don't read it as rejection. It's a man's way of setting boundaries and getting his head together.

## 307. LEARN HOW TO COMPROMISE

If you have been single for a while and supporting yourself, you have no doubt built a pretty remarkable life for yourself. Living alone means you have to do very little compromising in your personal life. If you think it's a concession to buy the Jimmy Choo knockoffs instead of the real thing, you're in for a surprise. Give and take is an important part of moving a serious relationship into marriage. You don't have to make trade-offs on the big things (here come the non-negotiables), but you have to learn to let little things go. You will not always get exactly what you want all of the time. Finding a middle course means looking out for his needs and interests and making room for them in your life.

## 308. HIS CHILDREN: THEORY VS. PRACTICE

If you don't have children and he does, you have some serious thinking to do. How do you feel about it? Are you willing to deal with the inevitable issues that will arise from his children and ex? Some women I work with aren't. They tell me that they don't want to date men with children. Some say it's because they are afraid of the ex-wife and her reaction to the situation. Or they may want children of their own and a man who already has kids may not want more children. Finally, some women have told me that they simply don't want to "embrace" another woman's children. You will have to meet his children at some point and see how you feel and how

## JANIS FACT

When it comes to marriage and men, it's all about timing. They wake up one morning and say to themselves, "I should be married and have a kid," and then, *BAM,* they're ready.

they feel. Having children already in the picture can hurt the chances of a relationship—it's something you are going to have to talk about with him. More important than that is seeing how he is with his children and what the relationship is like between him and his ex. If things seem tense and dramatic, it might be best to pull out. However, if the relationship seems amicable and you're willing to build a relationship with his kids, try to spend as much time as you can with them.

## 309. HIS CHILDREN: LEARNING TO UNDERSTAND

If you have fallen for a man with children and you don't have any, you may not completely understand what it's like to have that responsibility. You have to be aware that plans could change last minute. Instead of being disappointed and upset if your evening goes awry because of a sick child, try being understanding and helpful. Offer to pitch in. Jeremy, thirty-six, has a 9-year-old son who was in a bicycle accident. His ex had to take him to the emergency room and of course she called Jeremy. He had bought tickets to the opera for his girlfriend Rebecca, thirty-three, and had a special dinner planned at an awesome restaurant. He knew she would be disappointed, but what could he do? His son came first (and that's a quality you want in a man). He called Rebecca and gave her the bad news. "I was floored by her reaction," Jeremy told me. "She said, 'You know I was really looking forward to this evening, but you have to go to the hospital. Let me know if there's anything I can do for you.' What a woman!"

## 310. YOUR CHILDREN: THEORY VS. PRACTICE

If you've been married before and have children, creating a relationship with a new man will present some challenges. Your children come first, and you have to make that clear from the get-go. You are also going to have to talk to your children about your own plans for finding and building a relationship with a new man. This is an area that's out of my expertise and I urge you to seek professional help if you feel you need support.

If your children are old enough, explain to them why it's important for you to find someone to love. One of my women, Catherine, forty-six, has two children, ages nine and eleven. She says they are old enough to understand what their mom is doing. "My kids have been great. I tell them that I want to find someone who loves me and that will make their lives better. It won't take anything away from them or my love for them." She says she also wants men to meet her kids so they know what an important part of her life they are. "My children understand I deserve a life, but I never compromise my relationship with them for a man."

## 311. BUILDING TRUST IN A SEXUAL RELATIONSHIP

Sex is not a prerequisite of dating—when and how you decide to become intimate with your partner is *up to you.* Dr. Levine says you should *never* under any circumstances do anything sexual that you don't want to do. It's okay to stretch the limits of your sexuality if you want to, he says. But do not go past your limits or feel pressured to leave your comfort zone.

"One of the key elements in being sexual with a man you are building trust with is that you will not be hurt by him," he explains. It's even okay if the relationship doesn't work out, says Dr. Levine, as long as you feel you weren't taken advantage of sexually or otherwise. "Before making any decisions about intimacy, women have to think about whether being sexual will lead to getting hurt in some way," he cautions. He teaches his patients to build trust by taking samples of a potential mate's character and personality and looking at it for messages about his ability to be trust-worthy and caring. "For example, if you discover on the first date that the man wants to split up the bill based on who ate what, that's a bad sign." Dr. Levine says if he makes disparaging remarks about his ex-wife on sub-sequent dates, that's another indication that something is wrong.

## 312. DR. LEVINE'S RELATIONSHIP FLAGS

One practical way to look for signs of trouble or promise is to think about his actions in terms of green, red, and yellow flags. "Everyone has his or her own notion of what a deal breaker is," says Dr. Levine. You have to determine what yours are and go from there. And it's true—there

# Getting to "I do"

There is no magic trick to getting a man to move from saying he's committed to you and the relationship to meeting you at the altar. In fact, you can't "get" or "make" a man do anything he doesn't really want to do. That's why you have to stay firm, be honest, and stick to your goal. You never want to nag him or issue harsh ultimatums. If you are suited to each other and he's marriage-minded, it should not be difficult or even take very long to set and meet a marriage date. When it's right, it's fast. Both of you just know.

For instance, one of my male clients hired two matchmakers before me—and he went on fifty-nine unsatisfying dates. How crazy is that? He is about to be married to the first woman I introduced him to. She was right, he wanted to get married, and boom, it's happening. The lesson is if a man is stalling or pushing back he may not be ready. Don't waste your time. If he *is* ready, you will have no problem going from commitment to engagement to marriage. If not, it's better to leave with dignity—if he comes back, which happens more often than you may think, and you get married, great. If not, at least you are on your way to meeting someone else.

If he's reticent or you find you're performing contortions to make him happy and he's not budging on the marriage question, at the end of the day, you have to call it quits. If you've followed the guidance in this book and there's no ring and no definite date, he may not be the right person for you. It's not worth hanging on to someone who just doesn't want to get married.

I've given you enough cautionary examples of what happens when women stay in relationships that don't result in the commitment they want. Here's another one: Before I met Allen, I was with a commitment-phobic guy, or what I refer to as a "CP." He had been engaged four times and even literally left one woman at the altar. I said, "I can change him." But I couldn't. On the other hand, Allen knew he wanted to marry me the minute he saw me (if you recall what I wrote in the introduction). On our third date he said I was going to be the mother of his children!

The moment of knowing you want to marry someone has a lot to do with timing, to say the very least—and knowing when to move on is an important part of getting your timing in sync with Mr. Right.

are some things you have to make up your own mind about. But Dr. Levine says there are some signs that can be universally interpreted and you should watch out for them. It's a good idea to keep track of these flags as you date different people, according to the doctor. "Looking back at your previous relationships and seeing what yellow and red flags you ignored and what got you into trouble is a way of becoming more attuned to flags that may be going up in front of you right now. These flags will tell you whether building trust will be likely with this person. Green means it's very likely. Yellow means it could be unlikely or difficult. And red means no way!"

**Green flags:** Men who are warm and generous toward you, who are nice to children and speak well of women and show respect for them.

**Yellow flags:** He's been married three or four times or he's in his late forties or early fifties and never been married. He has some anger issues toward women.

**Red flags:** Stop! He's over thirty and lives with his mother or parents. His books are in alphabetical order and he gets upset if the arrangement is disrupted. He's quick to anger over minor inconveniences or annoyances. These examples may indicate extreme neuroses or issues with independence that could disrupt a relationship.

## *Manspeak*

"If she sets it up to happen, I'm there. If not, I'll try, but if she doesn't want to go forward, that's okay too. But by the third or fourth date if nothing is happening physically, and I don't necessarily mean intercourse, nothing's ever going to happen," says Ryan, thirty-five.

## 313. SOLVE SEXUAL PROBLEMS BEFORE YOU GET MARRIED

Money might be harder to discuss than sex for a lot of people, but sexual *problems* are another ball game altogether. But Dr. Levine says it's important to consider as you move toward marriage. "If you are having sexual problems with your partner before marriage, do not get married until they are straightened out," advises Dr. Levine. "If a guy is having a significant erection problem and it's an issue between the couple, you'd better straighten things out before you walk down the aisle," he says. He also says women have to be in touch with their own responses. If a woman is anorgasmic, which means without orgasm, it may be a problem that should be addressed before she gets married. "Especially if she has had no problem with men in the past, but only with her current relationship. That's not a good sign," says Dr. Levine. Sex therapists can be located through several professional organizations, and that information, along with Dr. Levine's contact information, is listed at the back of this book.

## 314. SAFELY SEXY

If you are having sex, use condoms. He can *say* he doesn't sleep around, but he may be lying. For example, if he's doing it with you on a first date, he's doing it, or trying to do it, with others. Eight out of twenty women tell me they use nothing but birth control pills, whether they are in or out of a serious relationship. The pill does not protect you from sexually transmitted diseases (STDs). Unless you know he is truly committed to you, it's a good idea to err on the side of condoms. They aren't foolproof, of course, but it's better than closing your eyes and keeping your fingers crossed.

Many couples have told me that when they made the decision to get serious they both got tested for STDs and HIV. It's not romantic, but it's a good idea. And it's responsible. If he balks at the suggestion, something's up.

## 315. SEX STOPPER

Don't trust yourself with your feelings around him? Think you might easily succumb before you're ready? My surefire solution for this when I was single was to go out unprepared to have sex. That means my legs were not perfectly shaved and I was sure to wear my granny pants. There's not a chance in hell that you should do it under those circumstances. That's because if you are ready to go, you have to make sure you're shaved, smooth, and wearing your best lacy bra and sexiest lace thong undies.

## 316. WRITE HIM A LOVE LETTER

The lost art of love letters should make a comeback, starting right here. If you have both made the decision to move forward, write him a letter telling him why you love him. List all the qualities you admire in him. Tell him your hopes and dreams for the relationship. Let yourself go a little. Be outrageous. Put it away for a day or two and re-read it. Then decide if you want to leave it for him on his pillow after you've gone to work. Or do you want to give it to him on your wedding night? Perhaps you want to keep it in a box and present it to him on your first anniversary.

## 317. MEET THE PARENTS

When you make a commitment to a man, you are also making a commitment to his family. You are promising his parents that you will cherish their darling son. Not every woman has a super close relationship with her in-laws. What's important is for you to understand the dynamics of his family. You can learn a lot about a man by the way he treats his mother and father.

# WRITE HIM A LOVE LETTER

_____

_____

_____

_____

_____

_____

_____

_____

_____

_____

## REVISIT AND REVISE

Review the goals you made in Chapter 1. Have they changed over the last several months? If so, revise them:

_____

_____

_____

_____

_____

_____

_____

_____

_____

_____

_____

.

# Ten

# True Love:
# Commitment and Marriage

Congratulations! Your hard work has paid off and you're engaged or you have entered into a serious long-term commitment. It's both exciting and frightening to find yourself embarking on this journey. You'll be creating an entirely new domain—the one you will operate in as a couple. Take time to enjoy the relaxed feeling that comes from being truly comfortable in a secure relationship. But never forget the personal care, romance, and social niceties that brought you here in the first place. Engagement and marriage may be the end of your search for the perfect man, but it's only the beginning of a relationship that will evolve through both challenges and remarkable moments.

Strong unions consist of many parts. The most important ingredient is, of course, the relationship itself. But practical issues must also be considered, such as finances, family planning, and family obligations, none of which seem particularly romantic. Figuring out how you will handle these issues is essential before you say "I do," especially if you have assets and a professional and personal life that extends beyond your future husband's. Many relationships and marriages, I'm sorry to say, have ended because the couples didn't openly discuss the big issues before they tied the knot.

Communication and tolerance are two other ingredients of a lasting, happy relationship. Two people who love each other and think they know everything about each other can often be surprised when they notice that they each have strong and very different ideas about life. This is particularly true if you meet and marry a man in a year or less. The getting-to-know-each-other process has been accelerated. Luckily, you took the time in the beginning of the book to sort through your feelings about many big life issues, and you likely feel compatible with your man on religion, politics, career choice, hobbies, and children. But that's not to say you won't be caught unawares when he announces he feels a bit differently than you thought about mingled bank accounts or the hours you keep at the office after you're married. So learn how to communicate and, more importantly, how to *listen*.

While openly talking about when you come home from the office or how much you plan to spend at the grocer's may well be necessary, so can *not* talking—especially when it comes to his little habits you find annoying. Sometimes saying nothing and letting unimportant irritants fall by the wayside is the best way to communicate with your mate. Success at building and maintaining a harmonious relationship comes from understanding and accepting your mate's peccadilloes, feelings, and opinions. That doesn't mean you have to like, agree with, or act on them 100 percent of the time. It simply means you should respect them when making your own decisions.

I'll also share some sage wisdom about the seemingly little things that I know make a marriage work. It's the kind of insight that is the traditional domain of the matchmaker, and I'm going to indulge in it here! None of them need a whole lot of explanation, but practiced as a whole they are important ways to build depth in a relationship. Simply being mindful of them helps make every minute count, and in this day and age that is *essential.* Let the advice and tips here serve as a jumping-off point for your own journey into marriage.

Here's wishing you endless love!

## 318. SHORT ENGAGEMENTS ARE THE BEST ENGAGEMENTS

Once you have made the decision to get married, don't wait. Long engagements are a waste of time: If you love each other and you're sure about the relationship, there's no point in waiting more than six to eight months to tie the knot. That's especially true if you're over thirty-five and want to start a family. You don't have the luxury of time, since you'll surely want some "alone time" before you start a family. At any rate, if you want to get married, why would you want to wait more than a year? You're either getting married or you're not!

Some women have told me that they waited longer than six months because a specific location that they wanted for their wedding was not available before a certain time. Frankly, there are many beautiful locations for weddings and booking a certain hotel or resort for your wedding isn't a good enough reason to hold up the proceedings. And it is possible to plan a wedding quickly. I've had couples who created beautiful ceremonies and receptions in three months in New York City, which is a highly competitive wedding market. In short, if you want to plan a wedding on short notice, you can! Don't let that be an excuse to wait.

## 319. LOCATION, LOCATION, LOCATION

If you have your heart set on a particular hotel, resort, or other wedding venue and it's booked for the month you would like, consider the following:

- June is a busy wedding month; consider spring (April, May) or fall (September, October). These times of year are beautiful, and often the weather is very cooperative.

- Consider a weekday or luncheon wedding if you have your heart set on getting married during high season at a popular venue. Most weddings are at night, and the venue may be able to accommodate you at an off time during high season.

- Holiday-time weddings (December and January) can be romantic, and often wedding chapels, churches, restaurants, and hotel ballrooms are already decorated for the season, saving you money on décor.

## 320. BELLS ARE RINGING

If you have a ring on your finger, tell anyone and everyone that you're engaged to be married. But be careful of "verbal engagements." They don't prove a thing. A friend called me about a year ago, breathless with excitement. "Janis, I'm getting married! I'm engaged!" she said to me. I asked her what her ring looked like, and she replied, "Well, we haven't picked one out yet." Uh-huh. Well, twelve months later, there's still no ring and my friend is still "engaged." Basically, her boyfriend told her what she wanted to hear and she's waiting around for him to live up to it, which I have a feeling he's not going to do. As I said earlier, the value of a ring is not monetary. It doesn't matter how big or flawless the diamond is. A ring has potent symbolic value. Its meaning is significant. A ring of gold represents a promise not easily broken. That is why an engagement is really only an engagement for marriage if a ring is offered and accepted in promise.

## 321. WEDDING PLANNING

Planning a wedding can and should be fun and exciting for all couples. Sometimes women get swept up in the excitement of wedding planning and forget about the man they are marrying. When planning your wedding, be sure to include your fiancé in the plans, with the exception of shopping for your gown. Make joint decisions on the guest list, venue, food, flowers, music, and décor. If he gives you the okay to make certain decisions on your own, that's fine. But give him the option of sharing his opinion or giving you the go-ahead to make the decisions yourself. Don't assume he's not interested in the finer points of reception planning. In most cases your wedding is the first major event you will be planning as a couple, and it's a great opportunity for you to start working together. You'll learn a lot about your husband-to-be by making decisions together.

## 322. STATIONERY SMARTS

When you are planning a wedding, you will need wedding invitations and announcement cards. Afterward, you will need thank-you cards for writing notes to those who were kind enough to give you a gift. And you'll need other cards and papers for invitations to parties and events that you'll doubtless be throwing with your new husband for friends and colleagues. Gorgeous stationery is an essential for every sophisticated couple. Here are some tips from New York stationer Bunny Shestack of Write and Invite on selecting the best of the best.

- Wedding invitations should match the colors and style of the wedding. If you are having a small, traditional wedding, white or crème paper with a crisp embossed border and simple script engraving is perfect.

- Engraving is beautiful. Bunny says many people are now going back to the old letter-press style. She says that the printer uses a soft, heavy paper, and the letters, which are set by hand, are pressed into it to create a raised effect. "It has texture and elegance," says Bunny. "It's not something you see every day and it makes a spectacular wedding invitation.

- Thank-you notes should be simple heavyweight linen card stock. "Your name should be simply engraved at the top of the card," says Bunny, "and make sure the envelope is lined in the same color your name is engraved in." Bunny says these note cards can carry you through many occasions and can be used for thank-you notes, handwritten invitations, or simple personal notes.

- Invitations for special events can have lots of personality and color, depending on what the celebration is for, according to Bunny. "Let your imagination run wild because there really are so many papers, typefaces, and special effects available," she says. Bunny believes that in the age of e-mail and cell phones, stationery should take a very special place in a couple's life. "There's nothing more personal or special than receiving a beautiful note or invitation in the mail," says Bunny. "It's still the ultimate way to communicate special information."

## 323. PRENUPTIAL AGREEMENTS

Prenuptial agreements are necessary for everyone. Mitchell Schrage, a matrimonial lawyer in New York, says there are three common reasons why couples draw up prenuptial agreements. The first is people coming into a marriage on unequal footing, meaning one person has substantially more assets than the other does. The second situation is a couple who really haven't known each other for a very long time. And the third is that one of the parties is paranoid and doesn't believe in love. Believe it or not, Mitchell says many men walk into his office and give this as their reason for wanting a prenup.

If that's the reason your fiancé is bringing you to his lawyer's office, that should be a red flag, ladies! "I have seen women who were desperate to be married and so were willing to take anything the fiancé-to-be was dictating," he says. "These kinds of agreements are so unfair that I didn't think the women should sign them. Love is blinding them," he says. His advice? If you both feel a prenup is necessary or your husband-to-be feels strongly about it, don't sign it unless there is some acknowledgment that if the relationship lasts for many years, as it should, there will be recognition of that in the form of financial assistance or property. In general, however, if you have financial or business assets at stake, it's not a bad idea to have an agreement in place. Mitchell says prenuptials are always tailored to the couple's specific needs. It might be that your parents or his want to protect the family business. Or there may be children involved, and their educational needs should be provided for.

If the balance of finances is in your future husband's hands, Mitchell says that you should never underestimate the value you bring to the marriage in other ways. You are contributing to your husband's life by raising children, making a lovely home, and taking care of family needs. "All of these things represent value," says Mitchell. And remember also that if you are going to draw up a prenuptial agreement, now becoming increasingly known as an antenuptial agreement, you will need to get your own lawyer so the two attorneys can work it out together for both of you.

Finally, check your state's laws—not every state recognizes prenuptial agreements.

## 324. CHILDREN AND THE MARRIAGE

If you have children and you are getting married, Mitchell says it is possible to protect their welfare via a prenuptial agreement. "We do prenuptials for a party with children that have provisions that say that no matter what happens the children will get a certain percentage of the estate," says Mitchell. After it goes into the prenup, you can create a trust or a will to back it up. This is an important consideration if you are bringing children into a new marriage. Mitchell also says some men who are going into their second marriage don't want children. "They like to see it in writing in the prenup, but it's not enforceable," says Mitchell. That means if the wife becomes pregnant, the man can't get out of his financial responsibilities toward the child.

## 325. LIVING TOGETHER

I am not big on the idea of unmarried couples living together. I think the public statement that marriage makes is an important aspect of a serious relationship. But if you insist on shacking up instead of tying the knot, it's imperative that you draw up what Mitchell calls, appropriately enough, a "living together agreement." According to Mitchell, a living together agreement does hold legal weight and is enforceable. You have to consider the same things as you would with a prenup (so why don't you just get married?). Financial responsibilities such as who will pay what bills need to be hashed out in writing. Property ownership, especially if you are going to buy land or a house together, needs to be established in case one of you wants to cash out. And if you are going to mingle bank accounts, watch out. You better have some protection in place. Don't depend on common-law status, which takes years to create and not all states recognize common-law marriage in any case.

## 326. TOP ISSUES TO CONSIDER IN PRENUPTIAL AND LIVING TOGETHER AGREEMENTS

1. Assets—determining what is an individual asset and what is a joint asset

2. Children—present and future, education

3. Debt and incurring debts for one another

4. Expectations—Is one of you going to be giving up a profession to care for children or the home?

5. Insurance policies

6. Lending or support to family members

7. Property ownership

8. Wills

## 327. GET YOUR FINANCIAL HOUSES IN ORDER

So you're getting married? Have you sat down with your fiancé and discussed finances? Have you talked about how you'll combine your income? How you'll pay your bills? Have you talked about your saving and investing goals, your philosophy about money, your spending habits, your debts?

The number one cause of divorce is disagreement about finances, so getting these issues out in the open and coming to an understanding before marriage can greatly increase your chances of staying out of divorce court.

It's extremely important to discuss money issues early in your marriage or even during your engagement. Financial issues can go to the heart of relationships. I can't tell you how many couples I have known that have gotten in trouble and even split up over money. That's why I tell every couple I have introduced who have gotten serious to discuss money issues. It's precisely why I asked you in Chapter 1's questionnaire to think about your own feelings about money.

Financial planning is a way of realistically providing for your present and future goals and needs. It is a process that is important for couples, especially if both of you are working professionals with savings and other assets and financial holdings. That's because issues such as cash flow and spending, savings, taxes, investment, retirement, estate, education, insurance, and legal issues require particular care within the context of relationships. It's a good idea to seek the advice of a qualified financial advisor. He or she can offer specific advice for your needs as a couple.

## 328. SOME FINANCE-RELATED ISSUES YOU SHOULD CONSIDER TOGETHER BEFORE YOU GET MARRIED

- How are assets held in joint ownership? There are several options, each with their advantages and disadvantages.
- Is there a plan if your household breaks up? (see **Tip 323**)
- How will assets be divided?
- Who will provide for children if you have them together?
- Do powers of attorney exist between you?
- Do you each have a will?
- Who will pay for what?
- How is money management carried out day to day?
- How is the future provided for?
- What has been decided regarding responsibilities to aging parents?
- What has been decided regarding ensuring well-being and education of any children?

## 329. LEAVING THE SINGLE LIFE BEHIND

Getting married doesn't mean an end to doing some of the things you enjoyed as a single woman, such as going to a movie with a girlfriend, shopping by yourself on a Saturday afternoon, or going out after work with colleagues. But your life will change dramatically, and if you are over thirty-five and used to living on your own, you are in for some big surprises. You will most likely want to spend your time differently than you spent it in the past, especially in the first years of marriage. You will also have to reevaluate your single habits, as will your husband. Everything from when you pay your bills to how you store milk in the refrigerator will be fair game. Be open to doing things in new ways—maybe they are better! And learn to be flexible about how you keep house and maintain your date book. When another person becomes part of your life, things can get turned around pretty quickly. Listen, absorb, and try it his way, and also ask him to try things your way.

## 330. KEEP ROMANCE ALIVE

Once you're married and back to the grind of work and life in general, romance can easily escape the two of you. Go out of your way to make time for it. Leave him love notes in his briefcase, and sprinkle in a few chocolate kisses while you're at it. Show him with words and actions that just because you're his wife now doesn't mean you no longer feel romantic about him—on the contrary! Kiss and cuddle. Give him a back rub and let him give you a massage. Tickle his feet and chase him around the bed. Giggle.

## 331. PLAN FOR THE FUTURE BUT LIVE IN THE PRESENT

No doubt you have established goals. You may want to buy a house or a car. Or you could have your eye on a move to a new state or a major career change. It's smart to talk about these big decisions, but don't let them consume and drive you so much that you forget where you are right now, today.

## 332. MAKE BIG DECISIONS WITHOUT LOSING SIGHT OF WHAT'S IMPORTANT TO EACH OF YOU

You will be making most decisions jointly now. When you are discussing big issues, think about them both in terms of what's good for you as a couple and in terms of what's good for you as an individual. For example, if your husband wants to take a job in another state because it means more money and opportunity for him, make sure it's also good for you and it will benefit the marriage. More money doesn't necessarily translate into a better marriage. "When Jason and I were married, he wanted to move to LA to work for a movie studio," says Meredith. "We did it even though I knew I'd be miserable and would have a tough time finding a job." Meredith didn't like Los Angeles and, as expected, she had a hard time finding work in her field. "There are a limited number of jobs in my area of finance in LA, so it was tough for me. I sat at home because it was hard to make friends in the city's car culture. Plus, I just didn't like it. Even though Jason was making a pile of money, he was working all the time and we never saw each other." If they had thought through the implications of the move, Jason and Meredith may not have made it in the first place. They are back in New York now, both are working in jobs they love, and they're happier than they ever have been.

### 333. CONSIDER FAMILY IN YOUR PLANS—BUT DON'T LET THEM MAKE THE RULES

It can be difficult to plan holidays and visits when you have two families to contend with instead of just your own. Thanksgiving, Christmas, Hanukkah, Mother's Day, Father's Day. Help! There are several ways you can work out "family planning" that should keep everyone but the most curmudgeonly sibling or parent happy. For big family holidays consider inviting both families to your house for a new twist on tradition. If you have the room and the families are nearby, it can be a great way for your respective parents to spend more time together and get to know each other better. If that's not feasible, make a decision well in advance of the holiday (at least a month) so you have plenty of time to break your decision to your families. And then switch off every year or every holiday. Listen to what your families think about what you should do, but don't feel obligated to fulfill the wants and needs of your relatives. You're a couple now and you can make decisions based on what you both desire. Your family will soon get used to it.

Make sure you ask your husband to give you the lowdown on his family members, and do the same for him. Sorting out your in-laws' likes, dislikes, quirks, and foibles will make dealing with them easier. And you'll be less prone to get upset when things you planned for them, or that they planned for you, don't turn out the way you expected.

## 334. BUILD NEW TRADITIONS TOGETHER

Don't think you have to replicate your families' way of doing things. It's important to develop customs and rituals together. That's how memories are made. If you want to go to Hawaii for Christmas, go for it! Your parents might be taken aback at first, but if you explain to them gently that you want to spend the holiday alone together, they will understand. Celebrations of any kind, whether it's a birthday or a long summer weekend, don't have to slavishly reproduce those you remember from childhood or growing up. Invent new celebrations that you can enjoy together and share with others.

## 335. CHILDREN—YOURS AND HIS—COMING TOGETHER

If he has children, remember that you will never become a replacement mother to them. You will have to negotiate a new and different kind of alliance with them than they have with their parents. Give them time to get to know you and don't put pressure on them to like you. And don't feel pressure to adore them. Like other relatives, children are complicated people with distinct personalities. You may or may not feel a natural affinity for them. Take it slowly and learn to tolerate them if you don't find an instant attraction.

Look for their best qualities, and don't let your feelings show (children are very perceptive about things like that). Most importantly of all, don't pressure your husband about your relationship with his kids. Even if you do like each other, expect to stay at a distance until they let you in. Accept your stepchildren's overtures of friendship graciously, but back off if you think they're getting wary of your motives. Children who are dealing with their dad's new wife often fear she will "take over" as their mother.

The same goes for your children and your new husband. Even if your children were fond of your husband before you were married, it might be a whole different ball game once you are in the same house together. Be sure to spend time with your kids, but also be sure they understand that part of your life is new and that you want to spend time with your husband as well.

The topic of children is really too big for this book, so seek advice from the experts. Be assured that women with children remarry every day, and most of the time they find a way to make the relationships work.

## 336. DATE YOUR HUSBAND ON A REGULAR BASIS

Keep the excitement of your relationship alive by going on regular dates with your husband. The key is to treat it just like a real date, the kind you went on when you were single. Blow him away with your makeup, hair, and outfit. Meet at a hot restaurant and make out on the way home! And, of course, on these dates you don't have to ask yourself if you should sleep with him or not. Have fun!

*Engagement and marriage may be the end of your search for the perfect man—but they're only the beginning of a relationship that will evolve through both challenges and remarkable moments.*

## 337. KEEP YOUR SEX LIFE ALIVE!

Another common occurrence in marriage is that you forget to have sex—or you're too tired or busy or something else gets in the way. Don't let it happen. If you have to, schedule it. "My husband and I schedule sex weekends," says Kara, thirty-six, a former client. "While we do make love in between these little weekends, it can sometimes be hurried or we do it when we're both tired." By making the extra effort of planning a romantic weekend, with the prime activity scheduled for the bed, Kara and Michael, forty, have something to look forward to. And the excitement builds as the weekend gets closer. "It's so much fun knowing that you will be getting away from everything with the idea of focusing on your love for each other," says Kara.

## 338. FAMILY PLANNING

If part of your marriage plans include starting a family, don't put it off too long. If you are in your twenties, you have some time to enjoy each other before you start trying to get pregnant. If you are in your thirties or forties, though, time really is of the essence. While there have been great strides in fertility treatments and options, it doesn't mean getting pregnant is a piece of cake after thirty-five. See your doctor and have a complete OB/GYN exam, including any tests that measure your ability to get pregnant.

If you are having a hard time, talk to your doctor about other options, including donor eggs. That's when you use another woman's eggs via in vitro fertilization. You carry the baby and it's 100 percent yours. He or she may have genetic information from the "biological" mother, but you are pregnant and your blood is helping the baby grow—just like a "natural" pregnancy.

Adoption is also an option. The many strides in fertility treatments have enabled more women than ever before to carry and give birth to children. The result is that there are more babies in the United States available for adoption. Of course, you can go overseas to adopt children also.

I know many women who have used all of these options to create beautiful families. But I will say again, the fact that there are more options does *not* mean you should procrastinate too long in starting. Fertility treatments can last months and adoption can be a long process. Once you have made the decision to have children, the sooner you start, the better off you will be.

## 339. THE HONEYMOON IS ABOUT THE TWO OF YOU

A honeymoon is your chance to relax and regroup after what has likely been a very hectic time in your lives. Planning a wedding, working, and setting up house together isn't easy—it's exhausting. The ideal honeymoon should last two weeks. If you can swing that much time, go for it. It's your chance to start your lives together in an idyllic setting away from cell phones and the demands of everyday life. Location is important, but not as important as being alone together.

## 340. BE CONSIDERATE

Sometimes you can forget the niceties and good manners that you practiced before you were married. When you are living together you may have a tendency to stop being considerate of each other in little ways that can make a difference. For example, when one of you asks the other to do something around the house or pick something up at the store, you may forget to say "thank you." Or you may leave the bedroom or kitchen messy. There are a million little things that diminish the quality of life in your home. Maintaining a loving atmosphere of respect and good manners makes each of you feel important to each other. And when these little things are lost, it's not uncommon for one of you to become disillusioned with the marriage.

## 341. LET EACH OTHER KNOW . . .

In today's world, consideration goes beyond simply good manners. Staying in touch and letting each other know what's going on is a cardinal rule in my house. After going through the terrible events of September 11, 2001, and the blackout of 2003 (cell phones did not work in either situation), it's important for each of you to let the other know:

- If you're going to be late coming home
- Where you are
- Where you're going to be in the immediate future
- What time you'll be home
- A meeting place in case you are separated in a catastrophic event
- A couple of places (with friends, family) where you can leave messages for each other, if necessary

## 342. STOP AND SMELL THE ROSES

Don't forget to take moments during the day or week to notice the things around you. Reflect on the good fortune you've received from finding a lifelong mate.

## 343. PATIENCE MAKES PERFECT

Sharing a home with another person can open a whole new world of little annoyances and quirks that may not have bothered you when he was living across town—but now have the potential to send you home to mother. Practice tolerance and moderation in your responses to little aggravations. Give *him* time to adjust to *you*! There are two sides to every coin—things you do may annoy him, too, but he may choose not to say anything about them.

## 344. KEEP THINGS IN PERSPECTIVE

You will be together a long time. Developing a long perspective about the relationship and its ups and downs helps you weather the trying times. Ask yourself: Is _____ really as bad as it seems? It's usually not.

## 345. SCREAM AND YELL

Studies have shown that couples who occasionally "get it all out" in the form of screaming matches or yell fests fare better than couples who instead have frequent "heart-to-heart" talks about their innermost feelings. I know long-married couples who have been together thirty years and longer and have never had one "dialogue" about the meaning of their union—and they are perfectly happy. Instead, they get annoyed with each other, shout or yell about it, and then go out to dinner as if nothing ever happened. Dr. Bonnie E. Weil is a therapist specializing in couples and the author of several books, including *Make Up, Don't Break Up*. She says that communication isn't everything. "Sometimes you can talk a relationship to death," says Dr. Weil. So give "Talking," with a capital T, a rest. And both of you think about shouting once in a while, just to see how it feels. If it works, use it on occasion; if not, see the next tip.

## 346. DON'T INSIST ON SOLVING EVERY PROBLEM

Not every problem in a marriage requires a solution. Focusing on little problems can sometimes make them take on a bigger and badder life of their own.

If something is irritating you, give it twenty-four hours before you say or do anything about it. Many times problems die away and cease to exist. Or they don't but you learn to live with them. Dr. Weil says a "temporary breakup" can help patch things up and reaffirm your commitment to each other. So go away for a while, whether it's a couple of hours or overnight ("going home to mother" is an old-fashioned idea that can really work) and chill out.

## 347. HAVE AN AFFAIR . . . WITH YOUR HUSBAND

Add some spice to your life—meet your husband in the middle of the day at a hotel room! Or "sneak off" on a Saturday and meet him at an out-of-the-way restaurant for some smooching and canoodling. The point is to keep excitement and the unexpected as part of your marriage. It's a great way to stay in love.

## 348. LET YOUR PARTNER HAVE AN EFFECT ON YOU

Yes, it's important to keep your individuality—keep up with your friends, participate in activities and hobbies you enjoy. Those are some of the things that make you lovable to your husband. But you are more than an individual now—you are also part of a couple. Let him "come into" your space and your heart. Let him influence your thinking—allow him to show you things in new ways. Try seeing the world through his eyes.

## 349. REMEMBER THAT LOVE AND MARRIAGE ARE GOOD FOR YOU!

Dr. Weil says that studies show marriage can lengthen life, boost physical and mental health, raise your income, reduce depression and sadness, and promote happiness and general well-being! My experience tells me she's right on.

## 350. BUILD HISTORY TOGETHER!

Create memories and shared experiences with your husband. In the literal sense, take lots of pictures, collect mementos, and save souvenirs from special occasions and vacations. Keep a memory box or scrapbook. Absorb the things you do together, whether it's going to the grocery store or attending the ballet. These moments make up a lifetime of shared experiences, and honoring them will help hold you together. Having "history together" is a powerful concept that has helped many couples weather difficult storms.

## 351. VALIDATE EACH OTHER

You may never agree with each other on some issues, but Dr. Weil says that being in agreement on everything is not the key to a happy marriage. Validating each other's ideas is. You can accept and respect your spouse's ideas on just about everything. If you simply accept your differences, you will decrease the chance that a little disagreement may escalate into destructive anger.

## 352. LIVE IN THE MOMENT

I have a friend who had a habit, learned from her mother, of saving things for a "special occasion." From a fine wine to a pretty dress—she would buy something and put it away for some unknown future event that the item would be worthy of. She had a closet full of unworn clothes and a wine rack full of fancy vintages. The right "occasions" never arrived. So her possessions sat until they were no longer useful. And she and her husband lost sight of the fact that every day together was special. The special occasion is *now;* it is today! Open that bottle of wine, wear that dress, and take that vacation. Life is too short to wait.

## 353. WORK AS A TEAM

Busy couples spend a lot of time apart, usually working. And when you're together you might be visiting family or socializing with friends. Make time to do things together as a team. That's different from going to the gym to work out in the same place or taking a walk. Those things are great but I'm talking about working on a single project together as a team.

I know a couple who fixed up a boat together. Every weekend they made time to go out and scrape and paint it, and basically put it back together nail by nail. Working together fosters a bond, builds trust, and lets you get to know each other in a very meaningful and practical way. When you work on any kind of project as a couple, it becomes "yours together."

## 354. MAKE TIME FOR LAUGHTER

At the end of the day, long term, you have to be able to laugh together. Your looks and bodies will change. People grow old. But the humor and fun you share can remain the same as the day you were married. Twenty or thirty years down the road, you still have to be able to wake up Sunday morning and laugh at the world around you.

## 355. UNSTICK YOURSELF FROM STUCK-IN-YOUR-WAYS WAYS!

Getting unstuck is especially important for people who are getting married in their forties and fifties. You've no doubt developed habits and ways of living that you think work just fine. But it may also mean you've become inflexible and rigid. Try this: If you've been doing something the same way forever, do it differently tomorrow. Take the same route to work? Change it. Make chicken soup with your mother's recipe? Use a different one. Insist on the same brand of shampoo? Buy another brand! Changing little habits will help open you up to other changes marriage will bring. Turn things on their head and shake them up a little bit!

## 356. DON'T GET SLOPPY

Never stop taking care of yourself. I know several marriages that ended because the husband or wife "let themselves go." Don't think you can get away with not taking a shower on Sunday or fixing your hair, or God forbid, gaining weight! A marriage license is not a permission slip that allows you to forget about your looks. Of course he loves you for who you are— and you will get older together and change. But that doesn't mean you can't always look good no matter your age or how long you've been married. Making yourself look good every day is a beautiful way of saying to him, "I care about you, dear—and myself."

## 357. KISS HIM GOODBYE—LIFE'S TOO SHORT NOT TO!

This is a simple rule, but an extremely important one. *Never ever* let him leave the house without kissing him good-bye. This is important all the time, but *especially* in today's world. Think about it—how many men and women were busy getting themselves ready for work or the kids off to school or just rushing around to make a meeting on September 11, 2001, and forgot or just didn't get to kiss their spouse goodbye? It's a tough way of talking about this topic, but believe me, not having kissed someone adieu is a regret you *never* want to have.

## 358. SAY "I LOVE YOU"—A LOT

See above! You really can't say "I love you" enough—there's no such thing. Say it now, tomorrow, and every day you're together.

## 359. HE COMES FIRST!

My family has always come first. That's just the way it is for me. I've canceled appointments, turned down wonderful and potentially lucrative business opportunities, and had to disappoint friends on various occasions to fulfill promises to my husband and daughters. Do I regret any of these decisions for a moment? No. Your relationship with your husband and family should take precedence over everything. They are your life. Your job isn't.

## 360. BE A GEISHA GIRL

A woman I helped to get married told me "all you have to do is be a geisha girl—feed 'em and fuck 'em and at the end of the day they'll be happy." Well! While I think there's a *little* more to it than that—and this advice may not be for everyone—her fun and sassy attitude helps keep her marriage alive. If you feel this example is a bit over the top, the message that's worth taking away is, look for inspiration in all kinds of places. This woman was inspired by an image of the geisha and it worked for her. What inspires you?

## 361. FIVE GREAT REASONS WHY MEN AND WOMEN TELL ME THEY LOVE BEING MARRIED

(Note the similarities!)

**Men say:**

1. Cleavage, cleavage, cleavage!

2. Worry-free sex practically anytime you want it

3. Makes me feel like a man; I'm her hero

4. It's great knowing you have someone to come home to

5. Someone really, really loves me

**Women say:**

1. He can help me fix all kinds of things that are broken, literally and figuratively

2. Lovemaking anytime you feel like it

3. I feel wanted and needed

4. It's great knowing you have someone to come home to

5. He's crazy about me!

## 362. STAY IN TOUCH!

Sex is important, but so are little day-to-day touches—a hug, a pat on the back, and a shoulder rub, for example. All of these "little" signs of affection mean a lot to most men. "I love to be cuddled," Jake, a man I recently helped to get married, told me. "I just really need a ton of affection," he says. That's not uncommon. Men really love to be touched and loved in all kinds of way. Stroke his head, run your fingers through his hair, caress his cheek. He will love it.

## 363. NEVER GO TO SLEEP ANGRY

This age-old wisdom has never gone out of style. Scream your head off, walk away, or throw a plate at the wall. Do whatever it is you do to "get it out of your system." But before you hit the sheets, kiss and make up. Enough said!

## 364. SAVOR THE PRECIOUS MOMENTS IN LIFE

Magical moments are few and far between. Don't let them go by unnoticed. Watch sunsets together. Hold each other close in front of a roaring fire. Look into his eyes and appreciate him for who he is.

## 365. HOLD HANDS

You will never be married too long or get too old to hold hands.

# Janis's "Best of" Resource Guide

ello! Welcome to the resource section, or what I call Janis's Best of . . ." My Cupids at Janis Spindel Serious Matchmaking, Inc. and I have done a lot of footwork for you! Many of the services listed are located in New York City because that's where I'm based, although I have clients all over the country. But what's wrong with taking a long weekend in this fabulous city and learning how to apply makeup or getting your hair and nails done? Do I even have to mention shopping? Besides, Mr. Right might be on the plane, train, or in the hotel lobby! Services, such as advice offered by image consultants, can be accessed long distance, by telephone or e-mail. And many products can be ordered via the Internet or telephone.

You will find very special people and unique places listed here. I have found that each delivers quality services and fine customer relations. I never recommend any store, product, or service provider unless I—and at least two other "guinea pigs" from my office—have personally tested them out. Please check my website, www.janisspindelmatchmaker.com, for continual updates to this list.

I've also included a place for you to write down your own favorite neighborhood finds. It's a good idea to keep important numbers at your fingertips. Building relationships with and loyalty to merchants leads to excellent service and appreciation from them.

Finally, you can write to me and share your success stories or inquire about the services of Janis Spindel Serious Matchmaking, Inc. by e-mailing me at: Janisbook@janisspindelmatchmaker.com. I look forward to hearing from you!

# List of Services

## BALLROOM DANCE LESSONS

Stepping Out Studios
37 West 26th Street
9th floor
New York, NY 10010
646-742-9400
www.steppingoutstudios.com

## COSMETIC DENTISTRY

Elisa Mello, D.D.S.
Ramin Tabib, D.D.S.
NYC Smile Design
8 East 84th Street
New York, NY 10028
212-452-3344
www.nycsmiledesign.com

Jennifer Jablow, D.D.S.
901 Lexington Avenue
New York, NY 10021
212-794-1100
www.doctorjablow.com

Invisalign Wall Street
Drs. Jennifer Salzer and Jessica Greenberg
111 Broadway, The Trinity Building
New York, NY 10006
212-871-9835
www.invisalignwallstreet.com

The Brace Place
Dr. Josh Epstein
800 Tennant Road
Manalapan, NY 07726
732-536-4422
www.braceplace.com

## DERMATOLOGY

Howard Sobel, M.D., F.A.A.C.S.
Dermatological surgeon
960 Park Avenue
New York, NY 10028
212-288-0060
www.drsobel.com

Neil Sadick, M.D.
Dermatology and Aesthetic Surgery
772 Park Avenue
New York, NY 10021
212-772-7242

*and*

833 Northern Blvd., Suite 130
Great Neck, NY 11021
516-482-8040
www.sadickdermatology.com

Heidi Waldorf, M.D.
Director of Dermatologic Laser Surgery and Cosmetic Dermatology
The Mount Sinai Medical Center
1190 Fifth Avenue
One Gustave L. Levy Place
New York, NY 10029
212-241-6500
www.mountsinai.org

Michele Sabino
Medical Aesthetician
1009 Fifth Avenue
New York, NY 10028
212-472-1800
Fax: 212-249-2370

## ELECTROLYSIS

Barbara Leibowitz Electrolysis
Herald Towers
50 West 34th Street
New York, NY 10001
212-239-0783
www.electrolysisnyc.com

## EYEWEAR

Alain Mikli
880 Madison Avenue
New York, NY 10021
212-472-6085
www.mikli.com

Felice Dee
Felice Dee Eyewear
69 East 71st Street 10021
212-717-7062
E-mail Felice Dee at: Felicedeeeyewear@aol.com

## HAIR SALONS

Christo Fifth Avenue
Christo, Artistic Director
Specialists in curly hair
574 Fifth Avenue, 5th Floor
New York, NY 10036
212-997-8800
www.curlisto.com

MV Salon
1467 Second Avenue
New York, NY 10021
212-472-7200
www.mvsalon.com

Extreme New York
1572 Third Avenue
New York, NY 10028
212-427-4608

Roy Teeluck Salon
38 East 57th Street
New York, NY 10022
212-888-2221
www.royteelucksalon.com

## IMAGE CONSULTANTS

Elena Castaneda
NYIC—New York Image Consultant
351 East 84th Street, #11A
New York, NY 10028
212-879-5790
www.newyorkimageconsultant.com

## LASER HAIR REMOVAL

Romeo and Juliette Laser Hair Removal
38 East 57th Street
New York, NY 10022
212-750-2000
www.romeojuliettelaserhairremoval.com

## LINGERIE

Bra Tenders Inc.
630 Ninth Avenue
New York, NY 10036
212-957-7000
www.bratenders.com

Le Corset
80 Thompson Street
New York, NY 10012
212-334-4936

## MAKEUP ARTISTS AND PRODUCTS

Laura Geller
Laura Geller Makeup Studios
1044 Lexington Avenue
New York, NY 10021
800-makeup-4
212-570-5477
www.laurageller.com

*Laura's products are also available through www.qvc.com.*

Vincent Longo
For product and service information call 1-877-Longo-99
www.vincentlongo.com

## MATRIMONIAL LAWYER

Mitchell R. Schrage
Mitchell R. Schrage and Associates
Tower 56
126 East 56th Street
New York, NY 10022
212-758-9000
www.mrsnylaw.com

## NUTRITIONISTS

Oz Garcia
10 West 74th Street
New York, NY 10023
212-362-5569
www.ozgarcia.com

Carmen Fusco
333 East 43rd Street, Suite #114
New York, NY 10017
212-983-6383
www.rejuvenex.net

Joy Bauer
116 East 63rd Street
New York, NY 10021
212-759-6999 x1
www.joybauernutrition.com

## PERSONAL SHOPPERS

Susan Tabak
Paris Personal Shopper
212-404-8398
www.parispersonalshopper.com

*Susan will take you on a shopping tour of this great city and show you the secret, sensational places where Parisian women shop.*

## PERSONAL TRAINERS

Allen Spindel
917-882-5200
www.spindelsportsacademy.com

*Allen holds a second-degree Black Belt in Hapkido from the Korea Kido Association. Additionally, Allen earned a bachelor's degree in physical education from Oklahoma City University and a master's degree in physical education from Emporia State University. He is a nationally certified personal fitness trainer and group fitness instructor and is a member of the National Strength and Conditioning Association.*

Radu
24 West 57th Street, 2nd Floor
New York, NY 10019
212-581-1995
www.radufitness.com

## POWER PILATES

**New York, NY**

Power Pilates Studio and Corporate Office
49 West 23rd Street, 10th Floor
New York, NY 10010
212-627-5852

Sichel Chiropractic & Power Pilates
136 East 57th Street, Suite 603
New York, NY 10022
212-371-0700

Power Pilates @ Equinox Greenwich Avenue
97 Greenwich Avenue
New York, NY 10014
212-352-8070

Power Pilates @ Equinox West 92nd Street
2465 Broadway
New York, NY 10025
646-505-1408

Power Pilates @ Equinox East 43rd Street
Power Pilates International Training Center
521 Fifth Avenue
New York, NY 10175
212-661-9488

Power Pilates @ Equinox Columbus Circle
10 Columbus Circle (60th Street)
New York, NY 10019
212-871-0425 (studio)

**Chicago, IL**

Power Pilates @ Equinox Chicago
1750 North Clark
Chicago, IL 60614
312-642-9360 (studio)

Power Pilates @ Equinox Chicago
900 North Michigan Avenue
Chicago, IL
312-335-8464

**Pasadena, CA**

Power Pilates @ Equinox Pasadena
260 East Colorado Boulevard
Pasadena, CA 91101
626-685-4800, ext. 7165

www.powerpilates.com


PRIVATE INVESTIGATIONS

Harbour Town Security Consultants
845-355-2057
212-227-9600
www.curiouscompany.com

*This is a private investigations firm, licensed and bonded in New York and New Jersey, which, for more than twenty years, has provided nationwide services to its clients, primarily the country's largest and most prestigious laws firms as well as federal and state government agencies (see them at www.targetresearch.com/htsc.htm).*

*HTSC's owners and directors, William Patten Jr. and Harlin Parker, bring together decades of experience in law enforcement, criminal defense, and civil affairs. They also operate Curious Company, a vetting service that provides you employment information, information about criminal convictions, DWI, or civil judgments against an individual.*

## SMOKING CESSATION PROGRAMS

American Lung Association
1-800-548-8252
www.lungusa.org
*The ALA has a Web-based quit smoking program.*

American Cancer Society
1-800-ACS-2345
www.cancer.org
*The ACS provides information and support for quitting smoking.*

## SPAS

Acqua Beauty Bar
7 East 14th Street
New York, NY
212-620-4329
www.acquabeautybar.com

Glow Skin Spa
30 East 60th Street, Suite 808
New York, NY 10022
212-319-6654
E-mail Glow at: info@glowskinspa.com

## STATIONERY AND INVITATIONS

Bunny Shestack
Write and Invite Ltd.
330 Seventh Avenue, 4th Floor
New York, NY 10001
212-594-5942, by appointment only

DK Schulman
Design/Calligraphy
225 East 73rd Street
New York, NY 10021
212-472-1596, by appointment only

## THERAPISTS

Richard A. Levine
Sex therapist
90 Eighth Avenue
Brooklyn, NY 11215
917-827-3731

Daniel Aferiat, CSW
Life Management Consultants
330 West 58th Street, Suite 410
New York, NY 10019
212-974-9722

## YOGA

Be Yoga
138 Fifth Avenue
New York, NY 10175

1319 Third Avenue
New York, NY 10021

160 East 56th Street
New York, NY 10022

50 S. Buckhout Street
Irvington, New York
212-935-9642 for information about and schedules at all locations
www.beyoga.com

OTHER

Little Shop of Plaster & Pottery
431 East 73rd Street
New York, NY
212-717-6636
www.littleshopny.com

*This paint-your-own-pottery shop offers singles' nights and complimentary wine at evening sessions—as do many shops of this kind across the country. Check this one out when you are in New York and be sure to research pottery painting shops in your own area. If they don't offer singles' nights, suggest that they do!*

Big Apple Greeters
1 Centre Street, Suite 2035
New York NY 10007
Visitor Info: 212-669-8159
Volunteer Info: 212-669-2364
General Info: 212-669-2896
Fax: 212-669-3685
www.bigapplegreeter.org/
E-mail: information@bigapplegreeter.org

Mille Fiori Floral Design by René Hofstede
227 West 29th Street, 2nd floor
New York, NY 10001
By appointment
212-714-2202
Fax: 212-714-2130
info@millefioriflowers.com
www.millefioriflowers.com

Wild Poppy
265 East 78th Street
New York, NY 10021
212-717-5757
wildpoppy@mindspring.com

## BOOKS

*Look and Feel Fabulous Forever: The World's Best Supplements, Anti-Aging Techniques, and High-Tech Health Secrets*
Oz Garcia, Sharyn Kolberg
ReganBooks, 2003

*The Balance: Your Personal Prescription for Supermetabolism, Renewed Vitality, Maximum Health, Instant Rejuvenation*
Oz Garcia
ReganBooks, 2000

*The Truth About Beauty: Transform Your Looks and Your Life from the Inside Out*
Kat James, Oz Garcia
Beyond Words Publishing, 2003

*How to Cook Everything: Simple Recipes for Great Food*
Mark Bittman
John Wiley & Sons, 1998

*The Joy of Cooking*
Marion Rombauer Becker, Irma S. Rombauer, Ethan Becker
Scribner, 1997

# Personal Favorites

## COSMETIC DENTISTRY

_____

_____

_____

_____

_____

_____

_____

## DERMATOLOGY

_____

_____

_____

_____

_____

_____

_____

_____

## ENTERTAINMENT (ROMANTIC RESTAURANTS, BARS, AND OTHER VENUES)

_____

_____

_____

_____

_____

_____

_____

## EYEWEAR

_____

_____

_____

_____

_____

_____

## HAIR SALONS

_____

_____

_____

_____

_____

_____

## IMAGE CONSULTANTS

_____
_____
_____
_____
_____
_____
_____

## JEWELRY

_____
_____
_____
_____
_____
_____
_____

## LASER HAIR REMOVAL

_____
_____
_____
_____
_____
_____
_____

## LAWYERS

_____

_____

_____

_____

_____

_____

_____

## LINGERIE

_____

_____

_____

_____

_____

_____

_____

## MAKEUP ARTISTS

_____

_____

_____

_____

_____

_____

## NUTRITIONISTS

_____

_____

_____

_____

_____

_____

## PERSONAL SHOPPERS

_____

_____

_____

_____

_____

_____

## PERSONAL TRAINERS

_____

_____

_____

_____

_____

_____

## PHOTOGRAPHERS

---

---

---

---

---

---

---

## PILATES/YOGA

---

---

---

---

---

---

---

## PRIVATE INVESTIGATIONS

---

---

---

---

---

---

---

SPAS

_____

_____

_____

_____

_____

_____

_____

STATIONERY AND INVITATIONS

_____

_____

_____

_____

_____

_____

_____

THERAPISTS

_____

_____

_____

_____

_____

_____

_____

## OTHER

_____

_____

_____

_____

_____

_____

_____

_____

_____

_____

_____

_____

_____

_____

_____

_____

_____

_____

_____

_____

_____

_____

_____

_____

_____

_____